Palgrave Studies of Entrepreneurship in Africa

Series Editors
Kevin Ibeh
Department of Management
Birkbeck, University of London
London, UK

Sonny Nwankwo
Office of the Academy Provost
Nigerian Defence Academy
Kaduna, Nigeria

Tigineh Mersha
Department of Management
and International Business
University of Baltimore
Baltimore, MD, USA

Ven Sriram
Department of Marketing
and Entrepreneurship
University of Baltimore
Baltimore, MD, USA

The Palgrave Studies of Entrepreneurship in Africa series offers an urgently needed platform to document, promote and showcase entrepreneurship in Africa and create a unique home for top quality, cutting-edge work on a broad range of themes and perspectives.

Focusing on successful African firms, small and medium-sized enterprises as well as multinational corporations, this series will cover new and ground-breaking areas including innovation, technology and digital entrepreneurship, green practices, sustainability, and their cultural and social implications for Africa. This series is positioned to eminently capture and energize the monumental changes currently taking place in Africa, well beyond the pervasive informal sector. It will also respond to the great thirst amongst students, researchers, policy and third sector practitioners for relevant knowledge and nuanced insights on how to further promote and institutionalize entrepreneurship, and optimize its benefits across the continent. The series will offer an important platform for interrogating the appropriateness and limits of Western management practices in Africa, examining new approaches to researching the fast-changing continent.

A diverse set of established experts and emerging scholars based in Africa and around the world will contribute to this series. Projects will also originate from entrepreneurship-themed tracks and Special Interest Groups at major Africa-focused conferences, notably the International Academy of African Business and Development, the Academy of Management Africa, and the Academy of International Business African Chapter. The foregoing breadth and diversity of themes, target authors and manuscript sources will produce a richly distinctive series.

More information about this series at
http://www.palgrave.com/gp/series/15149

Isaac Oduro Amoako

Trust, Institutions and Managing Entrepreneurial Relationships in Africa

An SME Perspective

palgrave
macmillan

Isaac Oduro Amoako
Liverpool Business School
Liverpool John Moores University
Liverpool, UK

Palgrave Studies of Entrepreneurship in Africa
ISBN 978-3-319-98394-3   ISBN 978-3-319-98395-0   (eBook)
https://doi.org/10.1007/978-3-319-98395-0

Library of Congress Control Number: 2018952368

Cover illustration: Roberto Binetti / Alamy Stock Photo

This Palgrave Macmillan imprint is published by the registered company Springer Nature Switzerland AG
The registered company address is: Gewerbestrasse 11, 6330 Cham, Switzerland

To my family

Acknowledgements

This book would not have been possible without the support of those with whom I have had the opportunity to work at Liverpool Business School, Liverpool John Moores University. I am particularly grateful to the Dean, Mr Tim Nichols, Academic Director, Dr Adam Shore, Director of Research, Professor David Bryde, Professor Bettany Shona, Professor Ian Fillis, Dr. Seamus O'Brien, and colleagues who have all been supportive of my passion for research. My next appreciation goes to the Head and the staff at the Centre for Enterprise and Economic Development Research (CEEDR) at Middlesex University where I received a scholarship for my PhD. I would particularly like to express my heartfelt appreciation to Professor Fergus Lyon, my Director of Studies and Dr. Leandro Sepulveda, my Second Supervisor, both at CEEDR. I am also thankful to the entrepreneurs who provided interviews for this book. Then thanks are due to my colleagues and friends; Dr. Frank Nyame Asiamah, Kingsley Obinna Omeihi, Dr. Loliya Akobo, Dr. Anne Broderick, Philomene Uwamaliya, Stephen Gyamfi and Vivien Bahire who read portions of the work and provided feedback. I would also like to thank the Series Editors- Professor Ibe, Professor Nwankwo, Professor Mersha and Professor Sriram whose feedback enabled me to improve on some sections of the book.

My final thanks go to my mother, Mary Yaa Adutwumwaa, my children Kwame, Yvonne, Noah, and Richmond, my granddaughter Marissa and my siblings Philip and Kofi whose support and encouragement enabled me to persevere during the many hours of writing.

26 June 2018   Isaac Oduro Amoako

Contents

List of Figures

List of Tables

List of Tables

1

Introduction: Trust, Institutions, and Managing Entrepreneurial Relationships in Africa

1.1 Introduction

Africa has recently achieved a remarkable economic expansion despite the global recession. Countries like Ethiopia, Ghana, Angola, Rwanda, Mozambique, and Zambia have enjoyed growth of between 7% and 9% year on year and have helped to triple the size of the African economy since 2000. Within the past decade, real income per person has jumped by 30% and about 350 million people are in the middle class and able to spend between $2 to $20 per day (Blerk 2018). The growth in Africa continues unabated as six of the 10 fastest growing economies in the world in 2018 are in the continent (World Economic Forum 2018). Currently, urbanisation is at 37% and Africa is comparable to China but is expected to be the fastest urbanising region in the world from 2020 to 2050. Africa is emerging as a magnet for investment, one that offers opportunities for growth for entrepreneurs, investors, businesses and other economies (BBC News 2018; Deloitte 2014). Africa has a population of 1.2 billion people and a gross domestic product (GDP) of US$2.6 trillion. On 21 March 2018, the African Continental Free Trade Area that offers Africans the right to move, work, invest, and

© The Author(s) 2019
I. O. Amoako, *Trust, Institutions and Managing Entrepreneurial Relationships in Africa*,
Palgrave Studies of Entrepreneurship in Africa,
https://doi.org/10.1007/978-3-319-98395-0_1

reside anywhere in the continent was agreed by 44 countries, in Kigali, boosting prospects for entrepreneurship and economic development (African Union Commission 2018). Interestingly, entrepreneurs and their small and medium-sized enterprises (SMEs) are at the heart of the economic boom. SMEs create around 80% of the region's employment, giving rise to demand for new goods and services (Africa Economic Outlook 2017). Not surprisingly, recently politicians, entrepreneurs, investors, and corporate executives have developed a keen interest in building networks and relationships with customers in the African continent, which is now regarded as an emerging market destination for businesses to invest, grow, and expand (BBC News 2018; George et al. 2016; Accenture 2010).

In spite of the considerable interest, entrepreneurs, investors, and corporate executives are deterred by the lack of trust in doing business in Africa due to widespread assumptions and reports in the West about the numerous weak institutional structures embedded in African economies (World Bank 2018; The Economist 2016; Bruton et al. 2010). Based on these assumptions and reports, strong institutions provide a sound economic environment and trust for entrepreneurship. As a result, in advanced economies with strong institutions, entrepreneurs have lower transaction costs and a strong trust to invest and innovate (North 1990). Conversely, in emerging economies with weak institutions, transaction costs are higher and so there is low trust to invest and innovate. According to these assumptions, economic and political institutional stability has led to the recent surge in entrepreneurship in Africa (World Bank 2018). Existing reports and conceptual developments on institutions and entrepreneurship have also mostly drawn on advanced Western economy contexts to focus on how state and market institutions could facilitate larger organisations' investments. However, these arguments about the role of institutions, trust development, and entrepreneurship do not reflect entrepreneurship theory or practices in emerging economies (Peng et al. 2008; Smallbone and Welter 2013) where entrepreneurs as actors, draw on cultural indigenous institutions to develop trust in the absence of strong state and market institutions (Welter and Smallbone 2011; Amoako and Lyon 2014). Entrepreneurship incorporates the discovery, creation, and exploitation of opportunities and the success or failure of these activities is attributed to the individual entrepreneur (Gartner 1988; Shane and Venkataman 2000), and the formal and informal institutional factors that shape opportunities (Chell 2000). While strong institutions provide a sound economic environment and trust for entrepreneurs in developed economies, in emerging economies with weak formal institutions, cultural institutions substitute for the weak institutions to provide trust to entrepreneurs to encourage them to invest and innovate.

In a study in the four largest emerging economies—Brazil, Russia, India, and China—also known as the BRICs, Estrin and Pervezer (2011) found that in the midst of weak state institutions, informal institutions might substitute for and replace ineffective formal institutions leading to enhanced domestic and foreign investment. Similarly, African entrepreneurs draw on indigenous cultural institutions to develop trust in entrepreneurial relationships in order to exploit opportunities embedded in the weak formal institutional environments (Tillmar and Lindkvist 2007; Amoako and Lyon 2014).

Yet, there is a chronic dearth of knowledge about how entrepreneurs in Africa draw on indigenous cultural institutions which work side by side with institutions of the modern states in Africa (Jackson et al. 2008; George et al. 2016). This book responds to these gaps by showing how African entrepreneurs operate in the context of weak state institutions by relying on indigenous cultural institutions to develop trust in entrepreneurial relationships.

This chapter, and indeed this book, re-examines the nature of institutions and how institutions shape entrepreneurial activity and trust development in African economy contexts. In these contexts, like other emerging economy contexts, the personal networks of the entrepreneur and norms governing interpersonal relationships play a crucial role in firm strategy and performance (Peng et al. 2008). Thus, in emerging economies, trust in networks of mutually supportive and cooperative relationships is important for market entry and the entrepreneurial process in general (Child and Rodrigues 2007).

The present chapter contributes to an understanding of the role of state and market institutions, indigenous cultural institutions, trust, and the entrepreneur in entrepreneurship in Africa. The chapter draws on the notions of institutions and institutional logics and connects them with broader conversations in entrepreneurship and trust theories to explore how both structure and agency influence entrepreneurship. By drawing on the institutional logics approach, the chapter is able to show how entrepreneurs draw on the logics of indigenous cultural institutions to develop networks, relationships, and trust in response to the weak institutional environment. This chapter, and for that matter this book, seeks to answer the key question: 'What are institutions and how do they influence trust development in entrepreneurial relationships in Africa?'

1.2   Definitions and Assumptions

The term 'Institutions' is defined as the 'taken-for-granted assumptions which inform and shape the actions of individual actors … at the same time, these taken-for-granted assumptions are themselves the outcome of social actions' (Burns and Scapens 2000, 8). Shane (2003) defines entrepreneurship as the ability to recognise and evaluate opportunity and mobilise resources to establish or grow a business in a given context. The entrepreneur refers to the individual who recognises and exploits opportunities to establish or grow a business in a given context. These two definitions integrate entrepreneurial action with context and the establishment or growth of a business. The author adopts a working definition of trust as 'a set of positive expectations that is shared by parties in an exchange that things and people will not fail them in spite of the possibility of being let down'. This definition highlights trust as an expectation based on accepted *cultural norms* and interactions within specific *contexts* (Zucker 1986; Zaheer et al. 1998; Möllering 2006). Institutional logics is defined as the 'socially constructed, historical patterns of cultural symbols and material practices, including assumptions, values, and beliefs by which individuals and organisations provide meaning to their daily activity, organize time and space and reproduce their lives and experiences' (Thornton et al. 2012, 2). A logic provides a set of coherent organising principles for a particular sphere of life and yet logics often overlap such that actors draw on multiple logics within and across domains (Friedland and Alford 1991; Besharov and Smith 2014). In this book, the author focuses on how societal-level logics of state and indigenous cultural institutions and norms influence entrepreneurs' decisions about trust development in entrepreneurial relationships in Africa. Drawing on the institutional logics approach, the following assumptions underpin this introductory chapter as well as this book.

First, the author assumes that trust has a significant impact on entrepreneurial behaviour and low levels of trust constrain entrepreneurship while high levels of trust enable entrepreneurship. Second, it is assumed that institutions and particularly societal-level institutional logics underpin trust development in entrepreneurship in a variety of ways due to factors such as geographic, historical, and cultural contexts in which entrepreneurs and organisations operate (see Besharov and Smith 2014). Third, the author assumes that societal-level institutional logics such as rules, legal institutions, cultural beliefs, norms, and practices shape entrepreneurs' cognition and decision making (Vickers et al. 2017; North 1990; Scott 2013; Thornton et al. 2012; Friedland and Alford 1991). Fourth, the author assumes that institutional logics offer strategic resources that connect organisations' strategy for trusting, networking, relationship building, and decision making (see Durand et al. 2013). Fifth, it is assumed that actors use logics to interpret and make sense of the world, although not always consciously, to support networking and trusting behaviour. At the same time, actors' networking and trusting practices and behaviour can both reinforce and challenge the assumptions, values, beliefs, and rules considered appropriate in a particular sphere of social life (see Besharov and Smith 2014). Sixth, it is assumed that organisations embody multiple logics and actors confront, reflect, and draw on the multiple logics in their practices, at the same time some logics may dominate others making them irrelevant to organisational functioning (Thornton et al. 2012; Besharov and Smith 2014). Together these six assumptions inform the theorising in the book that aims to offer an understanding about how entrepreneurs draw on institutions to develop trust in networks and relationships in order to access resources in African contexts.

In this book the author uses the abductive approach to combine existing literature and empirical data from entrepreneurs owning and managing 50 internationally trading SMEs in Africa to present frameworks for gaining insights into how institutions shape trust development from the perspective of the African entrepreneur.

The rest of this chapter is organised as follows. The next section summarises the literature on institutions, trust, and entrepreneurial relationships. The aims of the book, the author's motivation for writing the book, the context of the study, the methodology, the target audience, and the book's outline contents then follow.

1.3   Overview of Institutions, Trust and Entrepreneurial Relationships

Institutions are very important as they influence the nature and level of entrepreneurship and trust in any country or region (North 1990; Welter and Smallbone 2011). Institutions provide the incentive structures that define entrepreneurial opportunities in any given context (North 1990; Scott 2013). Some commentators therefore argue that the differences in institutions remain a key factor in explaining the variations in wealth and prosperity across different economies and countries (Acemoglu 2003). Institutions also enhance networks, social relationships, and social capital by promoting greater interactions, the free flow of information, and the formation of associations all of which increase the level of trust (Putnam 1993). Thus, networks and relationships are socially constructed and defined by institutions and culture in particular (Curran et al. 1995). Entrepreneurs develop trust and cooperation to exploit opportunities embedded in institutional environments through developing a variety of social and business networks and relationships (North 1990; Sarason et al. 2006; Granovetter 1985).

Trust plays two important roles in enterprise development and in entrepreneurial relationships. It reduces uncertainty through providing information and provides a coordination mechanism that helps to reduce opportunistic behaviour, and both of these functions help to reduce transaction costs (Welter et al. 2004). Hence, trust serves as a defining factor that enhances enterprise development and the building of networks and relationships between firms at both national and international levels (Welter and Smallbone 2011; Zain and Ng 2006).

The literature suggests that trust exists in two main forms namely personal trust and institutional trust (see Welter and Smallbone 2011). Personal trust is formed based on the initial knowledge of the exchange partner and may depend on the characteristics of a group such as ethnic, kinship, social bonds, and from emotional bonds between friends, family members, and other social groups (Welter and Smallbone 2006). On the other hand, the state, political, social, and cultural environments provide institutional trust (Zucker 1986; Scott 2013; Welter and Smallbone 2011). Hence in developed economies with strong institutions, trust can be based on, for example, the legal systems that are used to enforce contracts with individuals and partner firms.

However, in emerging economies like Africa the weak legal systems fail to enhance contract enforcement and institutional trust is low (Zaheer and Kamal 2011). Personal trust then becomes more important in emerging economy environments where formal sanctioning mechanisms are absent or fail. Furthermore, in cases where an exchange partner is not satisfied with the institutional arrangements or is unfamiliar with them, personal trust may complement institutional trust (Granovetter 1985; Welter and Smallbone 2006).

Trust remains a complex concept because its development processes are embedded in institutional contexts, particularly cultural institutions that shape trust development processes, perceptions of trust violations, and trust repair processes based on norms and expectations (Dietz et al. 2010; Bachmann et al. 2015). The challenge is that where there is a greater divergence of cultural backgrounds, trust development becomes complex. The cultural difference or 'psychic distance' (Child et al. 2002) between two parties in cross-cultural relationships can constrain trust development due to the inability to draw on common norms and expectations. As a result, actors from different cultures (Dietz et al. 2010) may have dissimilar trust expectations and different behavioural rules in conflict situations (Zaheer and Kamal 2011; Ren and Gray 2009). However, in general, existing studies have not paid much attention to the need to investigate trust development in different cultural contexts (Wu et al. 2014; Li 2016).

In the context of SMEs in emerging economies and Africa, given the absence of strong states and market support institutions, and the small sizes of economic transactions, informal contracts enforced based on trust in personalised relationships, networks, and indigenous institutions such as religion, family/kinship, and trade associations may be critically important and preferred (McMillan and Woodruff 2002; Amoako and Lyon 2014). However, this may differ in the context of larger organisations in which the size of economic transactions may require more detailed agreements and enforcement regimes based on intermediary institutions like the judiciary/courts and other regulatory bodies.

In summary, Africa has enjoyed significant economic growth recently and has become an increasingly important destination for investors and entrepreneurs to do business. However, the states and market institutions are less developed and entrepreneurs and their smaller businesses that are driving the economic boom rely mostly on indigenous cultural institutions, personal relationships, and networks to develop trust in order to do business (Amoako and Lyon 2014). There is therefore a need to understand how entrepreneurs draw on the logics of cultural-specific institutions to develop trust in entrepreneurial networks and relationships in the context of institutional weaknesses (see Jackson et al. 2008; George et al. 2016). This book attempts to bridge this gap by answering the core research question: What are institutions and how do they influence trust development in entrepreneurial relationships in Africa?

This book aims to contribute to:

1. A balanced approach to the study of entrepreneurship that recognises the role of state and market institutions while not underestimating indigenous cultural institutions, the entrepreneur, social capital, networking norms and trust, and the characteristics of the firm, all of which are very important to the entrepreneurial process.
2. A re-conceptualisation of our understanding of the role of institutions in entrepreneurship in Africa and other emerging economies. It highlights the importance of indigenous cultural institutions that provide the logics to promote trust development, networking, and relationship building in entrepreneurship in the context of weak formal institutions.

3. A cross-cultural understanding of common African indigenous institutions and particularly cultural-specific logics that shape trust development in entrepreneurial relationships. Understanding these institutions is important due to their potential to give rise to differences in expectations, explanations, and attributions for African entrepreneurial behaviour within relationships.

4. An awareness through example and discussion of how African entrepreneurs, as actors, develop and manage entrepreneurial relationships across cultures. It shows that entrepreneurs use the logics of weak state and market institutions, as well as those of local cultural institutions to develop trust in networks and relationships strategically in order to operate successfully in the contexts of weak state and market institutions in Africa.

5. A holistic view of trust focusing on the trustor (entrepreneur), trustee (partner entrepreneur or firm), their relationships, and the institutional contexts in which they operate. Such an holistic approach is currently lacking in trust research.

6. An understanding of the processes of trust development, interpretations of trust violation, and trust repair strategies, and how these processes are shaped by the logics of weak state and market institutions, indigenous cultural institutions particularly traditional legal systems, family/kinship, religion, gift giving, punctuality, trade associations, and industry norms in an African context. These institutions are important for understanding trust in African economies and across African cultures, the acceptable levels of trust violation and effective trust repair mechanisms in a relationship, and the cultural and market values that are important in trust repair processes.

7. An insight into the impact of trust violations on the entrepreneur. It shows that trust violations can lead to varying negative financial, psychological, and social costs to entrepreneurs and yet the literature has not paid attention to these issues.

8. An understanding of the wider implications of institutions and the importance for entrepreneurs, businesses and investors to understand local contexts and the institutional logics that enable trust to develop in entrepreneurship. It also shows the need to reform weak state and market

institutions while recognising, supporting, and considering local cultural institutions that support entrepreneurship. Furthermore, it emphasises basing national and international interventions on relevant local knowledge and practices in order to avoid misplaced development programmes instigated by donors and governments.

1.3.1 Motivation

The origin and development of this book is traced back over the past nine years during which the author researched, presented papers, and published on entrepreneurial trust and relationships building in Africa. It draws on the author's published PhD thesis that explored qualitative empirical data from 24 internationally trading entrepreneurs owning and managing SMEs in agriculture, services, and manufacturing sectors in Ghana (Amoako 2012). The thesis aimed to explore the role of trust in SME internationalisation in Ghana. The inspiration to expand the study to cover more countries in Africa originated from the author's conversations with publishers, fellow researchers, and entrepreneurs from Africa during international conferences, events, and research projects.

The author collected another set of empirical data from 26 entrepreneurs owning and managing internationally trading SMEs in Africa. The second set of empirical data was collected from entrepreneurs and managers, to gain insights into how institutional logics shape trust development and entrepreneurial relationship building in the region referred to by some entities as Sub-Saharan Africa.

1.3.2 Context

The economies of the so-called Sub-Saharan African countries are dominated by SMEs many of which operate in the informal sector that contributes about 55% of GDP and 80% of the labour force. The sector offers opportunities to vulnerable people, including women and the young (AfDB 2013). Yet, the term Sub-Saharan Africa is geographically confusing as four countries extend into the Sahara, but Djibouti, which is south of the Sahara is excluded from the list. To add to the confusion, different entities have assigned different countries to Sub-Saharan Africa. For example, the United Nations Development Programme (UNDP) lists 46 of Africa's 56 countries while the World Bank lists 48 countries. Critics therefore argue that the term is derogatory and used to stereotype Black Africa without being openly racist. After all there is no sub-Europe, sub-Asia, or sub-America so why Sub-Saharan Africa (Mashanda 2017)? Given the vagueness of the term, the confusion over the number of countries that constitute Sub-Saharan Africa, and the allegations of racist connotations of the term, the author uses the term Africa to refer to the countries in West, East, Central and Southern Africa. This book therefore does not include data from North Africa which is largely Arab and Berber but instead focuses on West Africa with predominantly Congo/Bantu, East Africa with largely Nilotic/Sudanic/Bantu, and South Africa with Bantu/Khoikhoi/Khiosan (Lituchy et al. 2013).

Africa is the second largest continent in the world with a land mass covering over 30 million square kilometres (George et al. 2016). There are 55 countries recognised by the African Union and United Nations (UN) in Africa. Western, Eastern, Central, and Southern Africa are made up of 47 countries that lie south of the Sahara Desert and have a total area of 23.6 million square kilometres. The four regions put together are therefore larger than the United States, Canada, and the European Union put together. Europeans agreed the Partition of Africa, which began with the Berlin Conference in 1884–1885 without recourse to ethnic affiliations. All the countries in the four regions were colonised, albeit briefly in the case of Ethiopia and Liberia. Currently all the countries are characterised by weak formal institutions even though some countries have relatively stronger institutions than others (Africa Economic Outlook 2017). The countries are also culturally diverse with unusually high levels of and large variations in ethnic diversity, cultures, and languages. As a result, even though the precise number is unknown, there are about 2000 distinct languages spoken in Africa (Heine and Nurse 2000). Given the many complex cultures and sub-cultures across Africa, the analysis and discussions focus on a number of key common institutions and institutional logics that are critically important in developing and managing entrepreneurial relationships across cultures in the continent. Additional context specific institutions and institutional logics may pertain to particular countries, industries, sectors, and markets and there is a need for further research to identify those that are critical for the development of trust and entrepreneurial trust building in the different contexts. The book therefore serves as the beginning of a research agenda that calls for further research into how entrepreneurs draw on indigenous institutions to develop trust in entrepreneurial relationships and indigenous management practices in African contexts.

1.4   Methodology

The author employs an abductive approach to combine deductive and inductive reasoning with theory development and theory construction. The abductive approach refers to the systematic combination of theoretical and empirical findings in order to refine or generate a theory. In this approach, the researcher goes back and forth between the theoretical framework, data sources, and analysis to systematically generate new theory (Tavory and Timmermans 2014). The abductive approach enabled the author to use existing literature and theories, observations, and semi-structured interviews from multiple cases to nurture theory development without being constrained by predefined methodological paradigms (Denzin 1978; Tavory and Timmermans 2014). The multiple case studies allowed the researcher to draw on multiple sources (Yin 2016) to study how entrepreneurs as actors develop trust and the role of institutions and entrepreneurial relationships in the context of SMEs operating in Africa. As a result, in every chapter, the author proposes frameworks and models based on iterative interactions between the existing literature and empirical evidence based on multiple cases to provide insights into trust, institutions, and managing entrepreneurial relationships in Africa; and this approach helps to refine existing theories on the subjects. The frameworks and models proposed are therefore starting points for further research. The existing literature includes studies from the wider literature and the author's published PhD thesis (Amoako 2012) as well as jointly published book chapter, conference papers and journal articles (Amoako and Lyon 2011; Yanga and Amoako 2013; Amoako and Lyon 2014; Amoako and Matlay 2015; Damoah et al. 2018; Amoako et al. 2018).

Chapters 2 and 3 focus on frameworks mostly developed from existing literature on institutions, entrepreneurship and trust in interorganisational relationships. Chapters 4 and 5 draw on the literature and empirical data collected between 2010 and 2017 from participant observation and semi-structured interviews with 50 entrepreneurs owning and managing SMEs in Africa to identify and discuss indigenous cultural-specific logics that influence the development of trust and management of entrepreneurial relationships in Africa respectively. SMEs reflect the impact of local institutions on trust development better than larger organisations. Given the size of the informal economy in Africa, 10 of the firms involved in the study are selected purposefully from the informal sector. The author used purposive sampling techniques to select the participants for the study Africa including Ghana, focusing on internationally trading entrepreneurs owning and managing smaller business that employ not more than 100 people based on the definition of SMEs in Ghana.

The original empirical data dominates Chaps. 6, 7, and 8 and was collected and used for the author's PhD thesis. The data was collected from 2010 to 2012 through participant observation and repeated face-to-face semi-structured interviews with 24 internationally trading entrepreneurs owning and managing SMEs across the agriculture, manufacturing, and services sectors in Ghana. However, for the purpose this book, more data was collected from 26 entrepreneurs and managers operating SMEs (firms employing less than 100 people) in agriculture, manufacturing, and services sectors in the informal and formal sectors across Gambia, Nigeria, Cameroon, Rwanda, Malawi, Zimbabwe, Congo DR, Kenya, Uganda, Tanzania, and Malawi. The author used a snowballing technique and conducted 20 face-to-face semi-structured interviews, mostly in workplaces, with the help of research assistants while Skype interviews were used for the remaining six semi-structured interviews since the entrepreneurs could not be reached physically. The semi-structured interviews in the various countries investigated the processes through which entrepreneurs developed trust and the role of formal and indigenous institutions in the process.

The book uses interpretivism to interpret empirical data. The interpretivist approach is based on the view that reality is socially constructed. In this approach, the perceptions and experiences of the research participants allow the researcher to construct and view the world, and therefore understanding the context of research is critically important (Willis 2007). Given that trust development in entrepreneurial relationships is shaped by institutional logics and particularly culture (Smallbone and Welter 2006; Saunders et al. 2010), the interpretivist approach enabled the author to gain insights into the meanings that entrepreneurs ascribe to how Africa's complex human institutions shape their decision-making processes in the process. The author used thematic analysis to organise the empirical data and to gain insights into the meanings of entrepreneurs' decisions and actions relating to trust development and how the process is embedded in institutional contexts (Braun and Clarke 2006; Granovetter 1985). The identified themes are presented based on interpretivist approaches.

Using abductive reasoning, the current literature was confronted to confirm or refute the case stories, and while certain concepts are confirmed others are refuted and new concepts identified which then led to the search for more literature to find a fit for the case themes. The levels of analysis focus on the individual entrepreneur, his or her personal and business relationships, state and cultural institutions and norms, as well as characteristics of SMEs that shape the trust development decisions of the entrepreneur. Logics allow for theorising the fragmented and contradicted nature of culture at different levels of analysis such as individual, organisational, and in specific contexts in which individuals operate (Thornton 2004).

This book targets a diverse audience: academics and students involved in entrepreneurship, trust, international business, marketing and cross-cultural management education and research across the world. The author is also optimistic that it will be useful to entrepreneurs themselves as it offers an understanding of the importance of entrepreneurial agency, networks, trust, and how local contexts influence strategy and entrepreneurship. It should also be useful to policy makers and the donor community who aim to promote sustainable development through relationships and collaborations in entrepreneurship, as well as the SME sector in Africa and other emerging economies. While acknowledging the challenges of writing for such a diverse audience, the author endeavours to pitch the discussion and arguments at an accessible level, even though some complexities and academic jargon may still be present throughout the book. The references at the end of each chapter present resources for further inquiry for those who may wish to extend their knowledge.

The introduction highlights why understanding trust, institutions, and managing entrepreneurial relationships in Africa is important. The rest of the book is divided into four main parts. Part I contains Chaps. 2 and 3. Chapter 2 examines the theory of institutions and entrepreneurship while Chap. 3 focuses on institutions, entrepreneurship, and interorganisational trust theory. Part II comprises Chaps. 4 and 5 and identifies a number of formal and cultural-specific institutions that influence trust development and the management of entrepreneurial relationships in Africa. Chapter 4 identifies African indigenous institutions and logics that underpin the development and management of personal and business relationships, while Chap. 5 focuses on how logics of weak state and market institutions and cultural-specific institutions in Africa—influence the development and management of personal and business relationships in Africa. Part III is made up of Chaps. 6, 7, and 8 and presents an in-depth analysis of the development of trust, perceptions, and interpretations of trust violations, and trust repair processes in an African context—Ghana. Chapter 6 highlights how the types of trust are developed in entrepreneurial relationships. Chapter 7 considers entrepreneurial perceptions and interpretations of trust violations in an African context while Chap. 8 examines entrepreneurial trust repair processes in an African context. In these chapters, the emphasis is on how the African entrepreneur operates in the context of weak formal institutions by drawing on indigenous institutions to develop trust in relationships in order to establish and grow businesses. Chapter 9, which make up Part IV, concludes the book by summarising the key issues in the previous chapters and discussing the implications for theory, practice, and policy. In the next chapter, Chap. 2, the author reviews the literature on institutions and entrepreneurship.

References

Accenture. 2010. Africa: The new frontier for growth. http://nstore.accenture.com/pdf/Accenture_Africa_The_New_Frontier_for_Growth.pdf.   Online Access 13 Feb 2012.

Acemoglu, D. 2003. Root causes: A historical approach to assessing the role of institutions in economic development. *Finance and Development* 40: 27–30.

African Development Bank Group. 2013. Championing inclusive growth across Africa: Recognizing Africa's informal sector, Tunis. https://www.afdb.org/en/blogs/afdb-championing-inclusive-growth-across-africa/post/recognizing-africas-informal-sector-11645.

African Economic Outlook. 2017. Entrepreneurship and industrialisation, African Development Bank, OECD, United Nations Development Programme, Abidjan, Paris and New York.

African Union Commission. 2018. African continental free trade area gathers strong impetus to boost economic growth, Press release N.XX/2018, Addis Ababa.

Amoako, I.O. 2012. Trust in exporting relationships: The case of SMEs in Ghana. Published PhD thesis, Center for Economic and Enterprise Development Research (CEEDR) Middlesex University, London, http://eprints.mdx.ac.uk/12419/.

Amoako, I.O., and F. Lyon. 2011. Interorganizational trust violations and repairs in a weak legal environment: The case of Ghanaian exporting SMEs. In *Conference paper presented at the 27th European Group for Organisation Studies (EGOS) Conference*, Gothenburg University, Sweden, July.

———. 2014. We don't deal with courts: Cooperation and alternative institutions shaping exporting relationships of SMEs in Ghana. *International Small Business Journal* 32 (2): 117–139.

Amoako, I.O., and H. Matlay. 2015. Norms and trust-shaping relationships among food – Exporting SMEs in Ghana. *The International Journal of Entrepreneurship and Innovation* 16 (2): 123–124.

Amoako, I. O., Akwei, C., & Damoah, I. S. (2018, forthcoming). "We know their house, family and work place": Trust in entrepreneurs' trade credit relationships in weak institutions. *Journal of Small Business Management.* https://doi.org/10.1111/JSBM.12488.

Bachmann, R., N. Gillespie, and R. Priem. 2015. Repairing trust in organizations and institutions: Toward a conceptual framework. *Organization Studies* 36 (9): 1123–1142.

BBC News. 2018. May in Africa: UK Prime Minister's mission to woo continent after Brexit (28 August 2018). http://bbc.co.uk/news/world-Africa-45298656

Besharov, M.l., and W.K. Smith. 2014. Multiple institutional logics in organizations: Explaining their varied nature and implications. *Academy of Management Review* 39K: 364–381.

Blerk, H. 2018. IPSOS NEWS: African Lions: Africa's rising middle class?, IPSOS, SA.

Braun, V., and V. Clarke. 2006. Using thematic analysis in psychology. *Qualitative Research in Psychology* 3: 77–101.

Bruton, G.D., D. Ahlstrom, and H.L. Li. 2010. Institutional theory and entrepreneurship: Where are we now and where do we need to move in the future? *Entrepreneurship Theory and Practice* 34 (3): 421–440.

Burns, J., and R. Scapens. 2000. Conceptualizing management accounting change: An institutional framework. *Management Accounting Research* 11: 3–25.

Chell, E. 2000. Towards researching the opportunistic entrepreneur: A social constructionist approach and research agenda. *European Journal of Work and Organizational Psychology* 90 (1): 63–80.

Child, J., and Rodrigues. 2007. The process of SME internationalisation: British firms entering Brazil, E&G Economia e Gestao. *Belo Horizonte* 7 (14): 1–178.

Child, J., S.H. Ng, and C. Wong. 2002. Psychic distance and internationalization: Evidence from Hong Kong firms. *International Studies of Management and Organization* 32 (1): 36–56.

Curran, J., R.A. Blackburn, and J. Kitching. 1995. *Small businesses, networking and networks: A literature review, policy survey and research agenda*. Kingston upon Thames: Kingston University/Small Business Research Centre.

Damoah, I.S., C.A. Akwei, I.O. Amoako, and D. Botchie. 2018. Corruption as a source of government project failure in developing countries: Evidence from Ghana. *Project Management Journal* 49 (3): 17–33.

Delloitte. 2014. The Delloitte consumer review Africa: A 21st century view. London: Delloitte.

Denzin, N.K. 1978. The logic of naturalistic inquiry. In *Sociological methods—A sourcebook*, ed. N.K. Denzin, 54–73. New York: McGraw-Hill.

Dietz, G., N. Gillespie, and G.T. Chao. 2010. Unravelling the complexities of trust and culture. In *Organizational trust: A cultural perspective*, ed.

M.N.K. Saunders, D. Skinner, G. Dietz, N. Gillespie, and R.J. Lewicki. Cambridge: Cambridge University Press.

Durand, R., B. Szostak, J. Jourdan, and P. Thornton. 2013. Institutional logics as strategic resources. In *Institutional logics in action*, part A (Research in the sociology of organizations, volume 39 part A), eds. Lounsbury, M., Boxenbaum, E., 165–201. Bingley: Emerald Group Publishing Limited.

Estrin, S., and M. Pervezer. 2011. The role of informal institutions in corporate governance: Brazil, Russia, India, and China compared Asia Pacific. *Journal of Management* 28 (1): 41.

Friedland, R., and R.R. Alford. 1991. Bringing society back in: Symbols, practices, and institutional contradictions. In *The new institutionalism in organizational analysis*, ed. W.W. Powell and P.J. DiMaggio. Chicago: University of Chicago Press.

Gartner, W.B. 1988. Who is the entrepreneur? Is the wrong question. *American Journal of Small Business* 12: 11–32.

George, G., J.N.O. Khayesi, and M.R.T. Haas. 2016. Bringing Africa in: Promising directions for management research. *Academy of Management Journal* 59 (2): 377–393.

Granovetter, M.S. 1985. Economic action and social structure: The problem of embeddedness. *American Journal of Sociology* 91 (3): 481–510.

Heine, B., and D. Nurse. 2000. *An introduction in African languages*. Cambridge: Cambridge University Press.

Jackson, T., K. Amaeshi, and S. Yavuz. 2008. Untangling African indigenous management: Multiple influences on the success of SMEs in Kenya. *Journal of World Business* 43 (3): 400–416.

Li, P.P. 2016. The holistic and contextual natures of trust: Past, present and future research. *Journal of Trust Research* 6 (1): 1–6.

Lituchy, T.R., B.J. Punnet, and B.B. Puplampu. 2013. *Management in Africa: Macro and micro perspectives*. London: Routledge.

Mashanda, T. 2017. Rethinking the term sub Saharan Africa, The Herald, Harare. http://www.herald.co.zw/rethinking-the-term-sub-saharan-africa/.

McMillan, J., and C. Woodruff. 2002. The central role of entrepreneurs in transition economies. *Journal of Economic Perspectives* 16: 153–170.

Möllering, G. 2006. *Trust: Reason, routine, reflexivity*. Amsterdam: Elsevier.

North, D.C. 1990. *Institutions, institutional change and economic performance*. Cambridge: Cambridge University Press.

Peng, M.W., D.Y.L. Wang, and Y. Jiang. 2008. An institution-based view of international business strategy: A focus on emerging economies. *Journal of International Business Studies* 39: 920–936.

Putnam, R.P. 1993. *Making democracy work: Civic traditions in modern Italy.* Princeton: Princeton University Press.

Ren, H., and B. Gray. 2009. Repairing relationship conflict: How violation types and culture influence the effectiveness of restoration rituals. *Academy of Management Review* 34 (1): 105–126.

Sarason, Y., T. Dean, and J.F. Dillard. 2006. Entrepreneurship as the nexus of individual and opportunity: A structuration view. *Journal of Business Venturing* 21: 286–305.

Saunders, Mark, Skinner Denise, Gillespie Nicole, Dietz Graham, and Lewicki Roy. 2010. *Organization trust – A cultural perspective.* New York: Cambridge University Press.

Scott, W.R. 2013. *Institutions and organizations: ideas, interests and identities.* 4th ed. Thousand Oaks: Sage.

Shane, S. 2003. *A general theory of entrepreneurship.* Northampton: Edward Elgar.

Shane, S., and S. Venkataraman. 2000. The promise of entrepreneurship as a field of research. *Academy of Management Review* 25 (1): 217–226.

Smallbone, D., and F. Welter. 2013. Entrepreneurship in emerging market economies: Contemporary issues and perspectives. *International Small Business Journal* 0 (0): 1–4.

Tavory, I., and S. Timmermans. 2014. *Abductive analysis: Theorizing qualitative research.* Chicago: University of Chicago Press.

The Economist. 2016. Special Report: Business in Africa, 1.2 billion opportunities. http://www.economist.com/news/special-report/21696792-commodity-boommay-beover-andbarriers-doing-business are-everywhere-africas.

Thornton, P.H. 2004. *Markets from culture: Institutional logics and organizational decisions in higher education publishing.* Stanford: Stanford University Press.

Thornton, Patricia H., William Ocasio, and Michael Lounsbury. 2012. *The institutional logics perspective: A new approach to culture, structure and processes.* Oxford: Oxford University Press.

Tillmar, M., and L. Lindkvist. 2007. Cooperation against all odds. Finding reasons for trust where formal institutions fail. *International Sociology* 22 (3): 343–366.

Vickers, I., F. Lyon, L. Sepulveda, and C. McMullin. 2017. Public service innovation and multiple institutional logics: The case of hybrid social enterprises providers of health and wellbeing. *Social Policy* 48: 1755–1768.

Welter, F., and D. Smallbone. 2006. Exploring the role of trust in entrepreneurial activity. *Entrepreneurship Theory & Practice* 30 (4): 465–475.

————. 2006. Exploring the role of trust in entrepreneurial activity. *Entrepreneurship Theory and Practice* 35 (1): 165–184.

Welter, F., and F. Smallbone. 2011. Institutional perspectives on entrepreneurial behaviour in challenging environments. *Journal of Small Business Management* 49 (1): 107–125.

Welter, F., T. Kautonen, and M. Stoycheva. 2004. Trust in enterprise development, business relationships and business environment – A literature review. In *Entrepreneurial strategies and trust: Structure and evolution of entrepreneurial behaviour in low trust and high trust environments in East and West Europe, part 1a review*, ed. H.H. Hohmann and F. Welter, 13–25. Bremen: Forschungsstelle Osteuropa.

Willis, J.W. 2007. *Foundations of qualitative research: Interpretive and critical approaches*. London: Sage.

World Bank Doing Business. 2018. Database accessed, May 2018. http://www.doingbusiness.org.

World Economic Forum. 2018. These will be Africa's fastest growing economies in 2018. http://www.we.forum.org/agenda/2018/01/what-does02018-hold-for-african-economies.

Wu, W., M. Firth, and O.M. Rui. 2014. Trust and the provision of trade credit. *Journal of Banking & Finance* 39: 146–159.

Yanga, M.L., and I.O. Amoako. 2013. Legitimizing dishonesty in organizations: A survey of managers in four Sub-Sahara African countries. In *(Dis)Honesty in management*, Advanced series in management, ed. Tiia Vissak and Maaja Vadi, vol. 10, 243–268. Bingley: Emerald Group Publishing Limited.

Yin, R. K. 2016. *Qualitative research from start to finish*, 2nd ed., 386 pp. New York: The Guilford Press. ISBN: 978-1-4625-1797-8.

Zaheer, A., and D. Kamal. 2011. Creating trust in piranha-infested waters: The confluence of buyer, supplier and host country contexts. *Journal of International Business Studies* 42: 48–55.

Zaheer, A., B. McEvily, and V. Perrone. 1998. Does trust matter? Exploring the effects of interorganizational and interpersonal trust on performance. *Organization Science* 9 (2): 141–159.

Zain, M., and S.I. Ng. 2006. The impact of network relationships on SME's internationalization process. *Thunderbird International Business Review* 48 (2): 183–205. https://doi.org/10.1002/tie.20092.

Zucker, L.G. 1986. Production of trust. Institutional sources of economic structure, 1840–1920. *Research in Organisation Behaviour* 8: 53–11.

Part I

Theories of Institutions, Trust and Their Impact on Entrepreneurship

2

Institutions and Entrepreneurial Relationship Development

2.1 Introduction

Institutional theory has been used since the 1990s to account for the influences of context on entrepreneurship (Bruton et al. 2010). Institutionalists explain that the appropriateness and activities of institutions heavily influence the development of entrepreneurship, entrepreneurial behaviour, and enterprise strategies adopted in any country (North 1990; Welter and Smallbone 2011). Institutions provide the incentives structures, opportunities, and constraints for entrepreneurs (North 1990; Boettke and Coyne 2009; Aidis et al. 2012). North (1990) proposes that institutions can be formal and informal. Formal institutions include: government policies that ensure economic freedom and secure property rights; fair taxation; a fair legal/judicial system and contract enforcement; and enterprise support institutions that offer advice, training, and financial support to start-ups, which all promote entrepreneurship (Sobel 2008; Reynolds et al. 1999). Yet, formal institutions only function successfully if individuals develop a basic level of trust in the reliability of exchanges, and in sanctions and penalties prescribed. Hence,

© The Author(s) 2019
I. O. Amoako, *Trust, Institutions and Managing Entrepreneurial Relationships in Africa*,
Palgrave Studies of Entrepreneurship in Africa,
https://doi.org/10.1007/978-3-319-98395-0_2

a consistent institutional framework requires both personal and institutional trust (Welter 2002). Informal institutions include codes of conduct, conventions, attitudes, values, and norms of behaviour. Broadly, culture and social relations constitute institutions (Thornton et al. 2011; Granovetter 1985). Thornton et al. (2011) assert that formal institutions are subordinate to informal institutions because the development of formal institutions is deliberately meant to structure the interactions of a society in tandem with the norms and values that make up the informal institutions. They argue further that this explains why attempts by policy makers to change formal institutions of society without efforts to change the informal institutions in compatible ways attain only marginal success.

Yet, Western literature, donor reviews, and policy documents that explore enterprise and economic activities in emerging economies, including Africa, ignore the important roles of informal institutions and instead emphasise that strong formal institutions are the prerequisites for enterprise and economic development. According to this view, entrepreneurs and investors are deterred from investing in emerging economies, particularly in Africa, due to weak formal institutions (see Bruton et al. 2010; World Bank 2018; The Economist 2016). However, these assumptions draw mainly from models in advanced economy contexts and do not fully reflect the nature and role of institutions in entrepreneurship in emerging economy contexts. In emerging economy contexts, the reliability of formal institutions and their prescribed sanctions and penalties is weak and hence institutional trust is low. As a result, informal institutions assume more importance and often substitute for and replace ineffective formal institutions leading to enhanced trust and entrepreneurship (see Welter and Smallbone 2011; Peng et al. 2008; Amoako and Lyon 2014; Estrin and Pervezer 2011). The embeddedness approach to the study of institutions and entrepreneurship highlights that entrepreneurs and firms' activities are connected to local contexts and often entrepreneurs rely on their embeddedness in formal and indigenous institutions to develop trust in relationships in order to develop businesses (Baumol and Strom 2007; Welter and Smallbone 2011). Embeddedness implies that individuals and organisations affect and are affected by their social contexts (Granovetter 1985). As a result, entrepreneurs exploit opportunities embedded in institutional environments by developing a variety of social and business networks that is built on trust and cooperation (Chell 2007; Thornton et al. 2011). Hence, entrepreneurs in emerging economies as actors do not necessarily succumb to institutional weaknesses but rather, as actors, they respond strategically and reflexively to do business in the midst of formal institutional weaknesses (see Peng et al. 2008; Vickers et al. 2017). For example, Wu et al. (2014) show that in China, where formal market institutions are weak, state controlled-listed firms receive preferential treatment when borrowing from the banks. In response, private sector organisations rely on trust in networks and ties to access trade credit from suppliers and customers. Thus, trust in social institutions enables entrepreneurs of private firms to overcome institutional barriers in financing their activities. Amoako and Lyon (2014) also show that in Ghana entrepreneurs owning and managing internationally trading small and medium-sized enterprises (SMEs) avoid the courts due to the weaknesses of the legal systems and instead rely on trust and relationships in indigenous institutions, such as trade associations, to resolve disputes and enhance trade in local and West African markets. Hence the entrepreneur's networks, relationships, and trust development enhance access to resources for smaller businesses operating in the context of weak institutions (Welter and Smallbone 2011; Wright et al. 2007).

Yet, existing entrepreneurship studies rarely present a balanced view of how entrepreneurs as agents respond to institutional constraints without unnecessary conformity and habitual behaviour. The lack of a balanced view, however, reflects a persistent debate in the social sciences about structure and agency. Structure broadly refers to 'society' and agency to the 'individual' and scholars regard them mainly as incompatible (see Giddens 1979). Some scholars take a structuralist view to explain human behaviour based on factors such as history, culture, institutions, and social class operating at the macro level and the level of analysis is society. Others take exception and instead take agency explanations as definitive, arguing that the human agent is the main actor and interpreter of social life hence the individual characteristics, goals, and beliefs form the basis of the analysis (see Elster 1982).

In the context of entrepreneurship, one group of studies focuses on agency and how individuals as heroes embark on the entrepreneurial process and thereby pays less attention to social cultural institutions, including networks and trust, that facilitate entrepreneurship (see Chell 2007).

In contrast, another stream of studies is based on how structure-institutions constrain or enable entrepreneurship while ignoring the role of the individual or organisation whose agency or actions create, maintain or change institutions (see Lawrence et al. 2011). Interestingly, the debate on institutions and entrepreneurial agency becomes more puzzling in the context of emerging economies such as Africa due to existing conceptual developments that are based mainly on assumptions about how formal institutions act as constraints or enablers while paying little attention to the role of cultural institutions and the entrepreneur (see Amoako and Matlay 2015).

In this book, the author argues that ignoring part of structure (informal institutions) or agency (entrepreneur) in the debate on entrepreneurship in emerging economies may lead to misplaced practices and policies that may focus on only the formal institutions that are weak. Such practices may not be as effective as those that consider both formal and informal institutions and the entrepreneur.

In this chapter, the author attempts to marry the structure and agency divide in entrepreneurship by re-examining how institutions shape entrepreneurial activity. To do so, he reviews the literature on institutionalist approaches to entrepreneurship to emphasise the role of formal institutions and informal institutions, particularly how culture and networks influence entrepreneurial strategy and decision making. Institutions are defined as the 'taken-for granted assumptions which inform and shape the actions of individual actors…at the same time, these taken-for-granted assumptions are themselves the outcome of social actions' (Burns and Scapens 2000: 8).

Drawing on the structure agency debate, the author attempts to put both the entrepreneur and cultural institutions back into the debate on entrepreneurship and thus answer the key question: 'What are institutions and how do they influence trust development in entrepreneurial relationships?'

This chapter shows that formal institutions such as legal systems and informal institutions such as culture, cognition, values, attitudes, norms and social networks, social capital, and trust impact entrepreneurship. Specifically, this chapter highlights that entrepreneurship involves the entrepreneur who as an actor draws on institutions to recognise opportunity and formulate strategy by building network relationships and trust to access resources in order to develop and grow a (SME) business.

This chapter contributes to theory, practice, and policy as it offers a balanced approach to the study of entrepreneurship by recognising the role of formal institutions while not underestimating the indigenous cultural institutions, the entrepreneur and social capital, and networking and trust, which are all very important to the entrepreneurial process.

The rest of the chapter is organised in the following manner. The next section (Sect. 2.2) examines the importance and nature of institutions. Section 2.3 looks at formal and informal institutions and how they influence entrepreneurship. Section 2.4 reviews the concepts of social networks and social capital and shows how networks, relationships, and trust enable the entrepreneur to mobilise resources for the entrepreneurial process. Section 2.5 discusses the attributes and role of the entrepreneur and nature and processes of entrepreneurship. Section 2.6 focuses on institutions and entrepreneurial relationships development in Africa. Section 2.7 re-examines institutions and entrepreneurship based on the institutional logics approach and Sect. 2.8 presents the conclusion.

2.2 Institutions: Why Are They Important and What Are They?

Institutions are very important as they influence the nature and level of entrepreneurship and trust in any country or region (North 1990; Welter 2011). The differences in institutions may remain a key factor in the differences in wealth and prosperity across different economies and countries and this is attributed to a number of reasons: institutions spur economic development through limiting costs of transactions, enhancing property rights based on the rule of law, reducing inequalities and oppression by the elites, and enhancing cooperation and social capital. Institutions limit costs by enhancing contracts, contract enforcement, and increased availability of information, all of which in turn reduce risk and uncertainty (Coase 1991). Reliable institutions enhance good returns on investment and property rights (North 1990). Institutions provide trust to entrepreneurs and investors who take risk by investing time and money in ventures in anticipation of the rewards that they can reap in future. These activities require long-term commitments and if entrepreneurs and investors do not have trust in the security of their investments, rewards, and profits, as there is no reliable institutional environment characterised by security and legal systems that prevent criminals or authoritarian rulers from seizing their assets, then they will be unlikely to invest (Estrin et al. 2013). Furthermore, institutions influence the scope of oppression and expropriation of resources by elites by reducing the dominance of powerful elites who dominate economic exchanges and thereby limit economic development (Birdsall et al. 2005). Institutions also enhance networks, social relationships, and social capital by promoting greater interactions, the free flow of information, and the formation of associations, all of which increase the level of trust (Putnam 1993).

Institutions formal, social and cultural confer legitimacy (Di Maggio and Powell 1983; Di Maggio 1988). Regulatory legitimacy requires firms to operate in accordance with the regulatory standards, rules, and laws that confer good citizenship on firms. Regulatory bodies include governments, trade associations, and professional bodies that set the 'rules of the game' and can therefore impose sanctions when expectations are not met (Scott 2003). Similarly, normative institutions are well-accepted, non-statutory, authority systems that actions of organisations and individuals must conform to (Scott 1995), and professions and industries develop norms that guide behaviour. Legitimacy confers many benefits including social worthiness, prestige, stability, social support, attraction of staff, survival capabilities, and mobilisation of resources (Di Maggio and Powell 1983; Di Maggio 1988; Oliver 1991). In the context of entrepreneurship, legitimacy refers to congruence between the culture and social values associated with the activities of an entrepreneurial firm and the norms of acceptable behaviour in the society in which the firm operates (Suchman 1995). Legitimacy therefore confers trust on entrepreneurs and businesses. The framework (Fig. 2.1) suggests that institutions shape entrepreneurs' social networks, relationships, trust, and entrepreneurship but the question is: 'What are institutions?' To provide answers, the next section examines the economic and sociological approaches to the study of institutions and entrepreneurship.

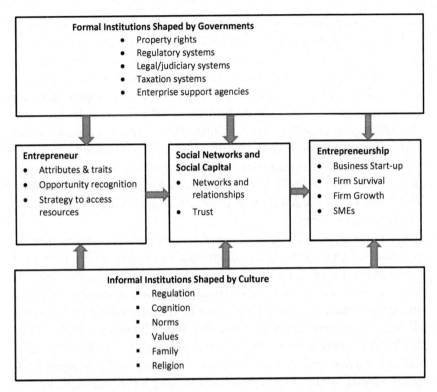

Fig. 2.1 Institutions influencing the entrepreneur and entrepreneurship. (Source: Own research)

2.3   Formal Institutions and Entrepreneurship

North (1990) is one of the key contributors to our understanding of institutions. North (1990) emphasises that the types of institutions and their quality influence how the members of a community attain their economic aspirations, entrepreneurship, and the growth of the economy (North 1990). North (1991) defines institutions as the humanly devised constraints that define political, economic and social interaction. Institutions constitute 'the rules of the game in a society, or more formally, are the humanly devised constraints that shape human interaction'. Institutions evolve incrementally over time and link the present to the past as well as the future, hence the performance of economies is path dependent on the past. According to North (1991) there are formal and informal institutions. Formal institutions include explicit regulations and rules such as constitutions, laws, economic rules, property rights, and contracts, all of which are written down. Formal institutions reduce risks and lower transaction costs for entrepreneurs (Baumol 1990). Institutions 'affect the performance of the economy by their cost on exchange and performance' (North 1991), and organisations and entrepreneurs are the players (North 1993). The institutional environment is the set of fundamental political, social, and legal ground rules that establishes the basis for production, exchange, and distribution. This refers to the guidelines that constrain an individual's behaviour or 'the rules of the game'.

Government remains the key formal (state) institution in any country and studies suggest that the size of government and its ability to control corruption influence an individual's decision to become an entrepreneur (Aidis et al. 2012). Government's implementation of regulatory policy and systems such as taxation and a stable macroeconomic environment all facilitate entrepreneurship (Akimova and Schwodiauer 2005; Sobel 2008). Conversely, regulations that are cumbersome and characterised by red tape increase the transaction costs of starting and managing businesses (North 1990; World Bank 2013), and heavy tax burdens and excessive regulation may drive many micro and small businesses 'underground' into the informal economy (Sepulveda and Syrett 2007). Another area where government can facilitate incentives for enterprise development relates to the provision of direct support through private and public enterprise agencies to enhance financial and technical assistance essential for entrepreneurial development (North 1990; Welter and Smallbone 2003).

According to North (1990), informal institutions are the implicit rules such as values, norms, sanctions, taboos, customs, traditions, and codes of conduct, all of which generally evolve from the society's culture (North 1990), and constitute many of the rules that shape individual behaviour (Helmke and Lentsky 2003). Informal institutions as unwritten rules that contain the interpretations of formal rules accepted by society and culture also contribute to the enforcement of formal institutions (Welter 2002). Regarding entrepreneurship, informal institutions are important as they shape entrepreneurial opportunities and the acceptable behaviour within a society. Together with formal institutions, they determine transaction and production costs and ultimately the feasibility, legitimacy, and profitability of enterprises. Together, formal and informal institutions provide the incentive structure of an economy which in turn influences the organisations that come into existence, the rewards and incentives that are available, and the direction of economic changes towards decline, stagnation, or growth (Etzioni 1987; North 1991).

Yet, there is a fundamental difference between institutions in advanced and emerging economies (Peng 2003; Smallbone et al. 2014). Predictable and strong governments, regulatory regimes, and legal systems that are taken for granted in developed countries are often lacking in emerging countries (Peng 2003; Amoako and Lyon 2014). However, the economic approach emphasises the importance of formal institutions while paying less attention to informal institutions that play important roles in enhancing entrepreneurship in different contexts (Su et al. 2015). A review of the literature shows that a large number of entrepreneurship studies based on economic theory dominate at the national/state level. Based on such studies, a strong relationship has been established between entrepreneurship and job creation, innovation, and economic growth (e.g. Baumol and Strom 2007). Yet the mainstream economic approaches are underpinned by assumptions of agency and rationality based on which entrepreneurship and the development of trust in entrepreneurial relationships are viewed as rational choices, calculated conscious decisions related to reason (Coleman 1988). However, studies show that entrepreneurs are not always rational actors in their decision making in their search for opportunities or resources (Mitchell et al. 2004).

These concerns are partly addressed by sociological approaches to institutions that focus attention on the embeddedness of actors and how social relationships and cultural institutions influence entrepreneurial agency.

One of the key institutions that is important for entrepreneurship is an efficient judiciary/courts system that ensures compliance with contractual relationships and the absence of rent seeking by actors of the state through bribery and corruption. The case of the UK small claims courts shows how strong formal institutions enable entrepreneurs to seek redress in court without necessarily incurring too much cost. Interestingly, these types of courts are not available in most emerging economies and entrepreneurs have to rely on trust in social networks and indigenous institutions to resolve commercial disputes.

Case Study 2.1 The Small Claims Court and SMEs in the UK
In the UK, entrepreneurs, SMEs, and indeed individuals have the option of going down the small claims track in the circuit court to recover or make claims if the amount is worth £10,000 or less. Yet, there are other options for collecting money including going to the county court or the High Court that may require seeking legal advice. The small claims court enables individuals to make a claim for faulty goods, and faulty services from companies and service providers including builders, dry cleaners, or garages and to recover wages or debts owed. Generally, people do not use solicitors and the time limit for the breach is six years. As part of the process, the complainant must try to resolve the problem before going to court. Complainants can also use third parties to mediate and usually there is a fee for mediation. Defendants are required to reply within 14 days and the amount to be claimed determines the court fees. However, the process may last between a couple of weeks to several months before the payment is received.

2.4   Informal Institutions Shaped by Culture

Sociological institutionalist approaches put much emphasis on society and particularly culture, networks, and relationships. Scott (1995) explains that institutions are multifaceted, durable structures comprising symbolic elements, social activities, and material resources that exhibit stability and yet are subject to both incremental and discontinuous change. Scott (1995) and Kostova (1997) suggest that institutions are comprised of regulatory, normative, and cultural-cognitive forms.

Hence Sociological institutionalist approaches to the study of entrepreneurship posit that entrepreneurs and their firms are embedded in cultural contexts and, as a result, are not atomistic. Culture is defined as the set of shared values and beliefs that (Hofstede 1980) serve as 'the unwritten book with the rules of the social game that is passed on to newcomers by its members, nesting itself in their minds' (Hofstede and Hofstede 2005, 36). The focus is that cultural institutions—distinct from political, social, economic, and technological factors—influence the creation of new ventures in a given country (Thornton et al. 2011). Cultural practices reflect particular ethnic, social, economic, ecological, and political complexities in individuals that may lead to differences in attitudes and entrepreneurial behaviour (Wu et al. 2014).

A way to understanding culture at the level of the individual is the framework suggested by Triandis (1972) which proposes that a given culture comprises objective and subjective elements. Objective cultural elements refer to the observable characteristics of culture that are displayed by the individual such as language, religion, and demographic traits. In contrast, subjective elements of culture are not observable outwardly and include the values, beliefs, norms, and underlying assumptions that underpin a culture and the thoughts, feelings, and actions of the members of a particular culture show these elements. The subjective elements of culture refer to the internal cognitive and emotional manifestations of the objective elements of culture.

Chao and Moon (2005) also suggest that the complex 'mosaic' of different cultural identities can be categorised into three groups: the demographic (age, gender, ethnicity, and nationality), the geographical (emphasising the role of place and locale), and the associational (related to a range of social groupings such as family, employer, industry, professional group, education, or hobbies). In each of these identities, there are sets of common beliefs and norms that shape entrepreneurial behaviour and mental models (Altinay et al. 2014), and networks and relationships based on sets of meanings, norms, and expectations (Curran et al. 1995), and this will be explored in more detail later in this chapter.

Culture is important in the decision to create new business (Aldrich and Zimmer 1986). Culture may influence entrepreneurial activity through its impact on agency—personal traits, cognition, social norms, and the decision to create a business—and the nature of networks (Welter and Smallbone 2011; Thornton et al. 2011). Furthermore, societies that

have positive attitudes towards entrepreneurship and believe that entrepreneurs are well respected and that starting a business is a good career
choice impact positively on the development of entrepreneurship.
Conversely, societies that are characterised by authoritarian and hierar-
chical cultures that do not promote, reward, or honour self-made success
will not promote entrepreneurship development (GEM 2017).

Hofstede's (1980) studies offer insights into how national cultures may
shape entrepreneurial networks. His framework suggests that power
distance, individualism-collectivism, masculinity-femininity, and long-
term versus short-term orientation and uncertainty avoidance all affect
entrepreneurship and interfirm relationships. According to his framework,
power distance demonstrates the level of power between the lowest in
society and the most powerful in society, and how people accept these
positions. Individualism reflects how people make decisions; a strong,
integrated group mentality involving unyielding loyalty and unquestion-
ing authority or, on the other hand, a very individualistic-oriented mentality. Masculinity refers to the extent to which masculine values such as
competition, assertiveness, and success are emphasised when compared
with feminine values such as quality of life and warm personal relationships. Uncertainty avoidance reflects how society deals with ambiguity
and shows how members of a society may either feel comfortable or otherwise in situations that are not structured in a way that is familiar to
them. Long-term orientation is characterised by attributes such as thrift
and perseverance that are two key values whilst short-term orientated individuals may put the emphasis on respect for tradition and social obligations. Hayton et al. (2002) posit that high individualism, high masculinity,
low uncertainty avoidance, and low power distance facilitate entrepreneurship. Shane (1994), however, associates entrepreneurship with high
individualism and low uncertainty avoidance. Undoubtedly, Hofstede's
(1980) study offers useful insights into the impact of culture on the development processes of entrepreneurial relationships. However, regarding
Africa, critics argue that the evidence is not clear due to what Jackson
(2004, 8) calls 'the lack of cross-cultural insight and model building'.
Hofstede's congruence approach ignores the stark difference between the
Western philosophy of life and the African philosophy of life.

2.4.1   Regulatory Institutions

The regulatory aspects involve the setting of rules, monitoring and sanctioning rule breakers (Scott 1995), and offering rewards and punishments that shape future behaviour. The regulatory elements within a particular country are made up of laws, regulations, rules, and government policies that encourage certain behaviours while restricting others (Scott 1995; Veciana and Urbano 2008). These include the political systems, government policies that ensure economic freedom and secure property rights, fair taxation, a fair and balanced legal/judicial system, contract enforcement, and the availability of enterprise-supporting institutions that offer advice, training, and financial support to start-ups (Sobel 2008).

2.4.2   Cognition and Entrepreneurship

The cultural institutions also include cognition. Cognition refers to sets of knowledge that are part of a shared social understanding and culture underpins cognition or systems of thought, and how members of a society think and feel (Haralambos and Holborn 2000). The mental model is composed of shared characteristics such as attitudes, behaviours, values, beliefs, and norms that are formed.

'through socialisation over a period of years within a culture, leading to development of comparatively predictable responses to social situations that are common to a group of people and these shape social and economic relationships' (Morrison 2000). Socialisation begins in the environment—family, school, work—where a child is raised (Hofstede 1984). This shapes social and economic relationships (Morrison 2000).

Individual cognition remains a key element in the entrepreneurship process as an entrepreneur's personal attributes may set him or her apart from other people. The cognitive filters allow economic actors to process different information and the propensity to process information (Gibson et al. 2009) and cultural norms and values impact these processes. For example, in economies that regard risk taking and failure as part of the process of innovation, people accept that failure is a necessary part of the entrepreneurial journey (GEM 2017).

2.4.3   Normative Institutions and Entrepreneurship

Scott (1995) posits that normative aspects comprise social norms, values, beliefs, and assumptions about human nature and behaviour that individuals hold and share socially through culture. Norms provide guidelines that shape behaviour and define acceptable and appropriate behaviour in particular situations (Haralambos and Holborn 2000). Norms can be defined as 'expectations about behaviour that are at least partially shared by a group of decision makers' (Heide and John 1992, 34) or as informal institutions involving enforcement mechanisms that are built around culture: traditions, customs, moral values, religious beliefs, social conventions, and generally accepted ways of doing things (Zucker 1977; Scott 1995; North 1990). Norms develop over time and may differ across groups and cultures (Fukuyama 1999) through socialisation, particularly during childhood, over a period of years within a culture. This may lead to the development of comparatively predictable responses to social situations that are common to a group of people (Haralambos and Holborn 2000). Formal or informal positive and negative sanctions accompanied by potential rewards for compliance and sanctions for violations help to enforce norms. Thus, norms constitute a major part of social control (Haralambos and Holborn 2000). However, not all norms are desirable since strong reciprocity in a group may lead to hostility or aggression towards non-members. Keefer (2002) refers to 'clientalism' and explains that narrow-radius norms that overcome collective action problems within families, social classes, or ethnic groups may have a negative impact on non-members of such groups. For example, when the building of trust and cooperation among groups are segregated based on ethnicity, class or occupation this may lead to negative benefits to the larger society such as discouraging trust with other groups.

Norms and traditions enable or constrain entrepreneurship through, for example, entrepreneurial decision making (Dana 2010), nature, and forms of contracts (Macneil 1980), expectations, reciprocity, cooperation, and trust in personal and interorganisational networks and relationships

(Amoako and Matlay 2015; Lyon and Porter 2009). Yet, trust and cooperation among groups if segregated based on ethnicity, class or occupation may discourage trust with other groups and which may in turn lead to negative benefits to society. These issues are explored in more detail in subsequent chapters.

2.4.4   Values and Entrepreneurship

Values provide more general guidelines for conduct while norms provide specific guidelines for behaviour (Haralambos and Holborn 2000). Values have been defined as 'a type of belief, centrally located in one's total belief system, about how one ought or ought not to behave, or about some end-state of existence worth or not worth attaining' (Snow et al. 1996, 124) or as 'global beliefs about behavioural processes' (Connor and Becker 1975, 551). Values therefore define what is important and worthwhile, and worth striving for in a society (Haralambos and Holborn 2000). Values underline attitudes—the internal states that express, overtly or covertly, positive or negative evaluative responses to an object, person, or condition (Snow et al. 1996). Norms are expressions of values and both differ from society to society (Haralambos and Holborn 2000). Thornton et al. (2011) suggest that different societies draw on different cultural values to enhance or constrain economic behaviour and entrepreneurship. For example, societal perceptions of failure have many implications for risk taking and the level of entrepreneurial activity in any society (Baumol 1993). This in turn informs how entrepreneurs ascribe attributions for setbacks that may be experienced, and how they change their behaviours as a result. However, culture shapes regulation, cognition, norms and values.

2.4.5   Family and Entrepreneurship

The family remains one of the key institutions that influence entrepreneurship. The literature posits that a family can bring clear values, beliefs, and a focused direction into a business (Burns 2016; Aronoff and Ward 2000). Strong family values shape the performance of business in many ways including decision making, strategic planning, motivating family members and employees to work harder, and constantly challenging the business to renew and enhance conventional thinking and innovation. Furthermore, strong family values can enhance the reputation of the business and promote trust, inspiration, motivation, and commitment among employees (Tokarczyk et al. 2007). Yet, conflicts in family business arise when family and business cultures differ. While, on the one hand, family values emphasise loyalty based on emotion, caring, and sharing, on the other hand, family values can bring a lack of professionalism, nepotism instead of meritocracy, rigidity, and family conflict into the workplace (Schulze et al. 2001; Miller et al. 2009). In contrast, business culture is unemotional, task orientated and based on self-interest; it is outward looking, rewarding performance and penalising a lack of performance (Burns 2016). The African family institution emphasises communalism and is starkly different from Western culture that emphasises individualism and as a result the African family's impact on entrepreneurship often differs from the Western family's impact and this is explored in detail in Chaps. 4, 5, and 6.

2.4.6   Religion and Entrepreneurship

Religion is another important institution that influences entrepreneurship and Weber's (1904) seminal study established that there is a relationship between religious (Christian) values and the development of Western capitalism. Dana (2010) posits that religious values underpin both the environment and the entrepreneurial event. Interestingly, religion is the origin of business concepts such as visions and missions (Vinten 2000). Yet, the relationship between religion and entrepreneurship is complex (Drakopoulou Dodd and Seaman 1998).

At the micro level, religion influences the psychological state of the embedded entrepreneur. Personal belief systems and values influence business (Vinten 2000). In particular, beliefs influence decision making regarding ethics, strategy, leadership styles, and perhaps performance (Vinten 2000; Worden 2005). Religion also shapes the nature of entrepreneurial networks (Drakopoulou Dodd and Gotsis 2007; Dana 2010).

At the macro level, religion shapes national cultures that may in turn influence the behaviour of entrepreneurs. For example, religious values that encourage thrift and productive investment, honesty in economic exchanges, experimentation, and risk taking promote entrepreneurship (Dana 2010). Religion may also shape the social desirability and the propensity to become an entrepreneur (Drakopoulou Dodd and Gotsis 2007). Hence, religion strongly influences believers' economic activities. Consequently, the level of entrepreneurship between believers from different religions may differ (Zingales 2006).

2.5   Social Networks and Social Capital

Regarding entrepreneurship as a social phenomenon enables us to draw on the concepts of embeddedness to analyse how social networks and social capital influence the entrepreneurial process. The social embeddedness approach is significant because it contests the rational choice view that assumes that the entrepreneur is a hero whose resourcefulness enables him or her to mobilise resources to innovate and create value without recourse to social relations (Chell 2007). Figure 2.1 shows that networks and trust enable the entrepreneur to embark on entrepreneurship.

Granovetter's (1985) seminal work on embeddedness theorises that economic activities are embedded in networks of social relationships. He argues that embeddedness in networks enables entrepreneurs to perceive opportunity, generate ideas, and mobilise resources to innovate (Shane 2003; Chell 2007). Entrepreneurs draw on their strong ties from family and personal friendships and weak ties from business networks to access resources outside their firms (Granovetter 1985), hence economic relations are sustained by social networks built on kinship, friendship, trust, or goodwill. The network approach reasons that other actors in the entrepreneur's social and business relations influence their activities (Granovetter 1985). Donckels and Lambrecht (1995) define networks as the organised systems of relationships within an external environment. Networks with key stakeholders such as customers, suppliers, and facilitators, including banks, universities, and trade associations, are essential in providing resources including information, knowledge, expertise, finance, access to markets, and many others that are critical for the survival of start-ups. Networks and relationships may offer resources in overcoming the limitations of institutional weaknesses and of being small, new, or growing ventures (Peng et al. 2008; Wright et al. 2007; Burns 2016). Yet, culture underpins the nature of networks and relationships used by entrepreneurs and organisations based on sets of meanings, norms, and expectations (Curran et al. 1995).

Scholars of social capital focus on the relevance of relationships as a resource for social action (Nahapiet and Ghoshal 1998). Burt (1997) defines social capital as an asset inherent in social relations and networks. Some prior studies have equated specialised networks, norms, and trust with 'social capital' (Lyon 2000). Even though originally social capital was seen as relational resources of individuals within their personal ties that may be used for development, studies broadly conceptualise social capital as assets of resources embedded in social relationships (Burt 1992). Understanding social capital is important as the ability of entrepreneurs to recognise opportunity and generate ideas and strategies to mobilise resources for developing businesses and to innovate are shaped by their embeddedness in networks (Chell 2007). The concept of social capital is studied from two different perspectives: structural or rational choice and embeddedness or relational approaches (Anderson 2002). In the rational choice perspective, social capital is concerned with social interactions and refers to the sum of relationships within a social structure. In this approach, social capital refers to a resource that the rational actor uses for self-interested ends. The embeddedness or relational approach emphasises that in addition to individual freedom of action, there is a need for reciprocity and mutuality due to the impact of implicit rules and social mores in embedded contexts. Consequently, the relational approach focuses on the direct relationships of the entrepreneur to others, and the assets of trust and trustworthiness embedded in these relationships (Anderson 2002). This study draws on both rational choice and the relational approach to emphasise the importance of the development of networks, relationships and trust to entrepreneurship in emerging economies such as China and Africa.

Case 2.2 Quanxi: Indigenous Personal Connection That Drives Business in China

The importance of networking and trust in promoting entrepreneurship in emerging economy contexts is exemplified by the Chinese concept of

Quanxi, which is an informal personal connection between two individuals based on cultural-specific norms of information sharing, mutual commitment, loyalty, obligation, and reciprocity. Quanxi types differ between family members, friends like classmates, and among business partners who may be strangers. Quanxi development involves identifying with common social identities such as coming from the same hometown, same school, working in the same firm or through a third party with whom either party have a Quanxi. In the context of business, potential partners without a common social identity but having shared values and aspirations can also express an interest in developing a Quanxi. The development of networks is based on familiarisation through the exchange of favours such as gifts and mutual information sharing and reciprocity. There are socio-cultural norms of obligation, affection, feelings, and trust inherent in Quanxi and understanding and adhering to these expectations is critical for the development and maintenance of long-term businesses relationships in China.

Source: Informal interviews with an anonymised Chinese friend.

2.5.1 Institutions and Trust in Entrepreneurship

Trust is important in entrepreneurship (Welter 2005). Apart from facilitating the development of entrepreneurial networks and relationships, trust provides incentives and confidence to invest and do business in any given economy (North 1990; Zucker 1986). Yet, institutions provide the different forms of embeddedness that encourage or discourage trustworthy behaviour and this is important for entrepreneurship and the efficient operation of an economy (Welter and Smallbone 2006; North 1990). State institutions such as the competence or corruption of court officials, the tax system, and other incentives from the institutional environment (Zucker 1986; North 1990) provide the logics and the degree of trust and the ability to trust (Welter 2005).

Nonetheless, as argued throughout this book, in emerging economy contexts, the institutions that facilitate trust development differ from those in developed economies. In developed economies with strong institutions, trust can be based on for example the judicial/legal systems that are used to enforce contracts with individuals and partner firms. However, in emerging economies like India, China and Brazil (see Estrin and Prevezer 2011), and Africa (see Fafchamps 2004; Amoako and Lyon 2014), enterprise support institutions such as judiciary/legal systems are inadequate, and personal relationships underpinned by indigenous, social, cultural institutions rather than state and market institutions enhance trust development (Wu et al. 2014; Amoako and Matlay 2015). In emerging economy contexts, trust serves as a substitute for the incomplete institutional framework (Welter 2002), and trust in informal cultural institutions is important in facilitating entrepreneurship.

Yet, challenges arise where there is cultural difference between two parties due to dissimilar trust expectations and different behavioural rules in conflict situations (Zaheer and Kamal 2011; Ren and Gray 2009). In such cases, cross-cultural relationships can be limited by the inability to draw on common norms and expectations (Dietz et al. 2010). However, currently there is a lack of understanding on how institutional contexts and particularly culture shape specific trust drivers (Li 2016; Bachmann et al. 2015). In the context of entrepreneurship, entrepreneurial activities are linked to local contexts and the entrepreneur relies on their embeddedness on local institutions in order to develop trust, in networks and relationships to develop businesses (Baumol and Strom 2007; Welter and Smallbone 2011). This book contributes to bridging this gap by analysing the complex processes through which cultural norms shape the development of trust in entrepreneurial relationships in Africa. Chapter 3 will explore this issue in more detail.

In spite of the immense contributions of institutionalist approaches to the study of entrepreneurship, critics argue that the traditional economic and sociological institutionalist approaches pay more attention to context and little attention to the role of the entrepreneur as an individual. The approach is therefore criticised for over-socialising entrepreneurship (Chell 2007), and for vouching for deterministic approach by emphasising on how institutions constrain or enable entrepreneurship (see Elster 1982; Greenwood et al. 2008). To address these criticisms the next section reviews some of the approaches to entrepreneurship that focuses on agency.

2.6   The Entrepreneur and Entrepreneurship

Central to entrepreneurship are the activities of the individual actor or the entrepreneur who drives the entrepreneurial process. Entrepreneurs who focus their activities on innovation in products and production techniques play a vital role in economic growth, productivity, and increase in social welfare (Baumol and Strom 2007). Schumpeter (1934) is a pioneer academic in entrepreneurship and he argues that the activities of the entrepreneur as an actor creates new firms with entrepreneurial characteristics and these firms displace existing firms that are less innovative resulting in a higher degree of economic growth. Economic development occurs whenever the role of the entrepreneur leads to an increase in income over a specific period. The entrepreneur does new things or does things already done in a new way (innovation).

2.6.1   Attributes of the Entrepreneur

The dramatic achievements of some entrepreneurs lead to notions that entrepreneurs must be different from other people and so there has been keen interest in identifying what makes entrepreneurs creative, innovative, daring, aggressive, optimistic, leaders, dissatisfied with the status quo, and so on (Stevenson and Jarillo 1990; Schumpeter 1934). Psychological theories of entrepreneurship focus on analysing the personal characteristics associated with inclinations of the individual to be an entrepreneur. The key personality traits identified include the need for achievement, an internal locus of control, innovativeness, tolerance of ambiguity, and risk taking. Internal locus of control refers to a belief that the outcomes of our actions are contingent on what we do while external locus of control suggests that the outcomes of our actions are contingent on events outside of our control. Entrepreneurs and business owners exhibit a higher belief that they can control life's events than other sectors of the population (see Rauch and Frese 2000). Entrepreneurs have a drive to achieve and excel and Johnson (1990) found that there is a relationship between achievement motivation and the decision to become an entrepreneur. Entrepreneurs have a tolerance of ambiguity and that describes how individuals perceive and process information about ambiguous situations when faced with unfamiliar, complex issues (Mohar et al. 2007). However, the personality trait model is criticised for overemphasising rationality and portraying the entrepreneur as a rational, heroic individual while ignoring the role of institutions and therefore undersocialising entrepreneurship (Busenitz and Barney 1997).

2.6.2   Opportunity Recognition

The entrepreneur is the actor who recognises opportunity in the entrepreneurial process. Shane (2003) explains that the entrepreneurial process involves, first, the ability to perceive new opportunities that cannot be proved during the moment when action is taken. In this book, the author defines opportunity as a chance to exploit a given situation that may lead to starting or growing a business. Drucker (1985) is a prominent proponent of the opportunity-based theory of entrepreneurship and he disagrees with Schumpeter's (1934) assertions that entrepreneurial activities cause change. Instead, Drucker (1985) argues that entrepreneurs search for and exploit change as an opportunity. In this theory, the entrepreneur focuses on possibilities rather than problems created by change. This approach reaffirms Kirzner's (1997) theory of entrepreneurial alertness. The opportunities result from changes in the environment but are not out there as objective entities for everyone to see (Veciana and Urbano 2008). The discovery of business opportunities involves alertness and boldness and the entrepreneur who has the necessary idiosyncratic knowledge discovers the opportunities (Kirzner 1973; Veciana and Urbano 2008). Kirzner (1997) reiterates that an entrepreneur is one who perceives profit opportunities and initiates action to fill currently unsatisfied needs or to improve inefficiencies. To act means to discover opportunity during uncertainty. However, opportunity recognition is just the beginning and the entrepreneur needs to formulate a strategy to mobilise the necessary resources in order to translate idea into a business. In this book, the author draws on Schumpeter, Drucker and Kirzner's theories to argue that entrepreneurs' risk taking, boldness, and alertness to profit opportunities, enable them to build networks and trust-based relationships based on strategy to facilitate access to critical resources.

2.6.3   Strategy to Access Resources

Entrepreneurship draws on the resources based view (RBV) to theorise that availability and mobilisation of resources are critical for the entrepreneurial process (Barney 1991). Entrepreneurs utilise different strategies to mobilise resources needed to exploit opportunities for their firms. Entrepreneurial resources include ideas, motivation, information, capital, access to markets, skills and training, and the goodwill inherent in bureaucracy (Kristiansen 2004). The resources affect the start-up, survival, and growth of the firm. There are three main strategies used by entrepreneurs to access resources. First, entrepreneurs often rely on their own resources such as skills, and capital to finance their ventures. Second, entrepreneurs apply combinations of available, undervalued, and less utilised resources free or cheaply to exploit opportunities (Baker and Nelson 2005). Finally, entrepreneurs utilise their personal and business networks to access resources outside their firms (Granovetter 1985).

Consequently, critics of the agency perspective argue that by focusing on entrepreneurs as heroes and ignoring the context, important factors such as trust, networks, and relationships that are critically important for mobilising resources for the entrepreneurial process may be ignored (see Chell 2007).

In summary, this section shows that the entrepreneur's attributes and traits, alertness, opportunity recognition and strategy to access resources lead to entrepreneurship. Yet, the institutional environment and social capital, networks, and relationships and trust all mediate the process. The next sub-section reviews the literature on entrepreneurship.

Entrepreneurship

Entrepreneurship is vital for economic growth as it leads to new businesses, innovation, and job creation (Birch 1979; GEM 2016). Entrepreneurship is regarded as the fourth factor of production after land, labour, and capital (Acs 2006). The word entrepreneurship originates from the archaic French word 'entreprennoure' which originally referred to a manufacturer, a master builder, or a person who takes up a project (Herbert and Link 2006). Interestingly, while there is consensus on the role of entrepreneurship in economic development, there is no agreement on the definition of entrepreneurship (Kobia and Sikalieh 2010).

Yet, there are some well-known definitions. For example, Shane and Venkataraman (2000) define entrepreneurship as the discovery, evaluation, and exploitation of opportunities. Shane (2003) later defines entrepreneurship as the ability to mobilise entrepreneurial ideas and resources to develop businesses within a given context. Drawing on these two definitions, in this book, the author defines entrepreneurship as the ability to recognise and evaluate opportunity and mobilise resources to establish and grow a business in a given context. This definition integrates entrepreneurial action with context and the need to mobilise resources and grow a business.

Entrepreneurship remains complex because the term involves not only the process of starting up a business entity but also entrepreneurial behaviour, development, and growth or expansion of a business entity. Nonetheless, there is an important distinction between independent early-stage entrepreneurial activity by individuals starting and managing a business for their own account and risk, and the pursuit of opportunity within existing organisations known as intrapreneurship. Entrepreneurship therefore is a multidimensional concept that involves many different actors and several levels of analysis and, in this book, the author draws on Schumpeter, Drucker and Kirzner's theories to argue that entrepreneurs' risk taking, boldness, and alertness to profit opportunities, enable them to build networks and trust-based relationships that facilitate access to critical resources.

Schumpeter's (1934) theory regards entrepreneurship as a force of creative destruction through which new firms with entrepreneurial characteristics displace existing firms that are less innovative giving rise to a higher degree of economic growth (Katsikis and Kyrgidou 2008). Schumpeter was the first scholar to highlight the close relationship between entrepreneurship and innovation, and his concept of creative destruction explains how innovations disrupt technologies, sectors, and industries leading to economic growth. Entrepreneurship is widely regarded as a positive force in market economies (Saunders et al. 2010).

Schumpeter (1934) therefore links innovation to the entrepreneur and differentiates between five main types of innovation: introducing a good; introducing a new method of production; opening a new market; conquering a new source of raw materials; and reorganising an industry in a new way. However, Schumpeter's (1934) theory has been criticised due to assumptions of rationality. Baumol (1990) also contends that the main limitation of Schumpeter's theory is its silence on how government policy influences entrepreneurship. This is essential since institutional environments affect the structure of payoffs and the rules of the game (North 1990).

Entrepreneurship though has a dark side including entrepreneurial failure and other destructive impacts. Entrepreneurial failure is an integral part of the entrepreneurship process, yet there is no clear meaning of what constitutes entrepreneurial failure. Failure can be subjective or objective and even though academics rarely separate failure of the business and failure of the entrepreneur, they are not the same. This is because failure of a business may not necessarily mean failure of the entrepreneur, as an entrepreneur whose firm has failed may move on and establish a successful business. Conversely an entrepreneur may fail and yet the business may be taken over and be successful under a different entrepreneur (see Jenkins and McKelvie 2016; Saravasthy et al. 2013). Interestingly, prior studies have focused more on external logics that cause business failure rather than on the failure of the entrepreneur and the impact on the individual entrepreneur. Entrepreneurial failure can have very serious consequences on the entrepreneur including negative emotions and grief (Shepherd 2003) accruing from personal loss and at times can strain relationships. Other negative impacts include financial loss, loss of skills, loss of social capital, stigmatisation, and devaluation of entrepreneurs (Cardon et al. 2011),

Furthermore, entrepreneurship can be unproductive and in some cases destructive (Baumol 1990). Entrepreneurs can choose between productive ventures that create economic and social value and unproductive ventures in which rent-seeking behaviour reduces the incentive to engage in productive economic activities. Rent seeking can also involve lobbying, litigation, tax avoidance and evasion, monopoly, stealing and raiding productive inputs, as well as shadow venture activities such as drug dealing, prostitution, and corruption. Rent seeking can also lead to destructive activities based on the illegalities and damaging effects of entrepreneurial activities on society and on the environment.

The destructive nature of entrepreneurship is particularly manifest in emerging economies such as Africa due to the existence of weak formal institutions that cannot often enforce the law. For example, activities of some oil and mining companies are causing mass deforestation of tropical forests and the contamination of river bodies across Africa, although they operate legally. There are other forms of destructive entrepreneurship and these take the form of criminal and illegal activities across the continent even though there are regulations that seek to prevent these destructive activities.

Given the potential unproductive and destructive nature of entrepreneurship, recently there has been an upsurge in social entrepreneurship that seeks to enable businesses to achieve the triple bottom line (TBL) by creating economic, social, and environmental value. Increasingly, social entrepreneurs are using entrepreneurial problem solving, creativity, and innovation in addressing the social, economic, and environmental problems of society and creating social and environmental value while remaining profitable to ensure sustainability (Doherty et al. 2014). Social entrepreneurship is increasingly playing a vital role in the transformation of economies and society in Africa and globally.

In recent years, there has been a tendency to regard entrepreneurship as a broader phenomenon that manifests itself in entrepreneurial mindsets, attitudes, and behaviour in non-economic arenas (Cieślik 2017). For example, in the areas of higher education, health, public administration, and the voluntary/charity sectors and politics, entrepreneurship is about the deployment of entrepreneurial skills and creative thinking to solve endemic problems.

In spite of the emphasis on entrepreneurship as an activity carried out mainly by individual entrepreneurs, recently there has been an interest in 'teampreneurship' that involves individual entrepreneurs working and learning in teams. The model is developed and championed by Team Academy (Tiimiakatemia), a Finnish entrepreneurship education programme that started about 20 years ago. The core philosophy of the programme is that students as 'teampreneurs' learn better via self-determined learning through which teams establish a business (see Lehtonen 2013).

2.6.4 Entrepreneurship and SMEs

Apart from the institutional environment and the competencies of the entrepreneur or teampreneur, the organisational arrangements of the firm are also important for entrepreneurial success. However, entrepreneurship exists in both large and small firms yet, in this book, the emphasis is on SMEs. Within SMEs, there is a non-separation of entrepreneurship and the small firm (Hill 2001). Entrepreneurial processes may often result in a business start-up in the form of a small business or may take place in an existing small firm and the entrepreneur will own, manage and grow the small firm in the midst of uncertainty and risk. However, it is important to state that not all SME owners/managers are entrepreneurs (Drucker 1985). In this book, the owner/managers who are interviewed are regarded as entrepreneurs given their zeal in risk taking regarding building trust-based relationships to grow their SMEs.

The literature identifies the main reasons for the interest in the SME sector shown by researchers and governments. SMEs play a key role in the global economy (Franco et al. 2014) and are regarded as the backbone of many economies as they contribute to job creation and act as suppliers of goods and services for larger firms (Walsh and Lipinski 2009), as well as promoting innovation, economic stability, and development (Cunningham 2011). The ILO (2000) demonstrates that the SME sector contributes significantly to national development goals in diverse ways. These include linkages through horizontal and vertical integration, equitable growth across regions, mobilisation of savings and financial resources internally for productive enterprises, and as a seedbed for medium and large firms. Consequently, the International Labour Organization (ILO) has recognised SMEs as a mechanism for new employment opportunities.

SMEs affect local economies significantly. Their impact on local economies emanates from their utilisation of resources, information, and markets in their immediate environment (Romanelli and Bird Schoonhoven 2001). Furthermore, the venturing process draws ideas for new products and services, and new sources of customer demands for existing products, from the immediate environment (Aldrich and Wiedenmayer 1993). Informal networks enable entrepreneurs to raise finance (Aldrich 1999) and the provision of business support and advice may originate from the immediate environment (Bennet and Smith 2002). This dependence on the local environment has led academics to view entrepreneurship as contextualised and therefore embedded (Jack and Anderson 2002; Granovetter 1985).

Interestingly, there is no uniformly acceptable definition of SMEs (Burns 2016). No single definition could cover all the divergent industries, therefore academics and policy makers use different qualitative and quantitative criteria to define SMEs (Bolton Report 1971). There is also a lack of clarity about firms regarded as SMEs as different countries adopt different measures. For example, in the United States, an SME refers to a firm employing not more than 500 employees (Burns 2016); in the European Union, SMEs employ fewer than 250 people (EU 1996). Similarly, definitions vary among African countries. For example, an SME describes a firm employing not more than 20 employees in Tanzania, 50 in Malawi, and 100 in Ghana. Therefore, critics argue that the many definitions cause practical problems (Burns 2016). Particularly, the lack of clarity renders SME policy formulation difficult. Therefore, to enhance simplicity and practical application in this book, the author adopts the definition from the Ministry of Local Government and Rural Development in Ghana that regards firms employing less than 100 people as SMEs. This is because the data for the author's PhD was collected from Ghana based on this definition.

SMEs differ from large firms. Typically, they use simple systems and procedures that facilitate flexibility, immediate feedback, a short decision-making chain, better understanding, and quicker response to customer needs than larger organisations (Singh and Garg 2008). One of the distinctive features of SMEs is the dominant role of the entrepreneur in the decision-making process of the firm (Carson and Gilmore 2000). In spite of these advantages, SMEs are constrained when compared with large firms. SMEs have severe limitations of resources and lack management competencies (Fillis 2002). They lack resources—time, cash, and technology—and therefore are characterised by a short-term planning perspective, are likely to operate in a single market, and are over-reliant on a small number of customers (Barry and Milner 2002; Burns 2016). Due to lack of cash, SMEs have difficulties in achieving economies of scale in the purchase of inputs, such as equipment, raw materials, finance, and consulting services (Buckley 1997).

Given the constraints faced by smaller enterprises, scholars posit that the development of networks, relationships, and cooperation may mitigate the liabilities associated with being small (Wright et al. 2007; Burns 2016). Thus, social networks and social capital are hugely important to SMEs.

The next two sections re-examine the debates on institutions, the entrepreneur and entrepreneurship in Africa and attempt to marry the two perspectives by using the institutional logics perspective.

2.7   Institutions and Entrepreneurial Relationship Development in Africa

Reports and studies suggest that African countries are characterised by weak and unsupportive formal institutional environments (The Economist 2016; Bruton et al. 2010). The poor institutional environmental factors including political instability, poor infrastructure, poor macroenvironments, lack of access to capital and corruption impede growth and internationalisation of African businesses (Ibeh et al. 2012). Yet recently, there have been improvements in formal institutional environments in a number of African countries including Ghana, Nigeria, Angola, Rwanda, Tanzania, Zambia, and Ethiopia and these and many other countries in the continent offer opportunities to entrepreneurs and investors. Yet African governments can do more to stimulate entrepreneurship. Sriram and Mersha (2010) emphasise that in addition to the role of entrepreneurs, government policy can stimulate entrepreneurship development in Africa.

Traditionally, Africa's business opportunities have been linked to the trade and export of raw and non-value-added commodities such as gold, timber, oil, coal, tea, coffee, leather, palm oil, and many others which were mostly exploited by national governments and multinationals. However, currently Africa offers countless business opportunities in non-traditional sectors such as agriculture, food processing, banking, consumer goods, infrastructure, and telecommunications (Accenture 2010). There are also other emerging areas including transforming local waste into greener alternatives, renewable energy, real estate development, fashion, start-up funding, healthcare, education, creative industries, and so on. African entrepreneurs and investors can focus on these opportunities to stimulate the economy instead of a reliance on the traditional lifestyle businesses that constitute the majority of SMEs in the continent.

Not surprisingly, Africa is now home to many successful and well-known entrepreneurs including Aliko Dangote (manufacturing, Nigeria), Mo Ibrahim (telecommunication, Sudan), Apostle Kojo Sarfo (motor vehicles, Ghana) and Elon Musk (technology, South Africa). While these entrepreneurs are operating larger businesses, the continent is teeming with countless entrepreneurs owning and managing innovative SMEs that are transforming the enterprise and economic landscape in Africa and beyond.

Prior studies on entrepreneurship in Africa found that successful African entrepreneurs tend to be male, middle-aged, married with a number of children, and on average more educated than the general population (Kiggundu 2002). Nevertheless, other studies report higher numbers of female entrepreneurial involvement in Africa (e.g. Mead and Liedholm 1998; Nziku 2012) and current entrepreneurial profiles range from young, old, males and females, highly educated to illiterates, all with a quest and passion to make a difference even though the vast majority operate in lifestyle businesses that are less innovative.

Entrepreneurs and their SMEs operate in many sectors, including waste and sanitation, information and communication technology, health and social care, agriculture, agro processing, manufacturing, communications, fashion, tourism, hospitality, financial services, consultancy, and so on. These enterprises continue to make significant contributions to social, economic, technological, and environmental development in spite of the prevailing institutional voids.

While previous studies found government attitudes and societal values in some African countries such as Ghana, Sierra Leone, and Ethiopia to be unsupportive of entrepreneurship due to the underlying socialist values of governments and capitalist values of entrepreneurship (see Buame

1996; Kallon 1990), times have changed and currently there are positive attitudes towards entrepreneurship in African economies (Saheed and Kavoos 2016). For example, since the year 2000, there have been a number of initiatives to facilitate entrepreneurship in Ghana. Furthermore, in 2017 the Ghanaian government launched the Ministry of Business Development whose flagship programme is the National Entrepreneurship and Innovation Plan (NEIP) with an initial seed capital of $10 million which will be scaled up to $100 million through private sector development partners (GoG 2017). Similarly, in Sierra Leone, the government's Agenda for Change (2008–2012) and Agenda for Prosperity (2013–2017), among others, aim to provide business development and career advice and guidance to its youth (UNDP 2018).

While improvements in the formal institutional environment may partly explain why entrepreneurship is vibrant in Africa (see World Economic Forum 2018), it is also obvious that informal institutions such as cultural norms, changing attitudes, personal networks, and trade associations enable entrepreneurs owning and managing SMEs to develop trust in order to establish and grow business ventures. Yet, these institutions have received very little attention from researchers (Amoako and Lyon 2014; Amoako and Matlay 2015; Jackson et al. 2008). Not surprisingly, there is very little understanding about how African entrepreneurs develop trust in networks and ties to enable access to resources for undertaking entrepreneurship in the context of weak state institutions.

2.8 Re-examining Institutions and Entrepreneurship

Given the context-based rationality of institutions, critics have argued for further development of institutional theory to take into account cognitive foundations of entrepreneurial behaviour (Welter 2002). In response, notions of institutional logics that reject both macrostructural theories and individualistic, rational choice perspectives are proposed as a more balanced approach (Thornton et al. 2012; Friedland and Alford 1991). Thornton et al. (2012: 2) define institutional logics as the 'socially constructed, historical patterns of cultural symbols and material practices, including assumptions, values, and beliefs by which individuals and organisations provide meaning to their daily activity, organize time and space and reproduce their lives and experiences'. The institutional logics perspective also assumes that institutions are historically contingent (Friedland and Alford 1991). Thornton et al. (2012) suggest that Western societies are based on seven core societal institutions and their logics: family, religion, state, market, profession, corporation, and community.

The author draws from Thornton et al.'s (2012) institutional orders and their logics to categorise institutional orders whose logics influence trust development in Africa into two main groups, namely logics of state and market institutions, and logics of indigenous cultural institutions. While the logics of state and market institutions focus on state institutions, particularly the legal/court systems and enterprise facilitating bodies, the logics of indigenous cultural institutions of African societies include traditional judicial systems, trade associations, language, family/kinship, religion, gift giving, and punctuality.

The institutional logic approach enables the author to highlight how cultural dimensions both enable and constrain social action (Thornton and Ocasio 2008) and how actors use logics to interpret and make sense of the world while the logics offer resources for relationship building, identity construction, and decision making. Based on this perspective, entrepreneurs as organisational actors make strategic choices to shift the rules and the norms that influence organisational choice, behaviour, and the distribution of resources (Vickers et al. 2017; Thornton et al. 2012). Thus, the embedded actor does not necessarily succumb to institutional structures but instead, acts in ways to counter the constraints and taken-for-granted assumptions prescribed by institutions; hence this approach presents a balanced view between institutions and entrepreneurial action (Vickers et al. 2017).

Furthermore, the author argues that contrary to current assumptions that Africa's weak institutions make the continent unattractive for entrepreneurship, the development of networks, relationships, and trust enable entrepreneurs to establish and manage businesses successfully just as in China and other emerging economies where investors are keen to invest.

2.9   Conclusion

This chapter shows that institutions are very important for entrepreneurship and economic development in any country. Yet, it also highlights that while state and market institutions have an influence on entrepreneurship, cultural institutions such as cognition, norms, values, attitudes and social networks and trust also influence the entrepreneurial process. This chapter shows further that entrepreneurship involves the entrepreneur who as an actor draws on institutions to recognise opportunity, formulate strategy (Thornton et al. 2012), and develop networks, relationships, and trust to access resources.

This chapter shows that both formal and informal institutions are important for entrepreneurship and economic development. In mature market economies, strong state and market institutions enhance entrepreneurship. Yet, socio-cultural institutions also shape entrepreneurial behaviour even though the reports and literature do not often highlight them. Culture plays an important role in entrepreneurship due to its impact on cognition—norms, values, beliefs—and trust development in entrepreneurial networking. While current reports and assumptions about entrepreneurship emphasise the role of state and market institutions, in emerging countries where these institutions are weak, cultural institutions and trust enable entrepreneurs to embark on entrepreneurship.

This chapter also sheds light on the role of the entrepreneur. The entrepreneurial process starts with opportunity recognition and the formulation of a strategy by the entrepreneur to access resources from him or herself or from networks, relationships with friends and acquaintances, or family/kinship. By including the entrepreneur in Fig. 2.1, this chapter shows that both institutions and the entrepreneur, as an actor, play a role in the entrepreneurial process. It also shows that networks, relationships, and trust enable the entrepreneur to access resources. The framework is particularly useful in analysing entrepreneurship in emerging economy contexts where, in the absence of strong state and market institutions, entrepreneurs rely on social and business networks, and relationships that are based on trust in order to do business (see Wu et al. 2014; Amoako and Lyon 2014). This may explain why even though there are weak formal institutions in emerging economies such as China, India, and Africa, entrepreneurship is vibrant. Yet, there is very little understanding of how culturally specific institutions influence entrepreneurial activity in Africa and this gap will be addressed in Chap. 4.

This chapter contributes to knowledge by showing that entrepreneurship involves the role of state and market institutions, cultural institutions and the entrepreneur who as an actor develops networks, relationships, and trust in order to access resources to develop or grow businesses. By so doing, this chapter helps to avoid the under- or oversocialisation of entrepreneurship.

References

Accenture. 2010. Africa: The new frontier for growth. http://nstore.accenture.com/pdf/Accenture_Africa_The_New_Frontier_for_Growth.pdf.   Online Access 13 Feb 2012.

Acs, Zoltan. 2006. How is entrepreneurship good for economic growth? *Innovations: Technology, governance, globalization* 1 (1): 97–107.

African Economic Outlook. 2017. *Entrepreneurship and Industrialization.* Abidjan/Paris/New York: African Development Bank, OECD, United Nations Development Programme.

Aidis, Ruta, Saul Estrin, and Tomasz Marek Mickiewicz. 2012. Size matters: Entrepreneurial entry and government. *Small Business Economics* 39 (1): 119–139.

Akimova, I., and G. Schwodiauer. 2005. The effect of trust on the performance of Ukrainian SMEs. In *Trust and entrepreneurship, A West-East perspective*, ed. H.H. Hohmann and F. Welter. Cheltenham: Edward Elgar.

Aldrich, H.E. 1999. *Organisations evolving.* London: Sage.

Aldrich, H.E., and G. Wiedenmayer. 1993. From traits to rates: An ecological perspective on organizational foundings. *Advances in Entrepreneurship, Firm Emergence, and Growth* 1: 145–195.

Aldrich, H., and C. Zimmer. 1986. Entrepreneurship through social networks. In *The art and science of entrepreneurship*, ed. D. Sexton and R. Smilor. New York: Ballinger Publishing Co.

Altinay, L., M.N.K. Saunders, and C.L. Wang. 2014. The influence of culture on trust judgements in customer relationship development by ethnic minority small businesses. *Journal of Small Business Management* 52 (1): 59–78.

Amoako, I.O., and F. Lyon. 2014. We don't deal with courts: Cooperation and alternative institutions shaping exporting relationships of SMEs in Ghana. *International Small Business Journal* 32 (2): 117–139.

Amoako, I.O., and H. Matlay. 2015. Norms and trust-shaping relationships among food-exporting SMEs in Ghana. In Special issue on the competitiveness of SMEs in the food sector; Exploring possibilities for growth, ed. B. Quinn, A. Dunn, R. McAdam, and L. McKitterick. *International Journal of Entrepreneurship & Innovation* 16 (2): 123–134.

Anderson, R.B. 2002. Entrepreneurship and aboriginal Canadians: A case study in economic development. *Journal of Developmental Entrepreneurship; Norfolk* 7: 45–65.

Aronoff, C.E., and J.L. Ward. 2000. *Family business values: How to assure legacy of continuity and success*, Family Business Leadership Series, 12. Marietta: Business Owner Resources.

Bachmann, R., N. Gillespie, and R. Priem. 2015. Repairing trust in organizations and institutions: Toward a conceptual framework. *Organization Studies* 36 (9): 1123–1142.

Baker, T., and R. Nelson. 2005. Creating something from nothing: Resource construction through entrepreneurial bricolage. *Administrative Science Quarterly* 50: 329–366.

Barney, J.B. 1991. Firms resources and sustainable competitive advantage. *Journal of Management* 17: 99–120.

Barry, H., and B. Milner. 2002. SMEs and electronic commerce: A departure from the traditional prioritization of training? *Journal of European Industrial Training* 26 (7): 316–326.

Baumol, W.J. 1990. Entrepreneurship: Productive, unproductive, and destructive. *Journal of Political Economy* 98 (5): 893–921.

———. 1993. Formal entrepreneurship theory in economics: Existence and bounds. *Journal of Business Venturing* 8 (3): 197–210.

Baumol, W.J., and R.J. Strom. 2007. Entrepreneurship and economic growth. *Strategic Entrepreneurship Journal* 1: 233–237. https://doi.org/10.1002/sej.26.

Bennett, R., and J.C. Smith. 2002. The influence of location and distance on the supply of business advice. *Environment and Planning* 34: 251–270.

Birch, D.G.W. 1979. *The job generation process*. Vol. 302. Cambridge, MA: MIT Program on Neighborhood and Regional Change.

Birdsall, N.D., D. Rodrik, and A. Subramanian. 2005. How to help poor countries. *Foreign Affairs* 84 (4): 136–152.

Boettke, P.J., and C.J. Coyne. 2009. Context matters: Institutions and entrepreneurship. *Foundations and Trends in Entrepreneurship* 5 (3): 135–209.

Bolton, J.E. 1971. *Report of the committee of inquiry on small firms*, Cmnd. 4811, London: HMSO.

Bruton, G.D., D. Ahlstrom, and H.-L. Li. 2010. Institutional theory and entrepreneurship: Where are we now and where do we need to move in the future? *Entrepreneurship Theory and Practice* 34 (3): 421–440.

Buame, S.K. 1996. *Entrepreneurship: A contextual perspective. Discourses and praxis of entrepreneurial activities within the institutional context of Ghana.* Lund: Lund University Press.

Buckley, P.J. 1997. International technology transfer by small and medium-sized enterprises. *Small Business Economics* 9 (1): 67–78.

Burns, P. 2016. *Entrepreneurship and small business, start-up, growth and maturity.* 4th ed. London: Palgrave Macmillan.

Burns, J., and R.W. Scapens. 2000. Conceptualizing management accounting change: An institutional framework. *Management Accounting Research* 11 (1): 3–25.

Burt, R.S. 1992. The social structure of competition. In *Networks and organizations structure, form and action*, ed. N. Nohria and R.G. Eccles, 57–91. Boston: Harvard Business School Press.

———. 1997. The contingent value of social capital. *Administrative Science Quarterly* 42 (2): 339–365. https://doi.org/10.2307/2393923.

Busenitz, L., and J. Barney. 1997. Differences between entrepreneurs and managers in large organizations: Biases and heuristics in strategic decision-making. *Journal of Business Venturing* 12 (1): 9–30.

Cardon, M.S., C.E. Stevens, and D.R. Potter. 2011. Misfortunes or mistakes? Cultural sensemaking of entrepreneurial failure. *Journal of Business Venturing* 26 (1): 79–92.

Carson, D., and A. Gilmore. 2000. SME marketing management competencies. *International Business Review* 9: 363–382.

Chao, G., and H. Moon. 2005. A cultural mosaic: Defining the complexity of culture. *Journal of Applied Psychology* 90: 1128–1140.

Chell, E. 2007. Social enterprise and entrepreneurship: Towards a convergent theory of the entrepreneurial process. *International Small Business Journal 25 (1): 5–26.*

Cieślik, J. 2017. *Entrepreneurship in emerging economies: Enhancing its contribution to socio-economic development.* London: Palgrave Macmillan.

Coase, R.H. 1991. Contracts and the activities of the firms. *Journal of Law and Economics* 34: 451–452.

Coleman, J.S. 1988. Social capital in the creation of human capital. *American Journal of Sociology 94*: 95–120. https://doi.org/10.1086/228943.

Connor, P.E., and B.W. Becker. 1975. Values and the organization: Suggestions for future research. *Academy of Management Journal* 18: 550–561.

Cunningham, J.B. 2011. Defining entrepreneurship. *Journal of Small Business Management* 13: 159–179.

Curran, J., R.A. Blackburn, and J. Kitching. 1995. *Small businesses, networking and networks: A literature review, policy survey and research agenda.* Kingston upon Thames: Small Business Research Centre, Kingston University.

Dana, L.P. 2010. Introduction: Religion as an explanatory variable for entrepreneurship. In *Entrepreneurship and religion*, ed. L.P. Dana, 1–24. Cheltenham: Edward Elgar Publishing Ltd.

Dietz, G., N. Gillespie, and G.T. Chao. 2010. Unravelling the complexities of trust and culture in Saunders. In *Organizational trust: A cultural perspective*, ed. M.N.K. Saunders, D. Skinner, G. Dietz, N. Gillespie, and R.J. Lewicki, 3–41. Cambridge: Cambridge University Press.

DiMaggio, P.J. 1988. Interest and agency in institutional theory. In *Institutional patterns and organizations: Culture and environment*, ed. L.G. Zucker, 3–21. Cambridge, MA: Ballinger.

DiMaggio, P.J., and W.W. Powell. 1983. The iron cage revisited: Institutional isomorphism and collective rationality in organizational fields. *American Sociological Review* 48: 147–160.

Doherty, R., H. Haugh, and F. Lyon. 2014. Social enterprises as hybrid organizations. *A review and research agenda International Journal of Management Reviews* 16 (4): 417–436.

Donckels, R., and J. Lambrect. 1995. Networks and small business growth: An exploratory model. *Small Business Economics* 7: 273–289.

Drakopoulou Dodd, S., and G. Gotsis. 2007. The interrelationships between entrepreneurship and religion. *The International Journal of Entrepreneurship and Innovation* 8 (2): 93–104.

Drakopoulou, Dodd S., and P.T. Seaman. 1998. Religion and enterprise: An introductory exploration. *Entrepreneurship: Theory and Practice* 23 (1): 71–86.

Drucker, P.F. 1985. *Innovation and entrepreneurship.* New York: Harper and Row. Entrepreneurship: Theory and practice, 35 (1) (2011): 165–184

Elster, J. 1982. Marxism, Functionalism and Game Theory. *Theory and Society* 11: 453–482.

Estrin, S., and M. Prevezer. 2011. "The role of informal institutions in corporate governance:" Brazil, Russia, India, and China compared. *Asia Pacific Journal of Management* 28 (1): 41–67.

Estrin, S., J. Korosteleva, and T. Mickiewicz. 2013. Which institutions encourage entrepreneurial growth aspirations? *Journal of Business Venturing* 28: 564–580.

Etzioni, A. 1987. Entrepreneurship, adaptation and legitimation. *Journal of Economic Behaviour and Organization* 8: 175–189.

European Commission. 1996. *Definition of SMEs*. Information Society Directorate General, European Commission, Brussels.

Fafchamps, M. 2004. *Market institutions in Sub-Saharan Africa: Theory and evidence*. Cambridge: MIT Press.

Fillis, I. 2002. An andalusian dog or a rising star: Creativity and the marketing/entrepreneurship interface. *Journal of Marketing Management 18 Foreign Affairs* 84 (4): 136–152.

Franco, M., M.F. Santos, I. Ramalho, and C. Nunes. 2014. An exploratory study of entrepreneurial marketing in SMEs: The role of the founder-entrepreneur. *Journal of Small Business and Enterprise Development* 21 (2): 265–283.

Friedland, R., and R.R. Alford. 1991. Bringing society back in: Symbols, practices, and institutional contradictions. In *The new institutionalism in organizational analysis*, ed. W.W. Powell and P.J. DiMaggio, 17th ed., 232–263. Chicago: University of Chicago Press.

Fukuyama, F. 1999. *Social capital and civil society*. Fairfax: The Institute of Public Policy, George Mason University. October 1, 99.

GEM. 2017. *Global entrepreneurship monitor 2017*. http://www.gemconsortium.org/report. Accessed 5 Jul 2017.

Gibson, C.B., M. Maznevski, and B.L. Kirkman. 2009. When does culture matter? In *Handbook of culture, organizations, and work*, ed. R.S. Bhagat and R.M. Steers. Cambridge: Cambridge University Press.

Giddens, A. 1979. *Central problems in social theory: Action, structure and contradiction in social analysis*. Berkeley: University of California Press.

Global Enterprise Monitor. 2016/2017. Global Report 2016/17. Global Entrepreneurship Monitor. http://www.gemconsortium.org.

GOG. 2017. National Innovation and Entrepreneurship Plan (NEIP): A government of Ghana Initiative, Accra. http://neip.gov.gh/#!/up.

Granovetter, M.S. 1985. Economic action and social structure: The problem of embeddedness. *American Journal of Sociology* 91 (3): 481–510.

Greenwood, R., C. Oliver, K. Sahlin, and R. Suddaby, eds. 2008. *Sage handbook of organizational institutionalism*. London: SAGE.

Haralambos, M., M. Holborn, and R. Heald. 2000. *Sociology, themes and perspectives*. 5th ed. Collins: London.

Hayton, J.C., G. Gerard, and S.A. Zahra. 2002. National culture and entrepreneurship: A review of behavioural research. *Entrepreneurship Theory and Practice* 26 (4): 33–52.

Heide, J.B., and G. John. 1992. Do norms matter in marketing relationships? *Journal of Marketing* 56 (9): 32–44.

Helmke, G., and S. Levitsky. 2003. Informal institutions and comparative politics: A research agenda. *Perspectives on Politics* 2 (4): 725–740.

Herbert, R.F. and A. N. Link. 2006. Historical perspectives on the entrepreneur. [Online] Available http://libres.uncg.edu/ir/uncg/f/A_Link_Historical_2006. pdf. Accessed 4 Mar 2014.

Hill, J. 2001. A multidimensional study of the key determinants of effective SME marketing activity: Part 2. *International Journal of Entrepreneurial Behaviour, Research* 7 (6): 211–235.

Hofstede, G. 1980. *Culture's consequences: International differences in work related values*. Beverly Hills: Sage.

———. 1984. *Culture's consequences*. Newbury Park: Sage.

Hofstede, G., and G.J. Hofstede. 2005. *Cultures and organizations: Software of the mind*. 2nd ed. New York: McGraw-Hill.

Ibeh, K., J. Wilson, and A. Chizema. 2012. The internationalization of African firms 1995-2011: Review and Implications. *Thunderbird International Business Review* 54: 411–427.

ILO. 2000. *About GENPROM why a gender promotion programme?, ILO web site International Labour Office*.

Jack, S.L., and A.R. Anderson. 2002. The effects of embeddedness on the entrepreneurial process. *Journal of Business Venturing* 17 (5): 467–487.

Jackson, T. 2004. *Management and change in Africa: A cross-cultural perspective*. London: Routledge.

Jackson, T., K. Amaeshi, and S. Yavuz. 2008. Untangling African indigenous management: Multiple influences on the success of SMEs in Kenya. *Journal of World Business* 43 (3): 400–416.

Jenkins, A., and A. McKelvie. 2016. What is entrepreneurial failure? Implications for future research. *International Small Business Journal 34* (2): 176–188. https://doi.org/10.1177/0266242615574011.

Johnson, B.R. 1990. Toward a multidimensional model of entrepreneurship: The case of achievement motivation and the entrepreneur. *Entrepreneurship Theory and Practice* 14 (3): 39–54.

Kallon, K.M. 1990. *The economics of Sierra Leonean entrepreneurship*. Lanhan: University Press of America.

Katsikis, I.N., and L.P. Kyrgidou. 2008. Entrepreneurship in teleology: The variety of the forms. *International Journal of Entrepreneurial Behaviour & Research* 15 (2): 209–231.

Keefer, P. 2002. *Clientelism, credibility and democracy*. Washington, DC: The World Bank.

Kiggundu, M.N. 2002. Entrepreneurs and entrepreneurship in Africa: What is known and what needs to be done. *Journal of Developmental Entrepreneurship* 7 (3): 239–259.

Kirzner, Israel. 1973. *Competition and entrepreneurship*. Chicago: University of Chicago Press.

Kirzner, I.M. 1997. Entrepreneurial discovery and the competitive market process: An Austrian approach. *Journal of Economic Literature* 35 (1): 60–85.

Kobia, M., and D. Sikalieh. 2010. Towards a search for the meaning of entrepreneurship. *Journal of European Industrial Training* 34 (2): 10–127.

Kostova, T. 1997. Country institutional profiles: Concept and measurement. *Academy of Management Proceedings* 1997: 180–184.

Kristiansen, S. 2004. Social networks and business success. *American Journal of Economics and Sociology* 63 (5): 1149–1171.

Lawrence, T., R. Suddaby, and B. Leca. 2011. Institutional work: Refocusing institutional studies of organization. *Journal of Management Inquiry* 20 (1): 52–58.

Lehtonen, T. 2013. *Tiimiakatemia: How to grow into a teampreneur*. Ed. T. Makkonen. Jyvaskyla: Publications of Jamsk University of Applied Sciences.

Li, P.P. 2016. The holistic and contextual natures of trust: Past, present and future research. *Journal of Trust Research* 6 (1): 1–6.

Lyon, F. 2000. Trust, networks and norms: The creation of social capital in agricultural economies in Ghana. *World Development* 28 (4): 663–681.

Lyon, F., and G. Porter. 2009. Market institutions, trust and norms: Exploring moral economies in Nigerian food systems. *Cambridge Journal of Economics* 33 (5): 903–920.

Macneil, I.R. 1980. Essays on the nature of contract. *South Carolina Central Law Journal* 10 (1): 159–200.

Mead, D., and C. Liedholm. 1998. The dynamics of micro and small enterprises in developing countries. *World Development* 26 (1): 61–74.

Miller, D., J. Lee, S. Chang, and I. Le Breton-Miller. 2009. Filling the institutional void: The social behavior and performance of family vs non-family technology firms in emerging markets. *Journal of International Business Studies* 40: 802–817.

Mitchell, R.K., L. Busenitz, T. Lant, P.P. McDougall, E.A. Morse, and B. Smith. 2004. The distinctive and inclusive domain of entrepreneurial cognition research. *Entrepreneurship Theory and Practice* 28 (6): 505–551.

Mohar, Y., M.S. Singh, and K.K. Kamal. 2007. Relationship between psychological characteristics and entrepreneurial inclination: A case study of students at University Tun Abdul Razak (UNITAR). *Journal of Asia Entrepreneurship and Sustainability* 3 (2): 1–10.

Morrison, A. 2000. Entrepreneurship: What triggers it? *International Journal of Entrepreneurial Behaviour and Research* 6 (2): 59–71.

Nahapiet, J., and S. Ghoshal. 1998. Social capital, intellectual capital, and the organizational advantage. *The Academy of Management Review* 23 (2): 242–266.

North, D.C. 1990. *Institutions, institutional change and economic performance*. Cambridge: Cambridge University Press.

———. 1991. Institutions. *Journal of Economic Perspectives* 5: 97–112.

———. 1993. *Instituciones, Cambio Institucional y Desempeño Económico*. México: Fondo de Cultura Económica.

Nziku, M. Dina. 2012. Tanzanian education and entrepreneurial influence among females. *Journal of Female Entrepreneurship and Education (JWE)* 12: 52–73.

Oliver, C. 1991. Strategic responses to institutional processes. *Academy of Management Review* 16: 145–179.

Peng, M.W. 2003. Institutional transitions and strategic choices. *Academy of Management Review* 28 (2): 275–293.

Peng, M.W., D.Y.L. Wang, and J. Yi. 2008. An institution-based view of international business strategy: A focus on emerging economies. *Journal of International Business Studies* 39: 920–936.

Putnam, R.D. 1993. The prosperous community: Social capital and public life. *The American Prospect* 13: 35–42.

Rauch, A., and M. Frese. 2000. Psychological approaches to entrepreneurial success: A general model and an overview of findings. *International Review of Industrial and Organizational Psychology* 15: 101–142.

Ren, H., and B. Gray. 2009. Repairing relationship conflict: How violation types and culture influence The effectiveness of restoration rituals. *Academy of Management Review* 34 (1): 105–126.

Reynolds, P.D., M. Hay, and S.M. Camp. 1999. *Global Entrepreneurship Monitor: 1999 Executive Report*. Kansas City: Kauffman Foundation.

Romanelli, E., and Bird C. Schoonhoven. (eds), 2001. The local origins of new firms. In *The entrepreneurship dynamic: Origins of entrepreneurship and the evolution of industries*. Stanford: Stanford University Press.

Saheed, A., and M. Kavoos. 2016. The present attitude of African youth towards entrepreneurship. *International Journal of Small Business and Entrepreneurship Research* 4 (1): 21–38.

Sarasvathy, S.D., A. Menon, and G. Kuechle. 2013. Failing firms and successful entrepreneurs: Serial entrepreneurship as a temporal portfolio. *Small Business Economics* 40 (2): 417–434.

Saunders, M.N.K., D. Skinner, G. Dietz, N. Gillespie, and R.J. Lewicki. 2010. *Organizational trust: A cultural perspective*. Cambridge: Cambridge University Press.

Schulze, W.S., M.H. Lubatkin, R.N. Dino, and A.K. Buchholtz. 2001. Agency relationships in family firms: Theory and evidence. *Organization Science* 12 (2): 99–116.

Schumpeter, J.A. 1934. *The theory of economic development*. Cambridge, MA: Harvard University Press.

Scott, W.R. 1995. *Institutions and organizations*. Thousand Oaks: Sage.

———. 2003. Institutional carriers: Reviewing modes of transporting ideas over time and space and considering their consequences. *Industrial and Corporate Change* 12 (4): 879–894.

Sepulveda, L., and S. Syrett. 2007. Out of the shadows? Formalisation approaches to informal economic activity. *Policy and Politics* 35 (1): 87–104.

Shane, S. 1994. Cultural values and the championing process. *Entrepreneurship: Theory and Practice* 18: 25–41.

———. 2003. *A general theory of entrepreneurship*. Northampton: Edward Elgar.

Shane, S., and S. Venkataraman. 2000. The promise of entrepreneurship as a field of research. *Academy of Management Review* 25: 217–226.

Shepherd, D.A. 2003. Learning from business failure: Propositions of grief recovery for the self-employed. *Academy of Management Review* 28: 318–329.

Singh, R.K., and S.K. Garg. 2008. Strategy development by SMEs for competitiveness: A review. *An International Journal* 15 (5): 525–547.

Smallbone, D., F. Welter, and J. Ateljevic. 2014. Entrepreneurship in emerging market economies: Contemporary issues and perspectives. *International Small Business Journal* 32 (2): 113–116.

Snow, R.E., L. Corno, and D. Jackson. 1996. Individual differences in affective and conative functions. In *Handbook of educational psychology*, ed. D.C. Berliner and R.C. Calfee, 243–310. New York: Simon and Schuster Macmillan.

Sobel, R. 2008. Testing Baumol: Institutional quality and the productivity of entrepreneurship. Status of the field and future research agenda. In *Strategic entrepreneurship: Creating a new mindset*, ed. M.A. Hitt, R.D. Ireland, S.M. Camp, and D.L. Sexton, 255–288. Oxford: Blackwell.

Sriram, V., and T. Mersha. 2010. Stimulating entrepreneurship in Africa. *World Journal of Entrepreneurship Management and Sustainable Development* 6 (4): 257–272.

Stevenson H.H., and J.C. Jarillo 1990. A paradigm of entrepreneurship: Entrepreneurial management. *Strategic Management Journal*, Summer Special Issue 11: 17–27.

Su, J., Q. Zhai, and H. Landstrom. 2015. Entrepreneurship research in China: Internationalisation or contextualisation? *Entrepreneurship & Regional Development* 27 (1–2): 50–79.

Suchman, M.C. 1995. Managing legitimacy: Strategic and institutional approaches. *Academy of Management Review* 20 (3): 571–610.

The Economist. 2016. Special report: Business in Africa, 1.2 billion opportunities. http://www.economist.com/news/special-report/21696792-commodity-boom-may-beover and barriers-doing-business-are-everywhere-africas.

Thornton, P.H., and W. Ocasio. 2008. Institutional logic. In *The SAGE handbook of organizational institutionalism*, ed. R. Greenwood, C. Oliver, R. Suddaby, and K. Sahlin-Andersson, 99–129. London: Sage.

Thornton, P.H., D. Ribeiroi-Soriano, and D. Urbano. 2011. Socio-cultural logics and entrepreneurial activity: An overview. *International Small Business Journal* 29 (2): 105–118.

Thornton, P.H., W. Ocasio, and M. Loundsbury. 2012. *The institutional logics perspective: A new approach to culture, structure and processes*. Oxford: Oxford University Press.

Tokarczyk, J., E. Hansen, M. Green, and J. Down. 2007. A resource-based view and market orientation theory examination of the role of the "familiness" in family business success. *Family Business Review* 20 (1): 17–31.

Triandis, H.C. 1972. *Analysis of subjective culture*. New York: Wiley.

UNDP. 2018. *Youth empowerment and employment programme*. Freetown: UNDP Sierra Leone.

Veciano, J.M., and D. Urbana. 2008. The institutional approach to entrepreneurship research. Introduction. *International Entrepreneurship Management Journal* 4: 365–379.

Vickers, I., F. Lyon, L. Sepulveda, and C. McMullin. 2017. Public service innovation and multiple institutional logics: The case of hybrid social enterprises providers of health and wellbeing. *Social Policy* 48: 1755–1768.

Vinten, G. 2000. Business theology. *Management Decision* 38 (3): 209–215.

Walsh, F.M., and J. Lipinski. 2009. The role of the marketing function in small and medium sized enterprises. *Journal of small business and enterprise development* 16: 569–585.

Weber, M. 1904, 2002. *The protestant ethic and the spirit of capitalism*, 3rd Roxbury ed. Los Angeles: Roxbury Publishing Company.

Welter, F. 2002. Trust, institutions and entrepreneurial behaviour. In *Entrepreneurial strategies and trust: Structure and evolution of entrepreneurial behavioural patterns in East and West European environments – Concepts and considerations*, eds. H.-H. Höhmann and F.Welter, 37–42, Arbeitspapiere und Materialien 37. Forschungsstelle Osteuropa, Bremen.

———. 2005. Culture versus branch? Looking at trust and entrepreneurial behaviour from a cultural and sectoral perspective. In *Trust and entrepeneur-*

ship: A West-East perspective, ed. H.-H. Höhmann and F. Welter, 24–38. Cheltenham/Northampton: Edward Elgar.

———. 2011. Contextualizing entrepreneurship—Conceptual challenges and ways forward. *Entrepreneurship Theory and Practice* 35 (1): 165–184.

Welter, F., and D. Smallbone. 2003. Entrepreneurship and enterprise strategies in transition economies: An institutional perspective. In *Small firms and economic development in developed and transition economies: A reader*, ed. D. Kirby and A. Watson, 95–114. Aldershot: Ashgate Publishing.

———. 2006. Exploring the role of trust in entrepreneurial activity. *Entrepreneurship Theory and Practice* 30 (4): 465–475.

Welter, F., and F. Smallbone. 2011. Institutional perspectives on entrepreneurial behaviour in challenging environments. *Journal of Small Business Management* 49 (1): 107–125.

Worden, S. 2005. Religion in strategic leadership: A positivistic, normative/ theological and strategic analysis. *Journal of Business Ethics* 57 (3): 221–239.

World Bank. 2013. *Doing business 2013: Smarter regulations for small and medium-size enterprises*, Doing business. Washington, DC: World Bank.

World Bank Doing Business. 2018. Database accessed, May 2018. http://www. doingbusiness.org.

World Economic Forum. 2018. These will be Africa fastest growing economies in 2018. https://www.weforum.org/agenda/2018/01/what-does-2018-hold-for-african-economies.

Wright, M., P. Westhead, and D. Ucbasaran. 2007. Internationalisation of Small and medium-sized enterprises (SMES) and international entrepreneurship: A critique and policy implications. *Regional Studies* 41: 1013–1029.

Wu, W., M. Firth, and O.M. Rui. 2014. Trust and the provision of trade credit. *Journal of Banking and Finance* 39: 146–159.

Zaheer, A., and D. Kamal. 2011. Creating trust in piranha-infested waters: The confluence of buyer, supplier and host country contexts. *Journal of International Business Studies* 42: 48–55.

Zingales, L. 2006. *God's and Mammon's, global agenda 2006*, 228–229. Davos: World Economic Forum.

Zucker, L.G. 1977. The role of institutionalization in cultural persistence. *American Sociological Review* 42: 726–743.

———. 1986. Production of trust. Institutional sources of economic structure, 1840–1920. *Research in Organisation Behaviour* 8: 53–111.

3

Trust in Interorganisational Relationships

3.1 Introduction

Trust serves as the glue that binds people together and it is critical in every human relationship ranging from spouses, families, friends, sports teams, and political parties to business. Lack of trust leads to suspicion and lack of collaboration and often lack of cooperation. In the context of business, trust offers many advantages such as binding all key stakeholders to the business and enabling long-term relationships, access to resources, and growth (Welter 2012; Burns 2016). Nonetheless, trust involves risks, uncertainty, and vulnerability associated with whether the other party has the intention and the will to act as expected (Mayer et al. 1995; Rousseau et al. 1998; Möllering 2006).

The main challenge in the study of trust relates to its complex nature and a review of the literature reveals that there is lack of consensus among researchers on a number of issues such as definitions, the number of dimensions, operationalisations and methodologies, its relationship with contextual factors such as networks and relationships, contracts, power and institutions. The lack of consensus results from divergent assumptions originating from the diverse disciplines

© The Author(s) 2019
I. O. Amoako, *Trust, Institutions and Managing Entrepreneurial Relationships in Africa*,
Palgrave Studies of Entrepreneurship in Africa,
https://doi.org/10.1007/978-3-319-98395-0_3

involved in the study of trust. For example, psychology (e.g. Rotter 1971) traditionally approaches the study of trust by focusing on internal cognitions of trustors and trustees, in terms of their attributes, but pays less attention to the role of the environment or contexts. Most economists, on the other hand, regard trust as rational and calculative with actors mostly focused on their own benefits; as a result, economist underestimate the context or institutions (e.g. Gambetta 1988; Williamson 1993). Sociologists and old institutional economists suggest rather that sometimes actors rely on institutions that guide individuals and affect or shape their motivation to trust without personal knowledge of the individual (Zucker 1986). This approach suggests that trust is routinised and embedded in social relations (e.g. Granovetter 1985) or in institutions (Zucker 1986) while underestimating the role of the trustor, trustee, and the power relations that may lead to trust asymmetry and greater vulnerability of one of the parties (Bachmann 2001). Process theorists, on the other hand, suggest that in situations where actors do not have prior interactions and cannot rely on institutions, trust development becomes a reflexive process that is learned through interactions based on mutual experience, knowledge, and rules that develop over time (Möllering 2006). Lewicki and Bunker (1996, 135) compare these fragmented approaches as being similar to blind men, each one 'describing his own small piece of the elephant'. There is therefore a major gap in the literature for a holistic approach that examines the trustor, trustee, context, and their relationship (Li 2016; Chang et al. 2016).

This chapter aims to review the literature to develop a conceptual framework that presents a holistic view of trust by examining the entrepreneur as trustor, his or her exchange partner as trustee, the external cultural norms that shape trust development, and their interactions in relationships. The analysis and discussions aim to marry the different approaches to the study of trust: (1) as a rational choice, (2) as routine and taken for granted, and (3) as a reflexive process.

The analysis and discussions in this chapter are based on three key research questions:

RQ1   *What is trust?*
RQ2   *How is trust developed?*

RQ3   *How is trust violated and repaired in interorganisational relationships?*

The author provides answers to these questions by reviewing the literature on trust theory to offer an understanding of trust, how it is developed, violated, and repaired. The chapter presents a holistic view of trust that incorporates the trustor, trustee, their relationships, interactions, and the institutions that shape trust development and the outcomes of trust. This chapter shows that trust originates from a trustor's propensity to trust and trusting behaviour as well as the trustee's trustworthiness based on ability, integrity, and benevolence (Mayer et al. 1995; Tanis and Postmes 2005; Kim et al. 2004). Nonetheless, the development of trust is also influenced by contextual factors, particularly institutions, networks, and relationships and interactions with exchange partners (Granovetter 1985; Möllering 2006; Zucker 1986; Bachmann and Inkpen 2011). Trust also exists at personal, organisational, and institutional levels and trust leads to outcomes including cooperation, access to resources and vulnerability due to trust violations, and the need for trust repair. Figure 3.1 presents a summary of this

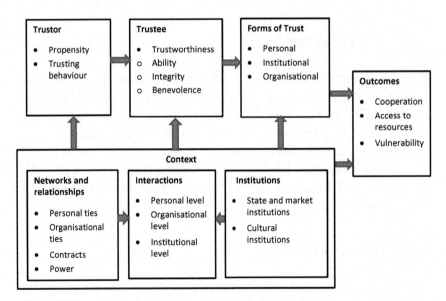

Fig. 3.1 Interorganisational trust in Entrepreneurial Relationships. (Source: Own research)

integrated approach to the study of trust and the author uses the framework in the review and discussions of trust theory in the rest of the chapter.

This chapter contributes to the literature in two main ways. It reviews the literature and highlights the current debates and gaps in interorganisational trust research in relation to entrepreneurship and small business management. Second, it presents a theoretical framework that offers a holistic view of trust development involving the trustor, trustee, institutions, relationships and interactions, and outcomes of trust.

The rest of this chapter is structured as follows. Section 3.2 answers the question of what constitutes trust by presenting the different definitions of trust based on different theoretical perspectives. Section 3.3 presents a model (Fig. 3.1) of interorganisational trust development in detail. Based on the framework, the literature review examines the roles of: contextual factors namely: networks and relationships, contracts, power interactions and institutions in trust development. This section also examines the role of the trustor and the trustee and ends by discussing trust outcomes. Section 3.4 reviews the literature on trust violations; Sect. 3.5 examines trust repairs and Sect. 3.6 concludes the chapter.

3.2   Trust: What Is It?

Trust has been widely studied by different disciplines. Yet, it remains a complex concept because it is multilevel, multidimensional, and plays many causal roles. Not surprisingly, it does not yet have an agreed definition as different disciplines have propounded different definitions, and even studies that use similar theoretical approaches have not necessarily used similar definitions (Rousseau et al. 1998). There is no single definition and as at 2014 there were over 121 trust definitions (Seppanen et al. 2007; Walterbusch et al. 2014) and the number continues to rise.

3.2.1   Definitions: Trust

Definitions of trust that draw on rational choice approaches focus more on the actor and rationality. For example, Mayer et al. (1995, 715) define trust as: 'the willingness to be vulnerable to the actions of another party based on the expectation that the other will perform a particular action important to the trustor, irrespective of the ability to monitor or control the other party'. Mayer et al. (1995) focus on the actor while paying less attention to the context. Similarly, in economics, Gambetta (1988, 217) is widely cited for his definition of trust as 'a particular level of the subjective probability with which an actor assesses that another actor or a group of actors will perform a particular action, both before he can monitor such action (or independently of his capacity ever to be able to monitor it), in a context in which it affects action'. Gambetta (1988) regards trust as a rational decision. However, one can argue that the rational choice approaches pay less attention to the norms that may underpin how different people see the same situation. Zucker (1986, 54) takes a sociological view and states that trust is 'a set of expectations shared by all those involved in an exchange'. This relates to both the idea of trust as a state of mind developed by an individual through interaction with others and trust as a reliance based on institutional safeguards (Bachmann and Inkpen 2011). Rousseau et al. (1998, 395) also combine the cognitive rational and sociological views, and define trust as 'a psychological state comprising the intention to accept vulnerability based upon positive expectations of the behaviour of another'. In contrast Möllering (2006) focuses on the process view in his definition of trust and emphasises uncertainty, risks, and vulnerability. Möllering (2006) defines trust as 'a reflexive process of building on reason, routine and reflexivity, suspending irreducible social vulnerability and uncertainty as if they were favourably resolved, and maintaining a state of favourable expectation towards the actions and intentions of more or less specific others'.

In this book, the author draws on all the above definitions to formulate a working definition of trust as 'a set of positive expectations that is shared by parties in an exchange that things and people will not fail them in spite of the possibility of being let down'. Based on this working definition, the author argues that entrepreneurs' trust development is based on their belief in the trustworthiness of the trustee based on interactions and accepted norms within specific contexts. This definition also recognises that trust is fraught with risks and vulnerability. Hence, within entrepreneurial relationships, trust calls for boldness and alertness (Schumpeter 1934, 1942; Kirzner 1979).

3.2.2 Trust: Rational, Routinised, or Reflexive and Process-Based?

Economic approaches draw on rational choice theory in the study of trust (Becker 1976). Rational choice theory assumes that decision makers are highly intelligent with clear objectives. Rational actors therefore are able to calculate and evaluate available alternatives and choose the best solution that optimises the decision maker's utilities (Misztal 1996). The rational choice paradigm regards trust as based on reason, and is conscious and calculated (e.g. Gambetta 1988; Williamson 1993). Williamson (1993) offers an economic calculative perspective of trust based on control, reciprocity, and conditional cooperation. According to Williamson (1993), the term calculative trust refers to the use of wisdom, rationality, and an economic calculative approach to trust and cooperation. Gambetta (1988) describes trust based on calculation as: some actor A, trusts some actor B when A calculates that the probability of B performing an action that is beneficial, or at least not detrimental, to A is high enough for A to consider engaging in some form of cooperation with B. Calculative trust is based on past experiences and trust development is based on the outcomes of risk taking or experience, equity preservation, and inter-firm adaptations (Williamson 1993). The approach suggests that actors are opportunistic, self-interested, and mostly focused on their own benefits. Hence, the rational choice approach has been criticised for overemphasising the role of the actor in placing trust (Zucker 1986; Möllering 2006).

Sociologists however disagree with economists on the calculative approach due to the habituation of trust based on norms and codes of conduct (Granovetter 1985; Zucker 1986). The critics argue that if trust is a matter of pay-off between trustor and trustee, then the trustee should rationally terminate the trust if there is no immediate pay-off. However, evidence suggests otherwise and Möllering (2006) explains that actors may sometimes be irrational and deliberately act in ways that enhances the utility of others. Even though irrational action may not be the dominant approach in social action, rational choice cannot explain all aspects of social action and that social norms, reciprocity, and cooperation may underpin trust (Elster 1989). Furthermore, actors may rely on systems of regulation, which guide individuals, shape their motivation and behaviour, and affect their behaviour to place trust without personal knowledge of the individual (Simmel 1950). However, critics argue that sociological approaches put too much emphasis on routines and the roles of institutions while marginalising agency, i.e. the trustor and trustee. Obviously, the role of the actor (trustor and trustee) is important since actors need to trust institutions before the institutions become a source of trust between actors (Möllering 2006). Calculation, routines, and cultural norms shape trust development: therefore, trust can be calculative but also routinised.

Apart from the rational and routine approaches, process theorists argue that trust is a reflexive process that is dependent on ongoing interactions between actors (Möllering 2006). In situations where actors do not have prior interactions and cannot rely on institutions, trust development becomes a process that is learned through interactions based on mutual experience, knowledge, and rules that develop over time. Even though such interactions may start relatively blindly or accidentally, these interactions may become self-reinforcing in a process of reflexive familiarisation and structuration (Möllering 2006, 80).

Regarding trust development in entrepreneurship, one can argue that entrepreneurs are not always rational actors in their decision making and in their search for opportunities or resources (Baron 1998). Academics have demonstrated that under certain circumstances heuristics and biases in strategic decision making influence entrepreneurs to develop and use non-rational modes of thinking (Busenitz and Barney 1997). Under certain conditions, entrepreneurs may also trust based on institutions when they do not have prior knowledge (Zucker 1986) whilst in other conditions they may have to develop trust based on their interactions when they do not have prior knowledge and cannot also rely on institutions (Möllering 2006). Figure 3.1 presents a model that shows an integrated approach to the study of trust, and the review, and discussions of trust theory in the rest of the chapter are guided by the model.

3.3   Trust Development

3.3.1   Trust and Context

Different contexts affect the processes of trust development by providing different forms of embeddedness that encourage or discourage trustworthy behaviour (Li 2016; Rousseau et al. 1998; Möllering 2006). In entrepreneurial trust development, context may refer to networks and social relations (Granovetter 1985), norms of contracts and power within specific networks and relationships (Amoako and Lyon 2014), specific interactions (Möllering 2006), industry-specific conditions as well as institutional environments particularly culture (Bachmann 2010; Saunders et al. 2010).

Networks, Relationships and Trust Building

The embeddedness or relational approach posits that in addition to individual freedom of action there is a need for reciprocity and mutuality due to the impact of implicit rules and social mores in embedded contexts. As a result, the relational approach emphasises the direct relationships of the entrepreneur to others and the assets of trust and trustworthiness that are embedded in these relationships (Tsai and Ghoshal 1998). Networks and relationships enhance trust building, cooperation and access to resources in the entrepreneurial process. The network approach emphasises that entrepreneurs are dependent on key relationships with actors within and outside the firm in the entrepreneurial process. This is significant given that entrepreneurs as individuals do not exist nor operate in a vacuum, but instead as actors who operate in social networks (see Granovetter 1985). Personal and organisational relationships constitute entrepreneurial networks (Hakansson et al. 1989). Personal networks comprise of relations between two individuals whilst interorganisational networks consists of autonomous organisations. However, inter-firm collaborations often originate from previously established networks of personal, informal relationships. Entrepreneurs rely on their strong and weak ties or personal and working relationships to gain information and resources.

Figure 3.1 shows the importance of networks and relationships to trust development.

In the context of Africa, entrepreneurs rely more on networks and relationships and trust with intermediaries, suppliers, and customers based on long-term relationships (Ghauri et al. 2003; Lyon 2005). Chapters 4 and 5 of this book explain these issues further.

Contracts and power are two other important factors that can complement trust in interpersonal and interorganisational relationships and these will be explored in this section.

Trust and Contracts The economic and sociological approaches to mitigating risks in economic exchanges have given rise to a debate on the relationship between contracts and trust in interorganisational relationships (Williamson 1979, 1985; Bradach and Eccles 1989; Rousseau et al. 1998). One key approach used by economists to explain the relationship between trust and contracts is transaction cost economics (TCE), spearheaded by Williamson (1985, 1993). The presence of opportunism subjects several exchange partners to risks and uncertainty, hence Williamson (1979, 1985) argues that substantial transaction cost in inter-firm relationships originates from the possibility of opportunism by any of the parties. Opportunism refers to 'calculated efforts (by an exchange actor) to mislead, distort, disguise, obfuscate, or otherwise confuse an exchange party' (Williamson 1985, 47). Williamson (1993) argues further that it is important for an exchange actor to devise contractual safeguards against such opportunism. In view of 'predatory tendencies' (Williamson 1993, 98), contracts or written agreements should be developed to monitor opportunistic behaviour of economic actors (Alchian and Demsetz 1972).

However, some researchers (e.g. Bradach and Eccles 1989; Nooteboom et al. 1997) oppose the TCE approach to trust and posit that it is trust rather than contracts that enhances economic exchanges. They suggest that trust economises on contract specification, enhances contract monitoring as well as offers material incentives for cooperation and reduces uncertainty. There is also disagreement on how trust complements or substitutes for contracts. While one group of studies suggest that the increase in the general complexity of contracts lead to increased trust (see Poppo and Zenger 2002), others (e.g. Malhotra and Murnighan 2002) assert that binding contracts that are aimed at promoting cooperative behaviour are more likely to decrease the level of trust and attitudes towards trust in collaboration. Macaulay (1963) and Beale and Dugdale (1975) also emphasise that, to some extent, presenting a contract signifies distrust and business people prefer not to have contracts. However, Nooteboom et al. (1997) suggest that trust can be either a complement or a substitute depending on the context.

In the contexts of smaller enterprises, in practice spelling out and enforcing exchange partners' obligations in all conceivable ways in a contract is particularly expensive (Hart 1989). Small firms often forget and ignore contracting issues and thereby cause more conflicts due to the imperfections and subjective interpretations of contracts in SME interfirm relationships (Frankel et al. 1996). Therefore, trust can mitigate the inherent complexity and risks and to cover expectations about what partner firms will do in situations where expectations cannot explicitly be covered. In the context of entrepreneurship, the importance of legal contracts as the basis of interorganisational relationships varies between cultures (Höhmann and Welter 2005). While written contracts are the most common form of institutionalised trust in Western economies (Lyon and Porter 2010), in Africa, studies (Amoako and Matlay 2015) suggest that trust and mostly oral contracts that are not enforceable in a court of law are the norm. In this book, the author examines contractual arrangements that entrepreneurs and smaller businesses use to manage familiar and unfamiliar relationships that may or may not be across cultures in Africa.

Trust and Power Trust and power seem to work in a similar way. Both mechanisms enable social actors to establish a link between their mutual expectations with each other based on a coordination of their actions (Bachmann 2001). Traditionally, power describes a phenomenon where someone imposes his or her will on others; and one person or group gives orders and the others obey (Taylor 1986). However, Foucault (1978) posits that modern power is in all social relations. He claims that 'power is everywhere not because it embraces everything, but because it comes from everywhere' (Foucault 1978, 92–93). Foucault (1978) argues that actors in specific relationships are positioned within network of power relations. Power is also present in all kinds of institutions, economic and social (Foucault 1980). However, in social relations, power is not used in the context of authoritarian rule but it facilitates the achievement of mutual goals for the actors in the social exchange process (Ap 1992).

Bachmann (2001) proposes that the risky nature of trust implies that trust remains a fragile mechanism even if it becomes established in a relationship; hence power is a more robust mechanism which even if misplaced does not entail as significant a loss as trust. Nonetheless, power like trust can break down, particularly when actors cannot enforce the sanctions inherent in the violation of power. In the context of entrepreneurial relationships, power exists in various forms and resides in resources such as knowledge, skills, tasks, money, strategy, and management, among others, and power can be exerted based on a larger firm's influence on decision making within a smaller firm. Thus, the level of trust and the degree of cooperation depend partly on the sizes of the firms as well as economic power and this may lead to asymmetric trust when there is greater vulnerability on the part of one of the exchange partners due to power and resource dependence (Pfeffer and Salancik 1978; Zaheer and Harris 2006).

Interactions and Trust Building

Process theories posit that in circumstances where actors do not have prior relationships, do not know each other, and at the same time cannot rely on institutions, trust as a process is learned through interactions, knowledge, mutual experience, and the rules that emerge over time (Ring and Van de Ven 1992; Möllering 2006). In such circumstances, actors as agency assumes an important role in trust development, maintenance, and the changing of it and may require a leap of faith in trusting strangers based on blind trust (Möllering 2006, 80). The process involves reflexivity due to the inherent uncertainty, risks, and vulnerability. In such circumstances, trust could be calculative, routinised, or a reflexive process contingent on ongoing interactions between the actors and, as a process, trust involves a leap of faith (Möllering 2006). Even though such interactions may start relatively blindly or accidentally, they may become self-reinforcing in a process of reflexive familiarisation and structuration (Möllering 2006, 80). Often organisational trustworthiness results from the interactions between individual actors who act as boundary spanners or from groups in multilevel networks (Zaheer et al. 1998; Gillespie and Dietz 2009), within organisations and institutions.

Institutions and Trust Development

Institutions affect trustworthy behaviour due to the incentives they make available and the sanctions they impose on trustees' mutual expectations in an exchange relationship (Welter and Smallbone 2006). In each country, the availability and nature of state and market support institutions as well as cultural institutions provide the different forms of embeddedness that encourage or discourage trustworthy behaviour (Welter and Smallbone 2006, 2011). Research suggests that state and market institutional orders, including government and state institutions such as legal and justice systems, the tax system, and other incentives offered by the institutional environment shape the level of trust and the ability to trust in a country (Zucker 1986; Welter and Smallbone 2010). There are thus fundamental differences between developed and developing economies regarding trust development in economic exchanges. The literature suggests that in developed economies, the presence of strong state and market institutions provide high levels of institutional trust that allows arm's-length exchanges with limited information about new partners, due to the presence of legal safeguards, and sanctions that may be applied should the relationship fail (Welter and Smallbone 2006, 2011). In contrast, in developing countries personal relationships enhance economic exchanges where there is a lack of strong institutions. However, this view is contested in this book as in the midst of weak state institutions, informal institutions may substitute for and replace ineffective formal institutions (Estrin and Prevezer 2011), leading to the development of 'parallel institutional trust' which enhances entrepreneurship (Amoako and Lyon 2014) and this will be discussed in detail in Chaps. 4 and 6.

Trust also acts as an informal institution due to its role as a sanctioning mechanism (Welter et al. 2004) and yet informal institutions influence trust development processes. In every culture, there are sets of common beliefs and norms that shape mental models and entrepreneurial behaviour (Altinay et al. 2014). Culture based on sets of meanings, norms, and expectations underpin behaviour and trust building in networks and relationships (Dietz et al. 2010; Curran et al. 1995; Amoako and Matlay 2015). Chao and Moon (2005) draw from the metaphor of a 'mosaic' of multiple cultural identities to describe the many different cultures of an individual or an organisation. These cultural 'tiles' include nationality, ethnicity, sector/industry, organisation, and profession and they shape entrepreneurial trust development (Altinay et al. 2014).

Recent research on trust emphasises that actors from different cultures may have different cultural values, hence, the level, nature, and meaning of trust may be different across different cultures (Dietz et al. 2010). The differences may lead to dissimilar trust expectations and different behavioural rules in conflict situations (Zaheer and Kamal 2011; Ren and Gray 2009; Saunders et al. 2010). Consequently, trust building between exchange partners from different cultures may be problematic (Dyer and Chu 2003). Yet, this challenge may not be limited to national borders but may include interfirm relationships such as strategic alliances, joint ventures, and flexible working relationships due to differences in organisational cultures (Zaheer et al. 1998).

One of the key challenges in the context of a globalised world where cross-cultural trust building in relationships is imperative for entrepreneurs, is that country and regional specific cultural and institutional environments render the adoption of universal concepts and models of trust challenging and untenable (Bachmann 2010). However, there is a dearth of studies that consider how particular cultural contexts shape specific trust drivers (Li 2016). Chapters. 4, 5, 6, 7, and 8 contribute to bridging this knowledge gap by examining how logics of specific, complex, sociocultural institutions shape trust building in business relationships in Africa.

Case 3.1 Culture and Trust Development in Africa
Different African cultures have different cultural norms guarding how to establish trust with visitors and strangers during a first encounter. Hence, it is very important for strangers to understand how to respond to the kind gestures of their hosts in order to establish that they are not enemies and can be trusted. Looking at the cultural norm for welcoming visitors, different African cultures welcome their visitors by offering different items such as drinks and food. For example, the Ibos in Nigeria traditionally offer cola to their visitors while the Akan people of Ghana traditionally offer water to their visitors. However, in Rwanda, traditionally, hosts offer milk to visitors. In spite of the differences in the items offered, in all three cultures it is important for the visitor or stranger to accept the cola, water, or milk offered in order to establish the initial trust that he or she is not an enemy and has good intentions. Yet, the same cultural symbol may mean different things in different cultures. For example, while water is the norm in Akan culture, if a visitor in Rwanda request water instead of milk it will suggest that the visitor does not trust the host and this will in turn lead to distrust from the host.
Source: interviews

3.3.2   Trustor: Propensity to Trust and Trusting Behaviour

Psychological theories regard trust as an attitude and an expectation at the individual level and propensity to trust describes the trustor's readiness to trust. The literature describes it in various ways; e.g. generalised trust propensity (Mayer et al. 1995). Mayer et al. (1995) define propensity to trust as the 'stable within-party factor that will affect the likelihood the party will trust' (Mayer et al. 1995, 725). It relates to the individual's awareness and tolerance of vulnerability (Bachmann and Zaheer 2013), and refers to the default level of trust placed in others. It is an attribute that is relatively stable and a generalised expectation about the perceived trustworthiness of others (Rotter 1967). Propensity to trust is a trait that allows a generalised expectation about the trustworthiness of others as it shapes the level of trust an actor has for a trustee prior to the availability of information about a particular trustee. Propensity to trust may serve as a cognitive filter that shapes the nature of reality based on the frames and inferential sets that individuals use in the selection and interpretation of information and in deriving meaning (Markus and Zajonc 1985). Hence, it relates to culture and emphasises the dimensions of trust-related personality. It also suggests that disposition rather than direct experience or availability of information on the trustworthiness of others determines the individual's level of trust (Blunsdon and Reed 2003).

People with different developmental experiences, personality types, and cultural backgrounds have different propensity to trust. Some scholars therefore suggest that propensity to trust influences the type of information that individuals attend to as those who have a lower disposition to trust are less positive and more suspicious of others and vice versa (see Bachmann and Zaheer 2013). People with low trust propensity will require far more evidence of trustworthiness to start trusting. Such people therefore need repeated evidence of trustworthy behaviour to alter their initial trust levels. Conversely, people with high trust propensity will require far less evidence of trustworthiness to start trusting (Bachmann and Zaheer 2013).

Hence, some individuals may over trust; that is they will repeatedly trust in situations that most people would not trust while others will not trust in situations that most people will trust. Over trust is 'a condition where one chooses, either consciously or habitually, to trust another more than warranted by an objective assessment of the situation' (Goel et al. 2005, 205). Over trust results in a condition of unguardedness that facilitates the exploitation of the trustor by the trustee. This is because actors who over trust are unlikely to engage in monitoring behaviour and may end up being more vulnerable to exploitation than actors who do not exhibit trust in the first place. Over trust may also lead to lock-in from high-trust relationships that may be unproductive (Gargiulo and Benassi 2000).

Conversely, actors may have distrust in a relationship, operating side by side with trust, independent of each other or comingle and influence one another (Zand 2016). Grovier (1994, 240) defines distrust as 'the lack of confidence in the other, a concern that the other may act to harm one, that does not care about one's welfare or intends to act harmfully, or is hostile'. Lewicki et al. (2006) suggest that cultural or psychological factors may cause biases in an individual towards initial distrust. Distrust causes suspicion and alienation and discourages offers of support, assistance, and constrains collaboration and the achievement of shared aims. Not surprisingly, distrust exists in weak relationships. This book focuses on trust even though occasionally the author refers to over trust and distrust.

Trusting behaviour refers to acting in a manner that shows some degree of trust or distrust of the trustee. Trusting behaviour originates from the trustor's beliefs about some of the consequences of trusting shaped by information from the trustee. The trustor's own assessment of the possible outcomes of promises that the trustee makes may also inspire trusting (see Swan and Nolan 1985). These may lead to perceptions of trustees' trustworthiness. Together these shape the intentions to trust and trusting behaviour. Trusting behaviour reflects expectations of the trustee's actions and the trustor accepts to rely on the trustee and thus becomes vulnerable. Even though being trustworthy influences trusting behaviour, it may not be a necessary condition for the trustor to place trust. Tanis and Postmes (2005) argue that it is expectations of reciprocity that appear to determine whether people will behave in trusting ways or not.

3.3.3   Trustee's Trustworthiness

Actors place trust based on the trustee's trustworthiness. Mayer et al. (1995, 717) define trustworthiness as: 'the characteristics and actions of the trustee that will lead that person to be more or less trusted'. Thus, trustworthiness relates to how the perceptions of the characteristics and behaviour of the trustee form the basis on which the trustor becomes willing to be vulnerable. Trustworthiness originates from trustees' perceived ability, benevolence, and integrity. The three dimensions of trustworthiness are different but related.

Mayer et al. (1995, 717–719) define ability as the skills, competencies, and characteristics that enable a party to have influence within some specific domain. Benevolence refers to the extent of the trustee's willingness to do good to the trustor (not be opportunistic) aside from the profit motivation. Integrity 'involves the trustor's perception that the trustee adheres to a set of principles that the trustor finds acceptable'. However, Mayer et al.'s (1995) dimensions of trustworthiness have been criticised by commentators due to the emphasis on individualism that is prevalent in the United States and the West in general (Möllering 2006). One may understand this criticism since trust dimensions in collectivist cultures differ from those in individualistic cultures. While trustors from 'individualistic cultures' are more concerned with a trustee's capability to honour promises, trustors from collectivist societies are more bothered with the trustees' predictability, motivations, and endorsements from 'proof sources' such as other trusted parties or/and groups (Doney et al. 1998). For example, instead of integrity, benevolence, and ability shown by Mayer et al.'s Western-focused model, honesty, sincerity, and affection are the dimensions of trust in China. Interestingly, Mayer et al.'s (1995) model does not address these issues.

Interestingly, scholars have paid little if any attention to investigating the dimensions of trustworthiness in entrepreneurship in Africa where entrepreneurs rely on relationships and cultural influences (Lyon 2005; Amoako and Matlay 2015). The culture in Africa is different from Western and Eastern cultures.

3.3.4   Forms of Trust Developed

The literature suggests that there are two main types of trust: personal trust and institutional trust (e.g. Lyon and Porter 2010). This raises questions about whether or not organisational trust exists since, originally, trust is an individual-level phenomenon. Critics argue that only individuals have subjective mental states, expectations, and attitudes (Zaheer et al. 1998). However, some scholars insist that formal organisations can be forms of institutions; in this way, institutional trust subsumes organisational trust (e.g. Welter and Smallbone 2006). Nonetheless, in this book, the author analyses trust at the personal, institutional, and organisational levels due to recent recognition of how organisational trust influences the structure and performances of relationships between organisations (Vanneste 2016).

Personal Trust

The nature of relationships influences the development of trust. Personal trust results from the outcomes of prior exchanges (Zucker 1986). The initial knowledge of the exchange partner and demonstration of trustworthiness are critical in gaining (personal) trust (Chang et al. 2016). It may also depend on the characteristics of a group such as ethnic, kinship, and social bonds and from emotional bonds between friends, family members, and other social groups (Welter and Smallbone 2006). Interpersonal trust refers to trust between two people, it describes the extent to which a person is confident and willing to act based on the words, actions, and decisions of another (McAllister 1995). Interpersonal trust may also originate from organisations based on trust between boundary spanners and from longstanding bilateral business relationships involving partners or friends. In such relationships, even though there may not be any explicit rules set out to govern the relationship, actors assume that the partner will behave as expected. Norms, values, and codes of conduct govern these relationships (Welter and Smallbone 2006). For interpersonal trust, an individual trusts or does not trust another individual (Vanneste 2016).

In the context of entrepreneurship, scholars suggest that entrepreneurs need to build interpersonal trust with key stakeholders such as customers and suppliers particularly during market entry (e.g. Aldrich 1999). However, the relationship between personal trust and institutional trust is complex. Institutional trust may complement personal trust in contexts with developed institutions (Zucker 1986). However, personal trust becomes more important for entrepreneurial success in societies such as Africa where formal institutions are weak. This is because personal trust can exist regardless of the legal and political context whereas institutional trust may require stability and predictability based on legitimate societal institutions reflected by societal norms and values (Welter and Smallbone 2006).

Institutional Trust: Trust Within and Between Institutions

Institutionalists conceptualise trust as a phenomenon within and among institutions, as well as the trust individuals have in those institutions (Möllering 2006). However, there is a disagreement on whether formal institutions can be trusted or not. Scholars such as Möllering (2006) indicate that interfirm relationships benefit from reliable institutions only if the actors trust those institutions. Others, such as Zaheer et al. (1998), suggest that trust exists only between people.

Institutional trust allows relationships to develop based on expectations that all parties uphold legal measures and common norms. The presence of a high level of institutional trust allows arm's-length exchanges with limited information about new partners in an exchange due to the presence of legal safeguards and sanctions that may be applied should the relationship fail (Welter and Smallbone 2006, 2011). In contrast, a lack of formal institutional trust hinders entrepreneurial relationship building and give rise to the need to compensate for trust development in other ways such as the use of informal institutions and social cultural, informal control mechanisms (Lyon et al. 2012).

Organisational and Interorganisational Trust: Trust Within and Between Organisations

March and Simon (1958) define organisations as a group of people. Organisational trust refers to trust reposed in organisations and in the processes and control structures of the organisation that enables the trustor to accept vulnerability when dealing with a representative of the organisation without knowing much about the particular representative (Zaheer et al. 1998; McEvily et al. 2003). Reputations and brands linked to trust in leaders or others in the organisation can lead actors to have this type of trust (Zaheer et al. 1998). Gillespie and Dietz (2009) and Dirks et al. (2009) corroborate that organisations are multilevel systems and the various components contribute to perceptions of an organisation's trustworthiness as well as to failures (Gillespie and Dietz 2009, 28; Dirks et al. 2009).

Trust between organisations has recently emerged as an important concept that influences the structure and performance of relationships between organisations (Vanneste 2016). Studies in entrepreneurship have shown that interorganisational trust has many advantages, for example it reduces uncertainty and complexity in business operations, reduces transaction costs in contracting, facilitates networking and allows business relationships with strangers (Welter and Smallbone 2006, 472). However, trust can be risky as it makes the trustor vulnerable due to potential trust violations which can cause great damage to relationships between exchange partners (Lewicki and Bunker 1996; Dirks et al. 2009) and adversely impacts on a firm's growth and even the survival of organisations (Bachmann 2001; McEvily et al. 2003).

In interorganisational relationships, one of the conceptual difficulties is to identify who trusts who. Zaheer et al. (1998) attempt to resolve this dilemma by suggesting that even though trust does not originate from firms but rather from individuals in an organisation, it is conceptually consistent to regard trust as being placed in another individual or a group of individuals such as a partner firm. Zaheer et al. (1998, 142) posit that in interorganisational exchanges 'interpersonal trust refers to the trust placed by the individual boundary spanner in her opposite member' in the partner organisation. On the other hand, interorganisational trust refers to 'the extent to which organisational members have a collectively-held trust orientation toward the partner' (Zaheer et al. 1998, 143). Zaheer et al.'s model suggests that trust at the interpersonal level has links to trust at the interorganisational level through the processes of institutionalisation (Zaheer et al. 1998, 143–144). During this process, individual boundary spanners establish informal commitments over time and these become taken-for-granted organisational structures and routines. Interpersonal trust of the boundary spanners becomes re-institutionalised and eventually influences the trust orientations of the other members of the organisations in their trust orientation towards the partner firms, thus showing the relevance of interpersonal trust in interorganisational exchanges. Therefore, interpersonal trust facilitates interorganisational trust and the attitudes of boundary spanners impact on norms of interfirm opportunism or cooperation. Vanneste (2016) also argues that interoganisational trust can also emerge from interpersonal trust through indirect reciprocity; a process that describes when kind and unkind acts are returned by others in organisational relationships.

Regarding SMEs' interorganisational trust in African contexts, the author argues in this book that the distinction between interorganisational trust and interpersonal trust is unclear since entrepreneurs remain the key boundary spanners and decision makers for their organisations. Therefore, entrepreneurs remain the origin and object of trust since interfirm relationships mostly come into being because of their strategic decisions (Inkpen and Currall 1997). This may differ in other contexts particularly in larger organisations where decision making is not vested in any single individual but rather in a number of managers.

3.3.5 Trust Outcomes

Cooperation

Studies suggest that interorganisational trust directly offers a variety of positive outcomes. In particular, trust enhances cooperation between individuals and organisations (Ring and Van de Ven 1992; Saunders et al. 2010; Amoako and Lyon 2014). However, trust may not be a necessary condition for cooperation as power can also induce cooperation (Mayer et al. 1995). In interorganisational relationships, the degree of cooperation depends partly on the size of firms as well as economic power (Zaheer and Harris 2006). The literature on buyer-seller relationships suggests that trust may have a direct positive impact on financial performance. For example, trust directly enhances financial performance (Zaheer and Harris 2006) and competitive advantage (Barney 1991), and trust indirectly influences performance through, for example, reducing transaction and relationship-specific costs by reducing conflicts

(Zaheer et al. 1998), opportunism, and control (Smith and Barclay 1997). However, in spite of the potential positive impact of trust on performance Katsikeas et al. (2009) remark that the relationship between trust and performance is complex and poorly understood, and trust may not improve outcomes under all circumstances.

Access to Resources

The resource-based view (RBV) suggests that availability and mobilisation of resources are critical for the entrepreneurial process (Barney 1991). Entrepreneurs deploy different strategies to mobilise resources needed to exploit opportunities. As stated in Chap. 2, one key strategy that entrepreneurs use is the development of personal and business networks to strategically access resources from the external environment (Granovetter 1985). However, trust fosters cooperation between individuals and organisations in networks and relationships (Ring and Van de Ven 1992; Lyon 2005; Amoako and Lyon 2014). Trust therefore allows entrepreneurs to access resources including ideas, motivations, information, capital, access to markets, skills and training, and the goodwill inherent in bureaucracy (Granovetter 1985). Trust is particularly important for SMEs as resources are limited and entrepreneurs and their firms often rely on partners to gain access to critical resources in order to manage uncertainty due to their limited expertise and capacity. However, the creation, upholding, and maintenance of trust involves costs in the form of a significant amount of time and resources such as gifts that may be expensive (Larson 1992; McEvily et al. 2003). Furthermore, trust entails risks and vulnerability and trusting may lead to the loss of resources when trust is violated.

3.4   Trust Violations

Trust is fragile and when violated can lead to considerable consequences (McEvily et al. 2003). Trust violations could be real or perceived based on instances of unmet expectations (Goles et al. 2009). At the personal level,

Palmer et al. (2000, 248) define trust violation as unmet expectations regarding another person's behaviour, or when a person does not act consistently with one's values. However, changes in supporting commitments for the trustee at some stage at which it becomes untenable to act as expected may cause trust violations (Möllering 2006). Yet, trustees may also at times disguise ulterior motives and falsely invoke the socially desirable notion of trust in their attempt to exploit others (Möllering 2006).

In the context of organisations, trust violations could refer to perceptions of unmet expectation of a product or a service (Goles et al. 2009). Institutional trust violations, on the other hand, could result from unmet expectations about particular institutions. However, academics have shown very little interest in violations of trust by organisations and institutions in entrepreneurship and this study aims to contribute to knowledge in these areas.

Unlike organisational and institutional trust violations, there has been a number of studies on interpersonal trust violations (e.g. Lewicki and Bunker 1996; Kim et al. 2004; Dirks et al. 2009). However, there are a few studies that investigate the trustor's perceptions of trust violations. One of the notable exceptions is Kim et al.'s (2004) study that draws on Mayer et al.'s (1995) dimensions of ability, integrity, and benevolence. The study suggests that perceived violations of ability and integrity lead to more decline in trust than perceived breaches in benevolence (e.g. Kim et al. 2004). The authors explain that trust violations that originate from perceived breaches of integrity or values may be generalised across other dimensions of trust due to stereotypes resulting from the belief that defective character transcends situations. This is because 'people intuitively believe that those with integrity will refrain from dishonest behaviours in any situation, whereas those with low integrity may exhibit either dishonest or honest behaviours depending on their incentives and opportunities' (p. 106). In spite of the insights that Kim et al.'s (2004) research offers on the subject, one can argue that since the study is based on controlled experiments their study downplays the complex relationships between calculation, cognition, and context. These assumptions about trust and its violations apparently ignore the differences between actors from different cultures (Dietz et al. 2010), as well as the potential subjective nature of interpretations of perceived trust violations by exchange partners across cultures, industries, markets, and relationships. These issues call for more investigations into trust violations in different contexts.

Understanding trust violations in interpersonal and interorganisational relationships is important since violations may lead to a reduction in subsequent trust and cooperation (Lewicki and Bunker 1996). In the context of organisations, trust violations may lead to considerable consequences such as raising concerns about why the victim may want to continue to buy from the offender (Goles et al. 2009). Business organisations that fall victim to trust violations may suddenly find themselves in a situation that threatens their very existence (Bachmann 2001). For example, when a supplier violates trust in a supply agreement, the firm that has fallen victim may suddenly find itself in a situation whereby it may not be able to meet customer demands and this may threaten its very existence. It may also lead to the victim engaging in negative word of mouth that may generate a multiplier effect that may go beyond the individual buyer's intent not to engage with that particular seller (Goles et al. 2009).

Trust violations originate from information that differs from trustor's expectations of behaviour of the trustees (Lewicki 2006; Kim et al. 2004). Trust violation may also originate from unreliability, harsh comments and criticism, or aggressive and antagonistic activities that occur as conflicts escalate (Lewicki 2006; Dirks et al. 2009). Perceived trust violations may originate from unsubstantiated allegations. However, exploration of perceptions of trust violations raises questions about whether both parties see the relationship and its violation in the same way. In relationships constituted on asymmetric power, the interplay of trust and control may shape not only the building and operation of trust (Bachmann 2001), but also perceived violations. A study of the context of trust violations also allows for the examination of power relations that shape organisational trust. While control may complement trust (Zucker 1986), the asymmetric nature of power in relationships (Inkpen and Currall 2004), means that violations may be perceived in very different ways by each party. There may be greater vulnerability on the part of one exchange partner in a relationship due to power and resource dependence (Pfeffer and Salancik 1978; Zaheer and Harris 2006), particularly so in contexts of SMEs involved in relationships with larger organisations. Furthermore, as common legal institutions and culturally specific norms are important in building trust, then there is also a need to understand how culture shapes perceptions of trust violations and the response to this. While this has been explored in theoretical contributions (Ren and Gray 2009; Zaheer and Kamal 2011) and controlled experiments there are very few examinations of trust violations in specific cultural contexts.

These issues therefore call for more investigations into how trust and the process of violation are embedded in existing social relations that may differ between cultures. The concept of trust violation is central to this book with a focus on how, in the weak institutional environments found in Africa, uncertainty and cultural differences can create greater threats to a relationship.

3.5   Trust Repairs

The key challenge following the violation of trust is finding ways to repair the damage and rebuild relationships. However, trust repair may be difficult due to the fragile nature of trust and the great damage that trust violations can cause to relationships between exchange partners (Lewicki and Bunker 1996; Dirks et al. 2009). Trust repair effort is defined as 'activities directed at making a trustor's trusting beliefs and trusting intentions more positive after a violation is perceived to have occurred' (Kim et al. 2004, 105). Kramer and Lewicki (2010) refer to this as seeking to restore the willingness of [a] party to be vulnerable in the future'. Interestingly, trust repair is an emerging area of research that currently has seen a few studies, mostly based on theoretical and controlled laboratory experiments (e.g. Lewicki and Bunker 1996; Kim et al. 2004; Gillespie and Dietz 2009; Dirks et al. 2011).

Lewicki (2006) cautions that repairing trust may take time due to the need for parties involved to re-establish the reliability and dependability of the perpetrator over a period of time. At the interpersonal level, Lewicki and Bunker (1996) propose a trust repair model suggesting that trustors may effectively contain conflict or rebuild trust in the shorter term by managing the distrust inherent in every relationship and repairing the trust violated. To repair trust, they outline a four-step process: (1) acknowledge that a violation has occurred; (2) determine the causes of the violation and admit culpability; (3) admit that violation was destructive; and (4) accept responsibility. However, the main challenge of the model emanates from the willingness of the violator to play an active role that in many cases may not be likely. The model also assumes that the trustor plays a passive role in trust repair. The role of the violator is important and in a later experimental study Dirks et al. (2011) confirm that the trustor's cognitions of repentance of the trustee play a role in trust repair.

In a similar study, Kim et al. (2004) found that apologies are only effective in repairing competence-based violations. Instead, they argue that denials are more effective for repairing violations of integrity and in contrast, actors may overlook violations of benevolence.

While the above models pay less attention to the role of context in trust repair processes, Ren and Gray's (2009) theoretical framework on trust repair emphasises the role of culture in trust repair processes. It particularly emphasises that culture impacts the norms that delineate the violations and prescribes the appropriate restoration process. Ren and Gray (2009) outline four restoration mechanisms namely (1) accounts, (2) apologies, (3) demonstration of concern, and (4) penance. They stress that the victim's perception of the type of violation and the national cultural values determine the processes of relationship restoration. Furthermore, they highlight that in collectivist societies, victims of trust violations in their attempt to repair trust are more likely to approach a third party. This observation supports Tinsley and Brodt's (2004) declaration that collectivists tend to use intermediaries in the process of repairing relationships by relying more on covert expressions and thereby avoiding direct confrontation with perpetrators of trust violations. The studies of Ren and Gray (2009) and Tinsley and Brodt (2004) suggest that cultural differences in cross-cultural entrepreneurial relationships add to uncertainty and create further challenges for repairing trust.

Concerning organisational trust repair, Gillespie and Dietz (2009) argue that in organisational contexts, the target for trust repair may be individuals or groups of individuals that make up an organisation. Consequently, trust repair at the organisational level creates a further degree of uncertainty and may be more difficult due to the multiplicity of organisational membership and the need for individuals to change their views towards the violating organisation.

Gillespie and Dietz's (2009) theorise further that interpersonal trust repair is not readily transferable to the organisational level because organisations are multilevel systems and the various components contribute to perceptions of an organisation's trustworthiness as well as to failures (Gillespie and Dietz 2009, 128). They argue that trust violations, which they also refer to as organisation failures, may result from malfunctioning of any of the components of an organisation. To repair organisational level trust, Gillespie and Dietz (2009) propose a four-stage model, viz.: (1) immediate response, (2) diagnosis, (3) reforming interventions, and (4) evaluation. They theorise further that trust-substantive measures such as regulation can repair trust through taking actions that would deter future breaches. Thus, confirming earlier studies that 'legalistic remedies' such as controls involving policies, procedures or monitoring (Sitkin and Roth 1993), punishment and regulation of the perpetrator, the voluntary introduction of monitoring systems, and sanctions (Nakayachi and Watabe 2005) all help to restore trust because they increase the reliability of the behaviour of the perpetrator. Existing research contributions therefore call for a greater understanding of these repair processes operating at the organisational level rather than the current focus on the interpersonal (Gillespie and Dietz 2009). This will require an understanding of the inter-relationship between interpersonal trust repair and organisational trust repair.

In this book, the interest in trust violations and trust repairs arises due to the need to maintain and repair trust in cases of violations in entrepreneurial relationships to facilitate access to resources and markets by smaller organisations in Africa in particular. Since conflicts may inevitably arise leading to the failure of some entrepreneurial relationships, trust repair may allow entrepreneurs to use alternatives to litigation through arbitration and bargaining as well as negotiation for the settlement of disputes without resorting to adversarial conflicts (Lewicki and Bunker 1996). In this book the author argues that by understanding the processes of trust repair in entrepreneurial relationships, entrepreneurs may be able to build and use relationships and networks to access critical resources for growing their businesses. The author therefore explores how cultural norms and power relationships shape the actions of both perpetrator and the violated parties. This chapter contributes to knowledge on these complex issues by specifically examining how Africa's complex socio-cultural institutions shape trust building, trust violations and trust repairs in business relationships.

3.6   Conclusion

This chapter reviews the literature and highlights that trust is needed due to the presence of risk and uncertainty in economic transactions. It also highlights the debates on definitions of trust, its development, violations, and repairs in interorganisational relationships. Psychological models suggest that trust may be shaped by propensity to trust, while economic models such as TCE emphasise that the decision to trust or not to trust originates from a careful rational reasoning of consequences (Gambetta 1988; Williamson 1993). On the contrary, sociological approaches suggest that trust development can be habitual and routine because trust is embedded in institutions and is taken for granted (Granovetter 1985; Zucker 1986). Trust may also be a process that involves reflexivity (Möllering 2006). This study therefore offers an integrated approach by adopting a working definition of trust as an 'an expectation that is shared by people in an exchange that things and people will not fail them in spite of the possibility of being let down'. This definition suggests that expectations based on the trustworthiness of the trustee, the nature of specific relationships, and accepted norms within each context influence the trustor's trusting behaviour. This definition also recognises that trust is fraught with risks and vulnerability.

This chapter contributes to knowledge through presenting a holistic model (Fig. 3.1) that incorporates the trustor, trustee, their relationships, interactions and institutions that shape trust development, and the outcomes of trust. The model suggests that trust originates from a trustor's propensity to trust and trusting behaviour as well as a trustee's trustworthiness based on his or her ability, integrity, and benevolence (Mayer et al. 1995; Kim et al. 2004). "The framework further shows that contextual factors namely: networks and relationships, contracts, power, interactions, and formal and cultural institutions influence the development of trust (Granovetter 1985; Möllering 2006; Zucker 1986; Bachmann and Inkpen 2011)".

Yet, the development of the model is informed by existing studies mostly conducted in the West and there is little understanding of trust development processes in other contexts including emerging economies such as Africa (Amoako and Lyon 2014; Wu et al. 2014). Scholars have therefore called for more investigations in other contexts to examine the nature of institutions, particularly networks and relationships, and cultural norms that influence trust development, trust violations, and trust repair (see Li 2016; Bachmann et al. 2015). There is also little knowledge of how context affects interpretations of what constitutes trust violations and the acceptable norms for repairing violations of trust in interorganisational relationships (Amoako 2012). Chapters 6, 7, and 8 will examine these issues in detail in an African context based on empirical studies in Ghana conducted by the author. The next chapter (Chap. 4) identifies the key common cultural institutions that facilitate trust development in entrepreneurial relationships in Africa.

References

Alchian, A., and H. Demsetz. 1972. Production, information costs and economic organization. *American Economic Review* 62: 77–95.

Aldrich, H.E. 1999. *Organisations evolving*. London: Sage.

Altinay, L., M.N.K. Saunders, and C.L. Wang. 2014. The influence of culture on trust judgements in customer relationship development by ethnic minority small businesses. *Journal of Small Business Management* 52 (1): 59–78.

Amoako, I.O. 2012. Trust in exporting relationships: The case of SMEs in Ghana. Published PhD thesis, Center for Economic and Enterprise Development Research (CEEDR) Middlesex University, London. http://eprints.mdx.ac.uk/12419/.

Amoako, I.O., and F. Lyon. 2014. We don't deal with courts: Cooperation and alternative institutions shaping exporting relationships of SMEs in Ghana. *International Small Business Journal* 32 (2): 117–139.

Amoako, I.O., and H. Matlay. 2015. Norms and trust-shaping relationships among food-exporting SMEs s in Ghana. Special Issue on the competitiveness of SMEs in the food sector: Exploring possibilities for growth, ed. B. Quinn, A. Dunn, and L. McKitterick. *International Journal of Entrepreneurship & Innovation* 16 (2): 123–134.

Ap, J. 1992. Residents' perceptions on tourism impacts. *Annals of Tourism Research* 19: 665–690.

Bachmann, R. 2001. Trust, power and control in trans-organizational relations. *Organization Studies* 22 (2): 337–365.

———. 2010. Towards a context-sensitive approach to researching trust in interorganizational relationships. In *Organizational trust: A cultural perspective*, ed. M.N.K. Saunders, D. Skinner, G. Dietz, N. Gillespie, and R.J. Lewicki, 87–106. Cambridge: Cambridge University Press.

Bachmann, R., and A. Inkpen. 2011. Understanding institutional-based trust building processes in inter-organisational relationships. *Organization Studies* 32 (2): 281–300.

Bachmann, R., and A. Zaheer. 2013. *Handbook of advances in trust research*. Cheltenham: Edward Elgar.

Bachmann, R., N. Gillespie, and R. Priem. 2015. Repairing trust in organizations and institutions: Toward a conceptual framework. *Organization Studies* 36 (9): 1123–1142.

Barney, J.B. 1991. Firms resources and sustainable competitive advantage. *Journal of Management* 17: 99–120.

Baron, R. 1998. Cognitive mechanisms in entrepreneurship: Why and when entrepreneurs think differently than other people. *Journal of Business Venturing* 13 (4): 275–294.

Beale and Dugdale. 1975. Contracts between businessmen. *British Journal of Law and Society* 2 (45): 45–48.

Becker, Gary S. 1976. *The economic approach to human behavior*. Chicago: University of Chicago Press.

Blunsdon, B., and K. Reed. 2003. The effect of technical and social conditions on workplace trust. *International Journal of Human Resource Management* 14 (1): 12–27.

Bradach, J.L., and R.G. Eccles. 1989. Price, authority, and trust: From ideal types to plural forms. *Annual Review of Sociology* 15: 97–118.

Burns, Paul. 2016. *Entrepreneurship and small business*. New York: Palgrave Macmillan Limited.

Busenitz, L., and J. Barney. 1997. Differences between entrepreneurs and managers in large organizations: Biases and heuristics in strategic decision-making. *Journal of Business Venturing* 12 (1): 9–30.

Chang, C.-C., S.-N. Yao, S.-A. Chen, J.-T. King, and C. Liang. 2016. Imagining garage startups: Interactive effects of imaginative capabilities on technopreneurship intention. *Creativity Research Journal* 28 (3): 289–297.

Chao, G., and H. Moon. 2005. A cultural mosaic: Defining the complexity of culture. *Journal of Applied Psychology* 90: 1128–1140.

Curran, J., R.A. Blackburn, and J. Kitching. 1995. *Small businesses, networking and networks: A literature review, policy survey and research agenda.* Kingston upon Thames: Kingston University, Small Business Research Centre.

Dietz, G., N. Gillespie, and G.T. Chao. 2010. *Unravelling the complexities of trust and culture.* In *Organizational trust: A cultural perspective,* ed. M.N.K. Saunders, D. Skinner, G. Dietz, N. Gillespie, and R.J. Lewicki, 3–41. Cambridge: Cambridge University Press.

Dirks, K., R. Lewicki, and A. Zaheer. 2009. Repairing relationships within and between organizations: Building a conceptual foundation. *Academy of Management Review* 34 (1): 68–84.

Dirks, K.T., P.H. Kim, D.L. Ferrin, and C.D. Cooper. 2011. Understanding the effects of substantive responses on trust following a transgression. *Organizational Behavior and Human Decision Processes* 114: 87–103.

Doney, P.M., J.P. Cannon, and M.R. Mullen. 1998. Understanding the influence of national culture on the development of trust. *Academy of Management Review* 23 (3): 601–620.

Dyer, J.H., and W. Chu. 2003. The role of trustworthiness in reducing transaction costs and improving performance: Empirical evidence from the United States, Japan, and Korea. *Organization Science* 14 (1): 57–68.

Elster, J. 1989. Social norms and economic theory. *Journal of Economic Perspectives* 3 (4): 99–117.

Estrin, S., and M. Prevezer. 2011. The role of informal institutions in corporate governance: Brazil, Russia, India, and China compared. *Asia Pacific Journal of Management* 28 (1): 41–67.

Foucault, M. 1978. *The history of sexuality: Volume 1: An introduction.* New York: Vintage Books.

———. 1980. *Trust and power.* In *Power/knowledge: Selected interview and other writing 1972–1977,* ed. C. Gordon, 109–133. New York: Pantheon Books.

Frankel, R., Whipple J. Smitz, and D.J. Frayer. 1996. Formal versus informal contracts: Achieving alliance success. *International Journal of Physical Distribution & Logistics Management* 26 (3): 47–63.

Gambetta, D., ed. 1988. *Trust: Making and breaking cooperative relations.* Oxford/New York: Basil Blackwell.

Gargiulo, M., and M. Benassi. 2000. Trapped in your own net? Network cohesion, structural holes, and the adaptation of social capital. In *Social capital and sustainability in a community threat,* ed. M. Edwards and J. Onyx. *Journal of Local Environment* 12 (1): 18.

Ghauri, P., Lutz L. Clemens, and G. Tesfom. 2003. Using networks to solve export marketing problems of small- and medium-sized firms from developing countries. *European Journal of Marketing* 37 (5/6): 728–752.

Gillespie, N., and G. Dietz. 2009. Trust repair after an organization level failure. *Academy of Management Review* 34 (1): 127–145.

Goel, S., G.G. Bell, and J.L. Pierce. 2005. The perils of Pollyanna: Development of the over-trust construct. *Journal of Business Ethics* 58: 203–218.

Goles, Tim, Simon Lee, Srinivasan V. Rao, and Warren John. 2009. Trust violation in electronic commerce: Customer concerns and reactions. *The Journal of Computer Information Systems* 49: 1–9.

Granovetter, M.S. 1985. Economic action and social structure: The problem of embeddedness. *American Journal of Sociology* 91 (3): 481–510.

Grovier, T. 1994. An epistemology of trust. *International Journal of Moral Social Studies* 8: 155–174.

Hakansson, H., J. Johanson, and F.J. Contactor. 1989. *Formal and informal cooperation strategies in international industrial networks*, 369–380. Massachusetts: Lexington books.

Hart, O. 1989. An economist's perspective on the theory of the firm. *Columbia Law Review* 89 (7): 1757–1774.

Höhmann, H.H., and F. Welter. 2005. *Trust and entrepreneurship: A West-East perspective*, 24–38. Cheltenham/Northampton: Edward Elgar.

Inkpen, A.C., and S.C. Currall. 1997. International joint venture trust. An empirical examination. In *Cooperative strategies: North American perspectives*, ed. P.W. Beamish and J.P. Killing, 308–334. San Francisco: New Lexington Press.

Inkpen, A.C., and S.C. Currall. 2004. The coevolution of trust, control, and learning in joint ventures. *Organisation Science* 15 (5): 586–599.

Katsikeas, C.S., D. Skarmeas, and D.C. Bello. 2009. Developing successful trust-based international exchange relationships. *Journal of International Business Studies* 40: 132–155.

Kim, P.H., D.L. Ferrin, C.D. Cooper, and K.T. Dirks. 2004. Removing the shadow of suspicion: The effects of apology versus denial for repairing competence-based versus integrity-based trust violations. *Journal of Applied Psychology* 89 (1): 100–118.

Kirzner, I.M. 1979. *Perception, opportunity and profit: Studies in the theory of entrepreneurship*. Chicago: University of Chicago Press.

Kramer, R.M., and R.J. Lewicki. 2010. Repairing and enhancing trust: Approaches to reducing organizational trust deficits. *Academy of Management Annals* 4: 245–277.

Larson, A. 1992. Network dyads in entrepreneurial settings: A study of the governance of exchange relationships. *Administrative Science Quarterly* 37: 76–104.

Lewicki, R.J. 2006. Trust and distrust. In *The negotiator's fieldbook: The desk reference for the experienced negotiator*, ed. A.K. Schneider and C. Honeyman, 191–202. Chicago: American Bar Association.

Lewicki, R.J., and B.B. Bunker. 1996. Developing and maintaining trust in work relationships. In *Trust in organizations: Frontiers of theory and research*, ed. R. Kramer and T.R. Tyler. Thousand Oaks: Sage.

Lewicki, R.J., E.C. Tomlinson, and N. Gillespie. 2006. Models of interpersonal trust development: Theoretical approaches, empirical evidence, and future directions. *Journal of Management* 32 (6): 991–1022.

Li, P.P. 2016. The holistic and contextual natures of trust: Past, present and future research. *Journal of Trust Research* 6 (1): 1–6.

Lyon, F. 2005. Managing co-operation: Trust and power in Ghanaian associations. *Organization Studies* 27 (1): 31–52.

Lyon, F., and G. Porter. 2010. Evolving institutions of trust: Personalised and institutionalised bases of trust in Nigerian and Ghanaian food trading. In *Organizational trust: A cultural perspective*, ed. M.N.K. Saunders, D. Skinner, G. Dietz, N. Gillespie, and R.J. Lewicki, 255–277. Cambridge: Cambridge University Press.

Lyon, F., M. Guido, and M.N.K. Saunders. 2012. Access and non-probability sampling in qualitative research on trust. In *Handbook of research methods on trust*, 85–93. Cheltenham: Edward Elgar.

Macaulay, S. 1963. Non-contractual relations in business: A preliminary study. *American Sociological Review* 28: 55–67.

Malhotra, D., and J.K. Murnighan. 2002. The effects of contracts on interpersonal trust. *Administrative Science Quarterly* 47: 534–559.

March, J.G., and H.A. Simon. 1958. *Organizations*. New York: Wiley.

Markus, H., and R.B. Zajonc. 1985. The cognitive perspective in social psychology. In *Handbook of social psychology*, ed. G. Lindzey and E. Aronson, 137–230. New York: Random House.

Mayer, R., J. Davis, and F. Schoorman. 1995. An integrative model of organisational trust. *Academy of Management Review* 20: 709–734.

McAllister, D.J. 1995. Affect- and cognition-based trust as foundations for interpersonal cooperation in organisations. *Academy of Management Journal* 38: 24–53.

McEvily, B., V. Perrone, and A. Zaheer. 2003. Trust as an organizing principle. *Organization Science* 14 (1): 91–103.

Misztal, B.A. 1996. Social norms and economic theory. *Journal of Economic Theory* 3 (4): 99–117.

Möllering, G. 2006. *Trust: Reason, routine, reflexivity*. Amsterdam: Elsevier.

Nakayachi, K., and M. Watabe. 2005. Restoring trustworthiness after adverse events: The signaling effects of voluntary 'Hostage Posting' on trust. *Organizational Behavior and Human Decision Processes* 97: 1–17.

Nooteboom, B., H. Berger, and N.G. Noorderhaven. 1997. Effects of trust and governance on relational risk. *Academy of Management Journal* 40 (2): 308–338.

Palmer, A., R. Beggs, and C. Keown-McMullan. 2000. Equity and repurchase intention following service failure. *Journal of Services Marketing* 14 (6): 513–528.

Pfeffer, J., and G.R. Salancik. 1978. *The external control of organisations: A resource dependence perspective*. Boston: Harper & Ro.

Poppo, L., and T. Zenger. 2002. Do formal contracts and relational governance function as substitutes or complements? *Strategic Management Journal* 23 (8): 707–725.

Ren, H., and B. Gray. 2009. Repairing relationship conflict: How violation types and culture influence The effectiveness of restoration rituals. *Academy of Management Review* 34 (1): 105–126.

Ring, P.S., and A.H. Van De Ven. 1992. Structuring cooperative relationships between organizations. *Strategic Management Journal* 13 (7): 483–498R.

Rotter, J.B. 1967. A new scale for the measurement of interpersonal trust. *Journal of Personality* 35 (4): 651–665.

———. 1971. Generalized expectancies of interpersonal trust. *American Psychologist* 26: 443–452.

Rousseau, D., S. Sitkin, R.S. Burt, and C. Camerer. 1998. Not different after all: A crossdiscipline view of trust. *Academy of Management Review* 23 (3): 393–404.

Saunders, M.N.K., D. Skinner, G. Dietz, N. Gillespie, and R.J. Lewicki. 2010. *Organisational trust: A cultural perspective*. Cambridge: Cambridge University Press.

Schumpeter, J.A. 1934. *The theory of economic development*. Cambridge, MA: Harvard University Press.

———. 1942. *Capitalism, socialism and democracy*. New York: Harper and Row.

Seppanen, R., K. Blomqvist, and S. Sundqvist. 2007. Measuring Inter-organisational trust – A critical review of the empirical research in 1990–2003. *Industrial Marketing Management* 36 (2): 249–265.

Simmel, G. 1950. The stranger. In *The sociology of Georg Simmel*, ed. K. Wolf. Glencoe: Free Press.

Sitkin, S., and N.L. Roth. 1993. Explaining the limited effectiveness of legalistic remedies for trust/distrust. *Organization Science* 4: 367–392.

Smith, J.B., and D.W. Barclay. 1997. The effects of organizational differences and trust on the effectiveness of selling partner relationships. *Journal of Marketing* 61: 3–21.

Swan, John E., and J.J. Nolan. 1985. Gaining customer trust: A conceptual guide for the salesperson. *Journal of Personal Selling & Sales Management* 5 (2): 39.

Tanis, M., and T. Postmes. 2005. A social identity approach to trust: Interpersonal perception, group membership and trusting behaviour. *European Journal of Social Psychology* 35: 413–424.

Taylor, C. 1986. Foucault on freedom and truth. In *Foucault: A critical reader*, ed. D. Hoy, 69–102. Oxford: Basil Blackwell.

Tinsley, C.H., and S.E. Brodt. 2004. Conflict management in Asia: A dynamic framework and future directions. In *Handbook of Asian management*, ed. K. Leung and S. White, 439–458. New York: Kluwer Academic.

Tsai, Wenpinand, and Sumantra Ghoshal. 1998. Social capital and value creation: The role of intrafirm networks. *Academy of Management Journal* 41 (4): 464–473.

Vanneste, B.S. 2016. From interpersonal to interorganizational trust: The role of indirect reciprocity. *Journal of Trust Research* 6 (1): 7–36.

Walterbusch, M., M. Grauler, and F. Teuteberg. 2014. How trust is defined.: A qualitative and quantitative analysis of scientific literature, Twentieth American conference on information systems, Savanah.

Welter, F. 2012. All you need is trust? A critical review of the trust and entrepreneurship literature. *International Small Business Journal* 30 (3): 193–212.

Welter, F., and D. Smallbone. 2006. Exploring the role of trust in entrepreneurial activity. *Entrepreneurship Theory & Practice* 30 (4): 465–475.

———. 2010. The embeddedness of women's entrepreneurship in a transition context. In *Women's entrepreneurship and the global environment for growth: An international perspective*, ed. C. Brush, E. Gatewood, C. Henry, and A. De Bruin, 96–117. Cheltenham: Edward Elgar.

Welter, F., and F. Smallbone. 2011. Institutional perspectives on entrepreneurial behaviour in challenging environments. *Journal of Small Business Management* 49 (1): 107–125.

Welter, F., T. Kautonen, and M. Stoytcheva. 2004. Trust in enterprise development, business relationships and business environments. In *Entrepreneurial strategies and trust. Structure and evolution of entrepreneurial behaviour patterns in low and high trust environments of East and West Europe. Part 1: A Review*, ed. H.H. Hohmann and F. Welter. Bremen: Forshungsstelle Osteuropa.

Williamson, O.E. 1979. Transaction-cost economics: The governance of contractual relations. *Journal of Law and Economics* 22: 233–261.

———. 1985. *The economic institutions of capitalism: Firms, markets, relational contracting*. New York: Free Press.

———. 1993. Calculativeness, trust and economic organization. *Journal of Law and Economics* 36: 453–486.

Wu, W., M. Firth, and O.M. Rui. 2014. Trust and the provision of trade credit. *Journal of Banking & Finance* 39: 146–159.

Zaheer, A., and J. Harris. 2006. Interorganizational trust. In *Handbook of strategic alliances*, ed. O. Shenkar and J.J. Reurer, 169–197. Thousand Oaks: Sage.

Zaheer, A., and D.F. Kamal. 2011. Creating trust in piranha-infested waters: The confluence of buyer, supplier and host country contexts. *Journal of International Business Studies* 42 (1): 48–55.

Zaheer, A., B. McEvily, and V. Perrone. 1998. Does trust matter? Exploring the effects of interorganizational and interpersonal trust on performance. *Organization Science* 9 (2): 141–159.

Zand, D.E. 2016. Reflections on trust and trust research: Then and now. *Journal of Trust Research* 6: 63–73. https://doi.org/10.1080/21515581.2015.1134332.

Zucker, L.G. 1986. Production of trust. Institutional sources of economic structure, 18401920. *Research in Organisation Behaviour* 8: 53–111.

Part II

Rethinking Institutions and Trust Development in Entrepreneurial Relationships in Africa

4

Institutions Influencing Trust Development in Entrepreneurial Relationships in Africa

4.1 Introduction

Africa's economy is experiencing significant transformation and growth. Currently, Africa offers tremendous entrepreneurial opportunities with the continent having the highest share of adults starting and managing new businesses in the world, and 80% of the population regarding it as a good career opportunity (African Economic Outlook 2017). However, Africa remains a complex market due to weak state and market institutions and widespread notions of corruption embedded in African state institutions and societies (The Economist 2016; World Bank 2018). Often, these institutional weaknesses are hyped up by existing literature, policy documents, and reports on Africa to justify the lack of entrepreneurship and investment by foreigners (Bruton et al. 2010; The Economist 2016).

In fact, the emphasis on weaknesses of state and market institutions is biased as it ignores the positive role played by indigenous African institutions such as trade associations, personal networks and other cultural institutions that enhance the development of trust in the absence of strong

© The Author(s) 2019
I. O. Amoako, *Trust, Institutions and Managing Entrepreneurial Relationships in Africa*,
Palgrave Studies of Entrepreneurship in Africa,
https://doi.org/10.1007/978-3-319-98395-0_4

institutions (Amoako and Lyon 2014; Amoako and Matlay 2015). The indigenous institutions work side by side with the institutions of the modern states in Africa (Jackson et al. 2008; George et al. 2016) to enhance the activities of local and foreign entrepreneurs who have an understanding of African business practices (Amoako and Matlay 2015; Jackson et al. 2008). While some literature mainly highlights the constraining influences of African cultural institutions (e.g. Dondo and Ngumo 1998), this chapter shows that far from being barriers to entrepreneurship development, African indigenous cultural institutions also enable entrepreneurship (see Buame 1996; Khayesi et al. 2017). In this chapter, the author shows that entrepreneurs on the continent rely mostly on indigenous institutions in their day-to-day activities and their wealth of local knowledge can benefit the global community of entrepreneurs and investors. Even though there are institutional barriers, entrepreneurs operating in Africa, as actors, do not necessarily accede to the weak institutions but instead rely on networks, relationships, and trust enabled by indigenous institutions to establish and grow businesses. In most instances, the indigenous institutions substitute for and replace the ineffective formal institutions leading to enhanced entrepreneurial activities (Estrin and Pervezer 2011; Amoako and Lyon 2014). There is increasing evidence that in spite of weak state and market institutions, and the contradictory roles of some indigenous cultural institutions, Africa offers opportunities to entrepreneurs and investors who are prepared to adapt their business models to the continent's markets (George et al. 2016; Delloitte 2014).

The weak institutions in Africa also provide official data supporting policy documents and reports that ignore the high levels of creativity and entrepreneurship in the informal sector, which accounts for about 55% of Africa's gross domestic product (GDP) and provides more than half of the goods and services traded outside the official economy (AfDB 2013). The informal sector predominantly relies on indigenous institutions and cultural norms to develop trust in entrepreneurial engagements but the sector and the indigenous institutions that drive its enterprise activities have not received much attention in the study of business management and entrepreneurship in Africa (Jackson 2004; Tillmar and Lindkvist 2007; Amoako and Matlay 2015).

By ignoring the roles of indigenous cultural institutions that enable entrepreneurship, the African entrepreneur, and the informal sector, the current Western and Eurocentric discourses about entrepreneurship practices in Africa have been criticised as resonating with colonial projects that highlight institutions that may not be compatible with African cultural contexts and paradigms (Jackson 2004; Zoogah and Nkomo 2013).

This chapter aims to draw attention to the important indigenous institutional influences on entrepreneurship in Africa by answering the question: 'What are the institutions that influence entrepreneurship and the development of trust in entrepreneurial relationships in Africa?'

To answer this question, the author draws on institutional theory particularly institutional logics perspective to show how African entrepreneurs use logics of state and market as well as indigenous cultural institutions in entrepreneurial decision making and activities (Thornton et al. 2012; Vickers et al. 2017; Friedland and Alford 1991). The term 'institutional logics' is defined as the 'socially constructed, historical patterns of cultural symbols and material practices, including assumptions, values, and beliefs by which individuals and organisations provide meaning to their daily activity, organise time and space and reproduce their lives and experiences' (Thornton, Ocasio and Lounsbury 2012: 2). Actors use logics to interpret and make sense of the world while at the same time the logics offer resources for relationship building and decision making (Thornton and Ocasio 2008).

This chapter highlights that entrepreneurs have a low trust in state and market institutions colonial heritage. As a result, entrepreneurs respond to the weaknesses of formal institutions using the logics of indigenous cultural institutions that have their origins in African societies. These cultural institutions run side by side with state institutions to enhance trust development in entrepreneurial relationships in Africa. Nonetheless, some of the cultural institutions pose challenges to entrepreneurs and these are also critically analysed and discussed in this chapter. Figure 4.1 presents a framework developed from the literature and empirical data to guide the discussions in the rest of the chapter.

This chapter contributes to the literature in three ways. First, by presenting a framework that attempts to offer an understanding of the roles of state and market and indigenous institutions in trust and

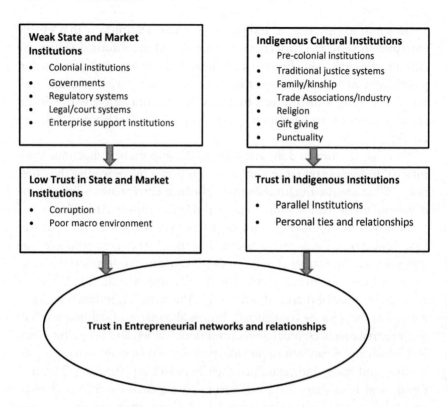

Fig. 4.1 Institutions influencing trust development in entrepreneurial relationships in Africa. (Source: Own research)

entrepreneurial relationship development in Africa. Second, it helps to reconceptualise our understanding of the role of institutions in entrepreneurship in Africa. Third, by identifying and critically analysing a number of key common African indigenous cultural institutions, it enhances our understanding of the processes of developing trust and cooperation with and among African entrepreneurs. This enhances cross-cultural entrepreneurial relationship development within and outside Africa.

The rest of this chapter is organised as follows. Section 4.2 identifies and discusses the weak state and market institutions in Africa. Section 4.3 presents a brief overview of low trust in formal institutions. Section 4.4 identifies and discusses indigenous cultural institutions shaping trust development in Africa. Section 4.5 discusses trust in parallel institutions and trust in personal ties and relationships and Sect. 4.6 concludes the chapter.

4.2   Weak State and Market Institutions in Africa

The institutional logics approach recognises that historical contingency may constrain or enable action (Thornton et al. 2012). Historical contingency explains the continued use of practices based on historical preferences. Thus, to understand the African institutions discussed in this book and how the logics of those institutions influence entrepreneurial practices, we need to take a step back into history. The next sub-section presents an historical overview of key institutions that evolved to enable or constrain trust development in precolonial and colonial entrepreneurial relationships in Africa.

4.2.1   Colonial Institutions Shaping Trust in Entrepreneurial Relationships in Africa

Africa was colonised by European countries namely Great Britain, France, Portugal, Germany, Denmark, Belgium, Italy, Spain, and the Netherlands. As a result, colonial institutions constitute the basis of the current post-colonial institutions of African states (Jackson 2004). Colonisation affects the quality of institutions and entrepreneurship in African countries (Treisman 2000; Acemoglu and Johnson 2003), due to the impact of the imposition of unfamiliar colonial capitalist institutions and structures in African contexts that were characterised mainly by peasant economic structures (Englebert 2000; Diop 1987).

The colonial governments established new or hybrid institutions which focused on assisting the administrations to plan and rule (Fallers 1955), and supported trade with the colonies. Yet, in most African countries, the imported, formal, capitalist institutions were not congruent with the indigenous institutions and thus hampered the development of trust in institutions of state.

The colonial institutions systematically prevented the development of indigenous entrepreneurship and particularly industries in order to keep the colonies as a protected market for European manufactured exports (Frimpong Ansah 1991; Jackson 2004). For example, by making the acquisition of trading licences from the colonial government difficult, the indigenes were prevented from entering most industries, importing machinery, exporting locally manufactured goods and, in effect, embarking on industrialisation. Ultimately, the indigenous Africans operated in traditional activities that were of no interest to the Europeans (Agbodeka 1992). Due to these restrictions, the indigenes achieved very little in creativity and innovation even though African cultures encourage individual entrepreneurship (Mbigi 1997). Thus, the colonial era when institutions mainly constrained the indigenous African people in entrepreneurship could partly explain the current low trust in state institutions.

Apart from institutions of state established by the colonial governments, other institutions such as captaincy also evolved to facilitate trading during the colonial era. For example, in West Africa, there were captains who served as master merchant-brokers. The captains supervised senior and junior as well as apprentice merchant-brokers. The institution of captaincy was widespread in the region and was the basis of social networking, sharing information, sustaining shared norms and values, sanctioning defaulters, mobilising collective action, and facilitating the generation of social capital amongst the trading parties (Kea 1982). To reduce uncertainty and opportunism and facilitate long-term exchanges, the merchant-brokers established credit systems based on networks and trust that benefitted the local traders and the Europeans (Cruikshank 1853). The extension of substantial credit from either party to the trading partner when required underpinned the trading relationships between the ship captains and their local actors: this was based on trust and therefore could last for years. However, incidents of trust violations such as defaults and cheating led to the abrogation of such trading relations that could lead to the forming of new relationships with others (De Marees 1987). Yet, the European ship captains had neither the resources nor the expertise to engage directly in trading with the African hinterland. They also lacked immunities to the many fatal diseases of Africa and hence, they sold their goods to and also bought their exports from local actors who relied on the existing indigenous structures to trade in the hinterland (Webb 1999). Therefore, precolonial social institutions facilitated colonial trade.

Apart from goods, colonial trade in Africa also involved the buying and selling of slaves that began in the fifteenth century after the Portuguese started exploring the coast of West Africa until the British Slave Abolition Act in 1833 and after the American civil war in the 1860s. Although there are no concrete records, it is estimated that about 12.5 million slaves landed alive on the other side of the Atlantic (Angeles and Elizalde 2017). However, the total number of slaves traded could be higher due to the many unrecorded deaths. Some scholars argue that the slave trade adversely affected the economic development of Africa for a number of reasons: for example, in the promotion of wars and unstable militarised societies (Becker 1977; Inikori 2003), and in the loss of skills, technological inventions, production capacity, and industry (Rodney 1972). Others include economic chaos and social political instability which prevented the transformation of the economy from agrarian to an entrepreneurial economy (M'baye 2006), and overdependence on selling of slaves, curtailing growth in other sectors of the economy (Klein 2010). Nonetheless, some commentators argue that the slave trade brought prosperity to Africa by increasing the imports of quality and luxury goods (Northrup 1978), and money made from slavery allowed importation of goods (Klein 2010). However, considering the moral, ethical, political, economic, and social implications of the slave trade the author argues that it was detrimental to African enterprise development and economic growth. With regards to trust, studies suggest that individuals belonging to ethnic groups who were targeted more during the slave trade show lower levels of trust in their relatives, neighbours, coethnics, and local governments today (Nunn and Wantchekon 2011).

Drawing on the notion of historical contingency, the author argues that Africa's lack of progress in entrepreneurship could be partly attributed to the imposition of dysfunctional colonial institutions that restricted its people from creative and innovative activities for centuries and partly to the slave trade, and not to the backwardness of its people.

Yet, attributing Africa's lack of progress to the imposition of colonial institutions remains debatable since modern states everywhere eradicate competing institutions in order to rise and the European notion of state and its institutions had been exported elsewhere without similar consequences (Spruyt 1994; Englebert 2000). Critics also argue that in most cases colonisation in Africa had limited impact due to the doctrine of indirect rule of some European colonial powers that in many instances strengthened the powers of tribal kings and chiefs (Mamdani 1996). This line of argument suggests that Africans had been unable to reform the dysfunctional colonial institutions and provide enterprise-friendly institutional environments. Interestingly, in this study, the interviews show that African entrepreneurs primarily blame the lack of entrepreneurship development on the activities of weak governments, corrupt politicians, and public officials who have failed, in the main, to reform the weak, dysfunctional, colonial institutions but have instead exploited and perpetuated them.

4.2.2   Weak Governments and Regulatory Systems

The government remains the key formal institution in any country. It remains the overseer of the institutions that offer secure property rights, economic freedom, a fair and balanced legal/judicial system, contract enforcement, fair taxation policies, business regulation, a stable macroeconomic environment, infrastructure, health, and primary education (Sobel 2008). The role of government is therefore key to trust development in state institutions in any economy. Even though entrepreneurs as risk takers mobilise resources such as financial capital and enter into ventures, these activities require long-term commitments and depend on property rights that are stable, secure, and effectively enforced (Estrin et al. 2013). Similarly, stable, predictable, and efficient regulatory regimes enable the development of entrepreneurship due to their impact on the reduction of transactional costs and the movement of an economy from being personalised-transactional oriented and relationship-based to an impersonal rule-based one (Welter and Smallbone 2011).

Based on the World Bank's measure of government's effectiveness, Africa has the lowest score. The measures focus on quality of public services, quality of the civil service and its independence from political pressures, quality of formulation and implementation of policy, and the government's credibility on commitments to its stated policy (World Bank 2017). With a few exceptions, there are setbacks in the consolidation of democracy in a number of countries—including Burundi, Congo DR, South Sudan, and Guinea—experiencing instability and political upheavals, yet about 20% of the countries are stable. Thus, state- and market-supporting institutions in most countries in West, East, Central and South Africa are fundamentally weak and different from those of Western economies. The weak formal institutions adversely influence the level of entrepreneurial engagement in the various countries. For example, there are widespread allegations of corruption and extortion of bribes from entrepreneurs. There is also a lack of proper implementation of laws and regulations enacted by the formal organisations in Africa (Bruton et al. 2010; Biggs and Shah 2006; Fafchamps 2004; World Bank Enterprise Surveys 2012). In spite of these highlighted challenges, it is important to acknowledge that these measures of good governance are based on models developed outside Africa and may not tell the African story well. It is therefore important to investigate alternative approaches based on African perspectives to propose solutions for good governance.

4.2.3 Weak Legal/Court Systems

The weaknesses of governments and regulatory bodies in Africa are amplified by the existence of weak legal/court systems (Fafchamps 2004; Biggs and Shah 2006; Amoako and Lyon 2014). Legal systems affect the choice of governance in interfirm relationships and ultimately impact on economic growth (Zucker 1986; North 1990). However, entrepreneurs from African countries overwhelmingly perceive the legal/court systems to be weak and unable to support contract enforcement for smaller businesses and entrepreneurs. The weakness of the legal systems is attributed mainly to bribery and corruption, complex legal processes, delays due to long processes, and high costs of legal and solicitor fees. Due to these weaknesses, entrepreneurs in most African countries rarely engage with the legal systems (Bruton et al. 2010; Amoako and Lyon 2014).

4.3   Low Trust in State and Market Institutions in Africa

Institutions provide the different forms of embeddedness that encourage or discourage trustworthy behaviour and they are important for the efficient operation of an economy (North 1990). Sadly, Africa's weak state institutions have largely supported and perpetuated corruption and poor macroenvironments in most of the countries (Bruton et al. 2010). Given the lack of trust in colonial institutions and prevalence of weak state and market institutions in most African countries, it is not surprising that generally there is low institutional trust in Africa.

4.3.1   Corruption

Corruption undermines formal institutional trust and entrepreneurship in Africa through a number of processes. The author defines corruption as any behaviour or conduct of an individual to use his or her position to request, agree to offer or accept cash, gifts, and favours to act illegally in the performance of his or her duties. In a corrupt environment, officials utilise their positions to acquire private gain at the cost of entrepreneurs (Estrin et al. 2013; Yanga and Amoako 2013). Corruption thrives in environments where conflicts of interest are not managed properly, and officials who oversee projects or resource allocation are able to either control or influence decision making in their favour (Yanga and Amoako 2013; Heyman and Lipietz 1999).

In the empirical study, some entrepreneurs made allegations about demands for monetary payments and gifts from some public officials in the ministries, police, tax and customs authorities and how these demands add up to transactional costs. Generally, entrepreneurs from Ghana, Nigeria, Cameroon, Congo DR, Kenya, Tanzania, Uganda, Zimbabwe, and Malawi believe that corruption is rife among state institutions such as the police and legal/court systems that are specifically designed to prevent it. Corruption influences officials to administer discriminatory and preferential treatment to people who agree to pay bribes based on unclear rules and regulations. Yet, the payment of bribes remains an ethical dilemma to entrepreneurs, as sometimes, one may not get the support needed from state institutions if bribes are not paid. While some entrepreneurs acknowledge that they pay the bribes, others do not bribe and cope with this challenge by either relying on third parties or developing relationships and friendships with intermediaries and at times with officials. Nonetheless, while smaller businesses can often evade these payments, medium enterprises that may have higher economic outputs attract the attention of the corrupt officials who may extort money from them (Yanga and Amoako 2013; Estrin et al. 2013). Yet in this study, African entrepreneurs questioned suggestions in foreign media and reports that corruption is an African phenomenon. Instead they argued that corruption exists in every country albeit in different forms and with different names.

Interestingly, Transparency International (2017) reports on corruption in African and other economies support both the allegations on the pervasive nature of corruption made by the entrepreneurs. Based on an index, Transparency International ranks 180 countries on how corrupt their public sectors are perceived to be according to experts and people in business based on a scale of 0–100, where 0 is highly corrupt and 100 is very clean. The Corruption Perception Index shows that out of a total of 54 African countries involved in the study, only three have a score above 50, with Botswana scoring 61%, Rwanda 55%, and Namibia 51%, ranking 34th, 48th, and 55th least-corrupt countries in the world respectively. Regrettably, 10 of the most corrupt countries in the world are in Africa with Somalia and South Sudan ranked 179th and 180th respectively. Not surprisingly, Africa has the lowest average score (32%) of all the regions of the world. Nonetheless, the report also provides evidence of widespread corruption in other countries and regions of the world. Even though it could be described as something else, it is exactly the same thing with those involved using public office and their positions to acquire private gains at the cost of society and entrepreneurs (Estrin et al. 2013; Gyimah-Brempong 2002). It is therefore naive to think that corruption is an African phenomenon.

Yet, the major difference is that while corruption exists in even developed economies like the UK: when MPs fiddled their expenses, civil societies and the judiciary rose up to fight corruption (McTague 2015), but this rarely happens in Africa. There is therefore a need to address the lack of civil engagement and the weak, corrupt police and legal systems that are incapable of spearheading the fight against corruption in Africa.

4.3.2 Poor Macroenvironments

Most African countries have volatile macroenvironments characterised by inadequate infrastructure (World Bank Enterprise Surveys 2012). High inflation, exchange rate fluctuations, and higher interest and tax rates are prevalent macroeconomic challenges that inhibit entrepreneurial activities in all sectors. Entrepreneurs particularly confront a lack of access to affordable credit. This is attributed to banks' requests for collateral, which most entrepreneurs do not have. Additionally, the cost of borrowing can be very high in some countries. For example, in 2016 interest rates on bank loans in Ghana and Nigeria were 33% and 25% respectively.

Yet, there have been major improvements in the macroeconomic environment of many African countries. The region has enjoyed a steady and sustained growth for the past decade with different countries enjoying varied rates of economic growth (see Sect. 4.1). Yet, foreigners often regard the volatile macroenvironment and lack of infrastructure as the main reason not to do business in Africa. However, native African entrepreneurs and some investors identify opportunities including the fast-growing and untapped markets with a growing middle class, improved regulatory regimes, tax reforms, and ICT/internet infrastructure embedded in the macroenvironments. Most African entrepreneurs are also motivated by access to indigenous cultural institutions that allow trust to develop (Tillmar and Lindkvist 2007; Amoako and Lyon 2014; Amoako and Matlay 2015) and these will be examined in the next section.

4.4   Indigenous Cultural Institutions Shaping Trust Development in Entrepreneurial Relationships

4.4.1   Indigenous Precolonial Institutions Shaping Trust Development

The African indigenous economy was a feudal socio-economic system predominantly based on networks and ties of ethnic, tribal, community, and family/kinship affiliations (Hyden 1986) where the chief or king traditionally played an important role in facilitating trade. Indigenous economies were built on agriculture, pastoralism, markets and trade, and profit-sharing schemes that foreigners ignorantly denigrate as primitive and leaning towards communism (Ayittey 2006). Economic activity was organised around kinship, the clan, community, tribe or ethnic group, and the chief or king (Osei-Hwedie and Rankopo 2012; Perbi 2004). Trust in personalised relationships underpinned by indigenous institutions supported trade and has persisted to date and continues to play an important role in trust development and entrepreneurship in African societies (Myers 1992; Amoako and Lyon 2014).

The literature suggests that indigenous institutions facilitated entrepreneurship before colonisation as African states such as ancient Ghana, Nok-Ife, Ethiopia, and Zimbabwe traded with each other and with foreign merchants (Diop 1987; Iliffe 1983; Ogonda and Ochieng 1992). For example, in East Africa, Wandiba (1992) suggests that various types of industries existed in precolonial Kenya. These included iron smelting and forging, house building, woodwork, pottery, leatherwork, and basketry. Similarly, in West Africa, the indigenous African technology of glass and bead making in Yorubaland and bronze in Benin existed in Nigeria and these technologies ushered in a social, religious, and economic transformation dating from the second millennium or earlier (Babalola 2017).

Africa also engaged in trade with the Egyptians and the Carthaginians. Cities on the East Coast of Africa traded with the Egyptians, Phoenicians,

Arabs, Persians, Indians, Siamese, and Chinese (Ogonda and Ochieng 1992). Similarly, the Sudan-Sohel region immediately south of the Sahara also had links with ancient trading blocks such as the Arab empires and feudal Europe. There was also a vibrant trade between West African communities and the Muslims from across the Sahara up to the Mediterranean. Muslim traders had links to the trans-Saharan and West African trade networks (Iliffe 1983). Trans-Saharan trade linked the whole of the Mediterranean, Arab, and European empires together, supplying gold from the Senegal and Ashanti regions in modern Ghana. The Mediterranean world supplied books, writing paper, cowries, tea, coffee, sugar, spices, jewellery, perfumes, bracelets, mirrors, carpets, and beads (Perbi 2004). There was also a vibrant regional trade among Africans. For example, between the first to the sixteenth centuries, merchants in ancient Ghana exchanged gold for slaves, beads, cotton, and cloth from their counterparts through a trade network stretching from modern Senegal to Benin state in Modern Nigeria. The northern Savannah region of West Africa also brought in millet, sorghum, wheat, livestock, gum, shea butter, ivory, ostrich feathers, cloth, and slaves. Through trade the ruling class obtained goods such as cloths, drugs, dates, and salt as well as items such as horses, copper, iron bars, and weapons (Amin 1972).

Indigenous institutions supported trade and economic exchanges in African societies during the precolonial and colonial era. Politically, African societies were characterised by a heterogeneity of significant political centralisation. For example, while the Shongai Empire in West Africa, Luba Kingdom in Central Africa, and Buganda in East Africa all had centralised political administrations headed by kings and chiefs, others such as the Nuer in Sudan had no centralised political organisation outside the villages (Murdock 1967).

Indigenous institutions provide most of the logics that enhance trust development in entrepreneurship across African countries and the next sub-section examines the key common ones. However, it is important to emphasise that there are countless cultural institutions and norms that may shape entrepreneurial trust development and they may differ based on markets, sectors, and countries.

4.4.2   Traditional Justice System

The majority of entrepreneurs rely on the logics of the traditional justice system based on customary law, and the system has been resilient in spite of the onslaught and subjugation by Western imposed formal justice systems (Myers 1992). The traditional justice system focuses on the restoration of impaired relationships at the physical level between individuals and all stakeholders involved but also at the spiritual level to restore severed relationships with family, neighbours, God or Allah, spirits, and ancestors depending on the nature of the case (Osei-Hwedie and Rankopo 2012). Interestingly, traditional methods prevail in many communities especially at the grassroots level. The process involves family heads, elders, queens, chiefs, and others who resolve, stop, and intercept conflicts. The traditional courts may initially start with the elders and the case can be escalated to the chief or paramount chief or king only if the elders fail to find a solution. The elder or traditional leader asks questions, seek advice from the members of the court, and give judgements that aim to reconcile the parties after they have given their accounts of what happened. The process is informal, less intimidating and less confrontational while aiming to restore trust, mend broken relationships, rectify wrongs, and restore justice. Internal and external control mechanisms involving shame and fear of supernatural forces and the behaviours and actions of others that may signify their approval or disapproval underpin the process (Okrah 2003).

The system, however, faces a number of challenges including negative attitudes received from 'modernised Africans' who despise traditional African spiritual practices such as rituals and witchcraft which complement conflict resolution. The constitutions of some African countries that regard the norms, values, and beliefs that form the basis of African customary law as inferior may limit the system. Furthermore, the close ties and social capital between families and kinsmen that underpin the system have reduced due to urbanisation. The system has also become vulnerable due to changes in the way African societies accumulate wealth these days. While in the past elders accumulated wealth through land and livestock, currently, younger people may be richer and a significant number of elders rely on younger people. As a result, bribery, corruption, and favouritism can affect dispute resolution by the elders (Kariuki 2015).

Drawing on the logics of the traditional African justice system, often entrepreneurs and their trading partners repair trust by resolving conflicts and disputes through a number of culturally specific institutions including the elders of family, community leaders and chiefs, trade associations, and religious leaders. Chapters 5, 6, 7 and 8 examine these issues in more detail.

4.4.3   Family/Kinship

The institution of family/kinship plays an important role in entrepreneurship in Africa. The most basic social structure in Africa is the extended family and there are close social ties and social capital among families, relatives, and the community. In African culture the community comes first, hence the philosophy of Ubuntu asserts that communalism, interdependence, sensitivity towards others, and caring for one another make up the traditional African way of life. As a result, perceiving human needs, interests, and dignity is fundamental to the African philosophy of life (Le Roux 2000). Within African societies, the philosophy of communalism that promotes trust, common good, and humanness persists. Furthermore, there is widespread respect for ancestors, elders, parents, fellow people, and the environment and these are embedded in norms, mores, taboos, and traditions (Bujo 1998) such as titles.

Traditionally, the social structure in Africa comprises of members of the extended family, heads of households, village chiefs, paramount chiefs, and the king (Osei-Hwedie and Rankopo 2012). The chief or king remains the head of the different families and the community and even though his or her authority has waned due to colonisation and modernisation, currently in many African countries ethnic chiefs and kings continue to wield significant power in allocating land, collecting taxes, and providing some basic public goods (Acemoglu and Robinson 2012; George et al. 2016).

The extended family develops the norms, values, and behaviour that society regards to be acceptable and members of the family have extended rights as well as extended obligations. However, currently due to colonisation, modernisation, and migration, the basic family system is changing from the extended family to the nuclear family (Osei-Hwedie and Rankopo 2012).

In African cultures, often the extended family intervenes to provide capital, education, and skills to family members as states provide little or no social support to care for children. Hence, a significant number of entrepreneurs regard family values, norms, and support to be important when starting, developing, and managing businesses and entrepreneurial relationships. Logics of family based on norms of mutuality, reciprocity, and care also influence the development of business relationships that resemble families. Yet, the norms of the African family system may pose immense challenges to African entrepreneurs and small and medium-sized enterprises (SMEs). For example, family members may make excessive demands on entrepreneurs due to poverty and inequalities in income distribution in African societies (Buame 1996; Kiggundu 2002; Kuada 2015). Family members may also show low commitment when they are employed in family businesses (Amoako 2012; Kuada 2015). Due to some of these challenges from African family norms, some commentators (see Okpara 2007) suggest that the African family system and cultures (see Dondo and Ngumo 1998) do not facilitate entrepreneurship. However, such arguments only present a partial picture since the African family system may or may not facilitate entrepreneurship development depending on the level of demands made on entrepreneurs based on the economic circumstances of particular families. Amoako and Lyon (2014) refer to these paradoxical norms as 'the paradox of the family'. Nonetheless, it is important to note that the constraining practices of family/kinship on developing enterprise and business relationships are not limited to Africa. For example, in Pakistan, due to patriarchal Islamic norms, women entrepreneurs are constrained by social cultural norms that dictate family roles (Rehman and Roomi 2012).

4.4.4   Norms of Trade Associations and Industry

Trade associations play important roles in enhancing trust development in entrepreneurial relationships in Africa. Yet, indigenous institutions underpin the overwhelming majority of trade associations. For example, in West Africa, the landlord *(efiewura)* system is an indigenous institution embedded in trade associations that involve agents (landlords) who sell goods on behalf of exporters in distant domestic and regional West African markets for a commission. Chapter 6 will explore this in more detail. The norms of specific trade associations are often associated with specific industries based on codes of conduct and practices that members adhere to.

Trade associations provide immense social capital by offering critical services to members including mobilising resources, regulating industries and markets, conflict resolution, advocacy, welfare, and networking. Yet these services may differ based on the context. For example, in East Africa, the Kenya Association of Manufacturers and the Leather Articles Entrepreneurs Association play active roles in building networks and mobilising resources for entrepreneurs operating in the leather industry. In Southern Africa, SIMODISA liaises with financial institutions including banks and venture capital associations to facilitate entrepreneurial financing and networking to enhance the rapid growth of enterprises. In West Africa, trade associations operate in all sectors and are often involved in conflict resolution, operating in parallel to the courts that entrepreneurs perceive to be corrupt, expensive and time consuming (Fafchamps 2004; Lyon and Porter 2009; Amoako and Lyon 2014). As a result, the associations provide 'parallel institutional trust' and cooperation; Chap. 6 will explore this in detail. Not surprisingly, the majority of African entrepreneurs belong to trade associations. In this book, trade association refers to an organisation formed to pursue the collective interests of businesses operating in an industry.

Members in specific industries and trades form and fund the associations mostly by the payment of membership fees. They may be led by a 'queen', 'chief' or chairperson who may be assisted by a secretary and a treasurer. Some of these associations may therefore be hybrid institutions that draw on Western organisational forms as well as local, traditional, and industry norms (Amoako and Lyon 2014). Members of the associations meet regularly to pursue their common good. Even though in most cases membership of trade associations are open to all, a few may restrict membership. For example, in northern Nigeria membership of some food associations is restricted to only males. This is due to the dominant cultural and religious norms in the north of Nigeria that may restrict females from engaging in some forms of enterprise activities. In some countries, a few trade associations may also operate as cartels by curtailing competition in particular sectors (Lyon 2005).

4.4.5 Religious Norms and Values

Religion remains an important cultural factor that provides logics in entrepreneurship in African societies. In a study of British Africans in the UK, Nwankwo et al. (2012) show that religion and spirituality offer space for entrepreneurship and enable Africans in the UK to overcome the institutional barriers to entrepreneurship. Currently among Africans, 21% are Muslims, 36% are Christians, and 40% are Animists. However, with the exception of a few hotspots such as northern Nigeria and Somalia the religious groups coexist peacefully. A significant number of African entrepreneurs use religious logics that emphasise the existence of supernatural powers that may protect or cause disaster. African entrepreneurs regard religious beliefs to be important in trust development in entrepreneurial relationships. Religious logics encourage honesty, reciprocity, and caring for one another, and therefore enhance trustworthiness. As a result, some entrepreneurs believe that partners who are religious and share similar faiths have similar values and will not deceive or cheat them since the Bible, Quran, and traditional religious values prohibit such acts.

Additionally, entrepreneurs draw on the logics of religion to rely on religious leaders and norms of religion to resolve disputes with business partners. Some of the entrepreneurs rely on ministers of religion—pastors, imams, and clerics—and traditional religious leaders instead of the courts to settle disputes and to enforce agreements between them and their partners. This is due to the complementary role of belief in supernatural bodies in traditional conflict resolution in Africa (Kariuki 2015).

Yet, there are fake religious leaders in Africa who use deception and fraudulent means to make claims about miracles and connections to the spirits in order to deceive and defraud entrepreneurs and other followers to enrich themselves. For example, De Witte (2013) explains how some Pentecostal pastors use an electric touch machine and other technologies to impart the 'holy spirit' and to mimic 'divine' voices in order to deceive their followers.

4.4.6   Norms of Gift Giving

Gift giving is a universal behaviour (Sherry 1983), but the norms of gift giving may differ from culture to culture. Gift giving is a very important part of African culture (Ayittey 1991; Kenyatta 1965). However, outside the continent there is little understanding about the practice of gift giving in African cultures and it is often misconstrued to perpetuate corruption. Gift giving enhances favours, obligations, and reciprocity among African communities. It fosters trust, peaceful coexistence, and harmony among African societies and it is legitimate (Yanga and Amoako 2013; Ayittey 1991; Kenyatta 1965). The author defines a gift as a present or an item given to someone to show favour, appreciation, or in expectation of reciprocity. This definition entails elements of sustaining social aspects and may be different from definitions in countries where gifts are expected to be free of reciprocity.

Gift giving influences trust development and the management of entrepreneurial relationships in Africa and entrepreneurs and managers use cultural logics to justify the practices of gift giving (Yanga and Amoako 2013). The gifts serve as acts of favour that help to build and cement relationships through indebtedness, reciprocity, and control and are acceptable within social and entrepreneurial relationships in the continent. Nevertheless, there is a debate about the role of gift giving in the perpetuation of corruption among state officials in Africa. While some entrepreneurs confirm the views of Ayittey (1991) and Kenyatta (1965) that gift giving is a legitimate African cultural norm that has nothing to do with corruption, others argue that it could promote corruption when dealing with public officials. Not surprisingly, some entrepreneurs adopt 'zero tolerance for gifts and tokens' and ensure that they do business without giving gifts, others at times offer gifts because there may be a correlation between how fast you can gain support from some state officials and how generous you are with gifts. Thus, the main problem with gift giving to public officials manifests when entrepreneurs have to wait 'forever' to access the services of public servants who expect them to offer gifts or bribes. In these instances, officials refuse to perform their duties because they have not received gifts (Yanga and Amoako 2013).

4.4.7   Norms of African Punctuality

Understanding norms of punctuality in Africa is critical to the development of trust and sustainable entrepreneurial relationships with African entrepreneurs. Africa's polychromic culture has a flexible approach to time use. Amoako and Matlay (2015) refer to instances when entrepreneurs and other economic actors may add one or two hours or a few days to the time or date agreed for a meeting and/or a transaction and therefore possibly missing the appointment or the deadline, as norms of 'African punctuality'. Norms of 'African punctuality' refers to culturally specific norms of flexibility about meeting deadlines and times for appointments, irrespective of how urgent these might be. These norms imply that, in Africa, being several minutes late for a meeting or missing a supply deadline by a few days may be acceptable. However, 'African punctuality' remains one of the least-understood cultural norms that has the potential to undermine trust development in entrepreneurial relationships with partners from different cultures. Norms of African punctuality play a significant role in the management of entrepreneurial relationships and in trust development and Chaps. 5, 6 and 7 will discuss these in more detail.

4.5   Trust in Indigenous Institutions in Africa

The discussions so far show that state and market institutions in African countries are weak (Fafchamps 2004; Amoako and Lyon 2014). Hence, entrepreneurs owning smaller businesses rely mainly on logics of indigenous institutions in developing trust to access resources, enforce contracts, and sanction defaulters. In both domestic and distant African markets, entrepreneurs draw on logics of indigenous institutions to develop parallel institutional trust and personal trust in networks and relationships. Personal trust becomes more important in environments where formal sanctioning mechanisms are absent or fail, and in cases where an exchange partner is not satisfied with the institutional arrangements or is unfamiliar with them, personal trust may therefore complement institutional trust (see Chap. 3). In Africa, parallel institutional trust and personal trust may therefore substitute for institutional trust. Parallel institutional trust refers to trust in indigenous institutions that run side by side with state and market institutions. This is because parallel institutional trust and personal trust can exist regardless of the legal and political context, whereas institutional trust may require stability and predictability based on legitimate societal institutions reflected by strong formal institutions (Welter and Smallbone 2006). Chapter 5 will discuss how state and indigenous institutions shape the development of parallel institutional trust and personal trust in more detail.

Case 4.1 Indigenous Institutions and SMEs in Africa

Alhaji Abiodun is the CEO of Alliasin Furniture Enterprise in Lagos, Nigeria. Currently he exports some of his products through agents to Cotonou and Accra in Benin and Ghana respectively. He has seven employees and five of them are his brothers while the two remaining workers are his cousins. He explains that he employs his family members because he trusts them first, then friends second, members of the mosque come third, and then people in the community come fourth. He explains that the furniture industry involves a lot of trust and most of the transactions are based on trade credit as the local banks do not support small businesses. Also transactions are based on oral contracts since some of his customers and suppliers are illiterates. Oral contracts are flexible, simple, and free as they do not involve any lawyers; instead entrepreneurs agree on transactions with strangers before two or three people who serve as witnesses. The trade credit system is based on trust and trade debtors are chosen based on a track record of honesty. He emphasises: 'You must be a honest person, sincere person, if you say I will come tomorrow, you will come tomorrow. Your word is important, once we can take your word for it and you don't have any bad record we will do business with you'. According to Alhaji, religion plays an important role in fostering trustworthy behaviour. He explains that religious people are honest and he likes doing business with people from his religion because 'our faith, belief and values are the same and a good Muslim will not cheat another Muslim'. Another important institution that supports his business is the trade association whose members meet once every month to network with one another. He explains that it is impossible to succeed in the furniture industry without being a member of a trade association. The association also serves other important purposes. For example, when a customer or supplier defaults (violates trust) he reports them to the trade association and the association leaders helps to resolve the conflict and repair trust. At times he reports defaulters to the head or chief imam of the local mosque. The chief imam is a respected cleric and he helps to resolve the problem. On other occasions he uses the local community chief, also known as the *bale*, and he explains that the local chiefs play an important role in conflict resolution and 'There is nobody the *bale* will summon that will not come. You have to come, so that is it'. Alhaji also intimated that he offers and receives gifts from customers and suppliers.

4.6 Conclusion

This chapter investigates institutional influences on trust development in entrepreneurial relationships in Africa (addressing the research question). The chapter presents a model that shows the institutions whose logics influence trust development in entrepreneurial relationships in Africa. The discussions explain that the imposition of colonial institutions that were not congruent with Africa's indigenous social structures impacted negatively on the development of trust in entrepreneurial relationships (Englebert 2000). The colonial institutions also restricted indigenous Africans' involvement in entrepreneurship and, by implication, creativity and innovation. Similarly, the slave trade caused instability and uncertainty that in turn led to mistrust among African societies (M'baye 2006; Nunn and Wantchekon 2011). This, rather than widespread suggestions that the people are backward or less creative, may explain why African entrepreneurship lags behind the rest of the world.

This chapter also critically evaluates the state and market institutions that are less efficient and may not necessarily be useful in the promotion of entrepreneurship in African economies. It highlights the weaknesses of state/market institutions and the importance of indigenous social and cultural institutions that promote trust, networking, and relationship building in entrepreneurship in the context of weak formal institutions.

Furthermore, this chapter identifies a number of cultural-specific African institutions that provide the logics that facilitate trust development in entrepreneurial relationships. These are the traditional justice system, trade associations, family/kinship, religion, gift giving, and punctuality. These indigenous institutions promote trust and trade in domestic and distant markets contrary to assumptions that indigenous institutions do not promote arm's-length exchanges (Amoako and Lyon 2014; Lyon and Porter 2009). Regrettably, most African governments and foreign enterprise support institutions do not recognise or support the indigenous institutions.

That is not to say that the informal institutions are without challenges too. Clearly, there are paradoxes relating to some indigenous institutions. For example, the African family system may enable but also constrain the development of trust in entrepreneurial relationships and enterprise development due to logics of sharing, reciprocity, obligations, and expectations for socially altruistic models of stewardship (Amoako and Lyon 2014; Drakopoulou-Dodd and Gotsis 2009). The African family system may endow entrepreneurs with resources such as start-up capital, information, networks, and cheap labour. Entrepreneurs in turn may have obligations to care and support family members (Ayittey 2006). However, some entrepreneurs who have established small businesses mainly by themselves and who often draw on agentic norms in the pursuit of wealth may reject their obligations to extended family members. However, by doing so these entrepreneurs reject the social capital inherent in family and kinship (Amoako and Lyon 2014). It is important to note that these contradictions and conflicts in family and business cultures (Drakopoulou-Dodd and Gotsis 2009) are not restricted to Africa.

This chapter contributes to the literature in three ways: (1) it presents a framework that visually portrays the formal and informal institutions that influence the development of trust in entrepreneurial relationships in Africa; (2) it analyses and reconceptualises the role of formal and informal institutions in entrepreneurship; and (3) it identifies and critically analyses the key, common, African formal and cultural-specific institutions and norms that shape trust development in entrepreneurial relationships. Understanding these formal institutions and cultural-specific institutional logics is critically important due to their potential to give rise to differences in explanations and attributions of trust, and therefore foster conflict and misunderstanding of African entrepreneurial behaviour within relationships.

The next chapter continues the analysis and discussion of how African entrepreneurs build, manage, and sustain their networks and relationships.

References

Acemoglu, D., and S. Johnson. 2003. Institutions, corporate governance. *Corporate Governance and Capital Flows in a Global Economy* 1: 32.

Acemoglu, D., and J.A. Robinson. 2012. *Why nations fail? The origins of power, prosperity, and poverty*. New York: Crown Publishers.

African Development Bank Group. 2013. Championing inclusive growth across Africa: Recognizing Africa's informal sector, Tunis. https://www.afdb.org/en/blogs/afdb-championing-inclusive-growth-across-africa/post/recognizing-africas-informal-sector-11645.

African Economic Outlook. 2017. Entrepreneurship and industrialisation, African Development Bank, OECD, United Nations Development Programme, Abidjan, Paris and New York.

Agbodeka, F. 1992. *An economic history of Ghana from the earliest times*. Accra: Ghana Universities Press.

Amin, S. 1972. Underdevelopment and dependence in Black Africa: Origins and contemporary forms. *Journal of Modern African Studies* 10 (4): 503–525.

Amoako, I.O. 2012. Trust in exporting relationships: The case of SMEs in Ghana, published PhD thesis, Center for Economic and Enterprise Development Research (CEEDR) Middlesex University, London, http://eprints.mdx.ac.uk/12419/.

Amoako, I.O., and F. Lyon. 2014. We don't deal with courts': Cooperation and alternative institutions shaping exporting relationships of SMEs in Ghana. *International Small Business Journal* 32 (2): 117–139.

Amoako, I.O., and H. Matlay. 2015. Norms and trust-shaping relationships among food exporting SMEs in Ghana. *International Journal of Entrepreneurship & Innovation* 16 (2): 123–124.

Angeles, L., and A. Elizalde. 2017. Pre-colonial institutions and socioeconomic development: The case of Latin America. *Journal of Development Economics* 10 (124): 22–40. https://doi.org/10.1016/j.jdeveco.2016.08.006.

Ayittey, G.B.N. 1991. *Indigenous African institutions*. New York: Transnational Publishers.

———. 2006. *Indigenous African institutions*. second ed. Ardsley: Transnational Publishers.

Babalola, A.B. 2017. Ancient history of technology in West Africa: The indigenous glass/glass bead industry and the society in early Ile-Ife, Southwest Nigeria. *Journal of Black Studies* 48 (1). https://doi.org/10.1177/0021934717701915.

Becker, C. 1977. La Sénégambie à l'époque de la traite des esclaves. *Revue Française d'Histoire d'Outre-Mer Paris* 64 (235): 203–224.

Biggs, T., and M.K. Shah. 2006. African SMES, networks, and manufacturing performance. *Journal of Banking and Finance* 30 (11): 2931–3256.

Bruton, G.D., D. Ahlstrom, and H.L. Li. 2010. Institutional theory and entrepreneurship: Where are we now and where do we need to move in the future? *Entrepreneurship Theory and Practice* 34 (3): 421–440.

Buame, S.K. 1996. *Entrepreneurship: A contextual perspective: Discourses and praxis of entrepreneurial activities: Within the institutional context of Ghana*. Lund: Lund University Press.

Bujo, B. 1998. *The ethical dimensions of community: The African model and the dialogue between North and South*. Nairobi: Kolbe Press.

Cruikshank, B. 1853. *Eighteen years on the Gold Coast of Africa*. Vol. 2. London: Hurst and Blacket.

De Marees, P. 1987. *Description and historical account of the Gold Kingdom of Guinea*. Trans. A. V. Dantzigand and A. Jones. Oxford: Oxford University Press.

De Witte, M. 2013. The electric touch machine miracle scam: Body, technology, and the (dis)authentication of the pentecostal supernatural. In *Deus in machina: Religion, technology, and the things in between*, ed. J. Stolow. New York: Fordham University Press.

Delloitte. 2014. *The Delloitte consumer review* Africa: A 21st century view. London.

Diop, Cheikh Anta. 1987. *Black Africa: The economic and cultural basis for a federated state*. Chicago: Chicago Review Press.

Dondo, A., and M. Ngumo. 1998. Africa: Kenya. In *Entrepreneurship: An international perspective*, ed. A. Morrison. Oxford: Butterworth-Heinemann.

Drakopoulou Dodd, S., and G. Gotsis. 2009. Enterprise values' in the New Testament and antecedent works. *International Journal of Entrepreneurship and Innovation* 10 (2): 101–110.

Englebert, P. 2000. Pre-colonial institutions, post-colonial states, and economic development in tropical Africa. *Political Research Quarterly* 53: 7–36.

Estrin, S., and M. Prevezer. 2011. The role of informal institutions in corporate governance: Brazil, Russia, India, and China compared. *Asia Pacific Journal of Management* 28 (1): 41–67.

Estrin, S., J. Korosteleva, and T. Mickiewicz. 2013. Which institutions encourage entrepreneurial growth aspirations? *Journal of Business Venturing* 28: 564–580.

Fafchamps, M. 2004. *Market institutions in Sub-Saharan Africa: Theory and evidence*. Cambridge: MIT Press.

Fallers, L. 1955. The predicament of the modern African chief: An instance from Uganda. *American Anthropologist* 57: 290–305.

Friedland, R., and R.R. Alford. 1991. Bringing society back in: Symbols, practices, and institutional contradictions. In *The new institutionalism in organizational analysis*, ed. W.W. Powell and P.J. DiMaggio, 17th ed., 232–263. Chicago: University of Chicago Press.

Frimpong-Ansah, J.H. 1991. *The Vampire state in Africa: The political economy of decline in Ghana*. London: James Currey.

George, G., J.N.O. Khayesi, and M.R.T. Haas. 2016. Bringing Africa in: Promising directions for management research. *Academy of Management Journal* 59 (2): 377–393.

Gyimah-Brempong, K. 2002. Corruption, economic growth, and income inequality in Africa. *Economics of Governance, Spring* 3: 183–209.

Heyman, C., and B. Lipietz. 1999. *Corruption and development: Some perspectives*. Pretoria: Institute for Security Studies, (40).

Hyden, Goran. 1986. African social structure and economic development. In *Strategies for African development*, 52–80. Berkeley: University of California Press.

Iliffe, J. 1983. *The emergence of African capitalism*. London: Macmillan.

Inikori, J.E. 2003. The struggle against the transatlantic slave trade: The role of the state. In *Fighting the slave trade: West African strategies*, ed. Sylviane A. Diouf, 170–198. Athens: Ohio University Press.

Jackson, T. 2004. *Management and change in Africa: A cross-cultural perspective.* London: Routledge.

Jackson, T., K. Amaeshi, and S. Yavuz. 2008. Untangling African indigenous management: Multiple influences on the success of SMEs in Kenya. *Journal of World Business* 43 (3): 400–416.

Kariuki, F. 2015. Conflict resolution by elders in Africa: Successes, challenges and opportunities. *Alternative Dispute Resolution* 3 (2): 30–53.

Kea, R.A. 1982. *Settlements, trade, and polities in the seventeenth century Gold Coast.* Baltimore/London: The Johns Hopkins University Press.

Kenyatta, J. 1965. *Facing Mt. Kenya.* New York: Vintage.

Khayesi, J.N.O., A. Sserwanga, and R. Kiconco. 2017. Culture as facilitator and a barrier to entrepreneurship development in Uganda. In *Entrepreneurship in Africa*, ed. A. Akinyoade, T. Dietz, and C. Uche. Leiden: African Dynamics, Volume 15, Brill.

Kiggundu, M. 2002. Entrepreneurs and entrepreneurship in Africa: What is known and needs to be done. *Journal of Development Entrepreneurship* 7: 239–258.

Klein, H.S. 2010. *The Atlantic slave trade.* 2nd ed. Cambridge: Cambridge University Press.

Kuada, J. 2015. Entrepreneurship in Africa—A classifactory framework and a research agenda. *African Journal of Economic and Management Studies* 6 (2): 148–163.

Le Roux, J. 2000. The concept of 'ubuntu': Africa's most important contribution to multicultural education? *MulticulturalTeaching* 18 (2): 43–46.

Lyon, F. 2005. Managing co-operation: Trust and power in Ghanaian associations. *Organization Studies* 27 (1): 31–52.

Lyon, F., and G. Porter. 2009. Market institutions, trust, and norms: Exploring moral economies in Nigerian food systems. *Cambridge Journal of Economics* 33 (3): 903–929.

M'baye, B. 2006. The economic, political, and social impact of the Atlantic slave trade on Africa. *European Legacy* 11 (6): 607–622.

Mamdani, M. 1996. *Citizen and subject: Contemporary Africa and the legacy of late Colonialism.* Princeton: Princeton University Press.

Mbigi, L. 1997. *Ubuntu: The African dream in management.* Randburg: Knowledge Resources.

McTague, T. 2015. All MPs' expenses receipts to be published after judges throw out bid to keep them secret, Mail Online, 28th April 2018.

Murdock, G.P. 1967. *Ethnographic atlas.* Pittsburgh: University of Pittsburgh Press.

Myers, L.J. 1992. *Understanding an Afrocentric world view: Introduction to an optimal psychology.* Dubuque: Kendall/Hunt.

North, D.C. 1990. *Institutions, institutional change and economic performance.* Cambridge: Cambridge University Press.

Northrup, D. 1978. *Trade without rulers: Pre-colonial economic development in South-Eastern Nigeria.* Oxford: Clarendon Press.

Nunn, Nathan, and Leonard Wantchekon. 2011. The slave trade and the origins of mistrust in Africa. *American Economic Review* 101 (7): 3221–3252.

Nwankwo, S., A. Gbadamosi, and S. Ojo. 2012. Religion, spirituality and entrepreneurship: The church as entrepreneurial space among British Africans. *Society and Business Review* 7 (2): 149–167.

Ogonda, R.T. and Ochieng W.R. 1992. "Land, natural and human resources, In W.R. Ochieng' and R.M. Maxon Eds. *An economic history of Kenya.* Nairobi: East African Educational Publishers.

Okpara, F.O. 2007. The value of creativity and innovation in entrepreneurship. *Journal of Asia Entrepreneurship and Sustainability* 3 (2): 1–14.

Okrah, K.A. 2003. *Nyasapo (the Wisdom Knot): Toward an African philosophy of education.* New York: Routledge.

Osei-Hwedie, K. and M.J. Rankopo. 2012. Indigenous conflict resolution in Africa: The case of Ghana and Botswana, *IPSHU English Research Report Series*, 29 (3), 33–51. Institute of Peace Studies, Hiroshima University.

Perbi, A.A. 2004. *A history of indigenous slavery in Ghana: From 15th to 19th century.* Accra: Sub Saharan Publishers.

Rehman, S., and M.A. Roomi. 2012. Gender and work-life balance: A phenomenological study of women entrepreneurs in Pakistan. *Journal of Small Business and Enterprise Development* 19 (2): 209–228.

Rodney, W. 1972. *How Europe underdeveloped Africa.* London: Bogle-L'Ouverture Publication.

Sherry, John. 1983. Gift giving in anthropological perspective. *Journal of Consumer Research* 10: 157–168.

Sobel, R. 2008. Testing Baumol: Institutional quality and the productivity of entrepreneurship. *Journal of Business Venturing* 23: 641–655.

Spruyt, Hendrik. 1994. Institutional selection in international relations: State anarchy as order. *International Organization* 48 (Autumn): 527–557.

The Economist 2016. Special report: Business in Africa, 1.2 billion opportunities, http://www.economist.com/news/special-report/21696792-commodity-boom-may-beover-and-barriers-doing-business-are-everywhere-africas.

Thornton, P.H., and W. Ocasio. 2008. Institutional logic. In *The sage handbook of organisational institutionalism*, ed. R. Greenwood, C. Oliver, R. Suddaby, and K. Sahlin-Anderssson, 99–129. Thousand Oaks: Sage Publications.

Thornton, P.H., W. Ocasio, and M. Lounsbury. 2012. *The institutional logics perspective: A new approach to culture, structure, and processes*. Oxford: Oxford University Press.

Tillmar, M., and L. Lindkvist. 2007. Cooperation against all odds, finding reasons for trust where formal institutions fail. *International Sociology* 22 (3): 343–366.

Transparency International. 2017. Corruption Perception Index 2017. Berlin.

Treisman, Daniel. 2000. The causes of corruption: A cross-national study. *Journal of Public Economics* 76 (3): 399–457.

Vickers, I., F. Lyon, L. Sepulveda, and C. McMullin. 2017. Public service innovation and multiple institutional logics: The case of hybrid social enterprises providers of health and wellbeing. *Social Policy* 48: 1755–1768.

Wandiba, S. 1992. Craft and manufacturing industries, In W.R. Ochieng' and R.M. Maxon Eds. *An economic history of Kenya*. Nairobi: East African Educational Publishers.

Webb, J.J. 1999. On currency and credit in the Western Sahel. In *Credit currencies and culture: African financial institutions in historical perspective*, ed. E. Stiansen and J. Guyer, 38–55. Uppsala: Nordiska Afrikainstitutet.

Welter, F., and D. Smallbone. 2006. Exploring the role of trust in entrepreneurial activity. *Entrepreneurship Theory & Practice* 30 (4): 465–475.

Welter, F., and F. Smallbone. 2011. Institutional perspectives on entrepreneurial behaviour in challenging environments. *Journal of Small Business Management* 49 (1): 107–125.

World Bank. 2017. *Government effectiveness index, worldwide governance indicators*. Washington, DC: The World Bank Group.

World Bank Doing Business. 2018. Database accessed, May 2018. http://www.doingbusiness.org.

World Bank Enterprise Surveys. 2012. World Bank. Washington DC. http://www.enterprisesurveys.org/.

Yanga, M.L., and I.O. Amoako. 2013. Legitimizing dishonesty in organizations: A survey of managers in four Sub-Sahara African countries. In *(Dis)Honesty in management*, Advanced series in management, ed. Tiia Vissak and Maaja Vadi, vol. 10, 243–268. Bingley: Emerald Group Publishing Limited.

Zoogah, D.B., and S. Nkomo. 2013. Management in Africa: Macro and micro perspectives. *Management Research in Africa* 53: 9.

Zucker, L.G. 1986. Production of trust. Institutional sources of economic structure, 1840–1920. *Research in Organisation Behaviour* 8: 53–111.

5

Managing Entrepreneurial Personal and Working Relationships in Africa

5.1 Introduction

Africa has recently experienced a remarkable economic growth and real income per person has increased significantly, giving rise to opportunities for growth to entrepreneurs, investors, and businesses (Delloitte 2014). The continent is now regarded as an emerging market and a destination for businesses to invest, grow, and expand (BBC News 2018; George et al. 2016; Accenture 2010) and this has, in turn, given rise to a need to understand how to develop and manage entrepreneurial networks and relationships with businesses and customers in the continent. Small and medium-sized enterprises (SMEs) and entrepreneurs are the main drivers of the economic boom, creating around 80% of the region's employment (World Economic Forum 2015), and as a result, networking with African SMEs and entrepreneurs offers opportunities in and outside Africa (Biggs and Shah 2006).

Network theory asserts that networking enables entrepreneurs and firms to access resources more cheaply than they could be obtained from markets and to secure resources such as reputation that are not available

© The Author(s) 2019
I. O. Amoako, *Trust, Institutions and Managing Entrepreneurial Relationships in Africa*,
Palgrave Studies of Entrepreneurship in Africa,
https://doi.org/10.1007/978-3-319-98395-0_5

in markets at all (Witt 2007). The development and management of diverse networks and relationships could enhance the growth of organisations (Kale and Singh 2007; Bruton et al. 2010). Particularly a new, small and entrepreneurial firm could obtain unique knowledge, competencies, and resources to alleviate in-house resource constraints (Birley 1985; Street and Cameron 2007; Aarstard et al. 2016).

Networks are particularly important for firms doing business in emerging economies such as Africa where state and market institutions are weak (Meyer et al. 2009). In these contexts, the personal networks and norms governing interpersonal relationships play a crucial role in firm strategy and performance (Peng et al. 2008). For example, Sakarya et al. (2007) explain that establishing networks with firms and other institutions could help mitigate the lack of information in emerging economies of Africa. Tesfom et al. (2004) also show that by relying on networks of intermediaries, suppliers, and customers based on long-term relationships, Eritrean entrepreneurs collaborate to penetrate international markets. The role of networks in Africa is important as state and market institutions are not strong and often resources for start-up and business growth are limited. In Senegal, entrepreneurs rely on personalised networks and relationships within groups to provide resources to support each other (Mambula 2008). Similarly, networks relationships with spouses and family members also provide resources for entrepreneurs in Ghana (Buame 1996; Amoako 2012). Yet, networks that the entrepreneur belongs to can also constrain entrepreneurship. For example, family members may demand more and contribute less to family businesses in terms of effort and commitment and this may lead to the collapse of businesses (Sorensen 2003).

Yet, the development of networks in Africa entails a further challenge relating to how culture influences networks (Klyver et al. 2008). Sets of meanings, norms, and expectations of society and industries, as well as trust, are all aspects of culture that underpin networks (Curran et al. 1995; Amoako and Matlay 2015).

As a result, where there is cultural difference or 'psychic distance' between two parties, developing cross-cultural relationships can be constrained due to different cultural norms and expectations (Zaheer and Kamal 2011; Dietz et al. 2010). For this reason, scholars involved in social network analysis have called for the examination of such processes globally (Klyver et al. 2008; Georgiou et al. 2011). However, many of the existing studies in this area have been done in mature markets and there is very limited knowledge about the patterns of entrepreneurial networks in Africa—and how they are shaped by the logics of cultural institutions (Tillmar 2006; Jenssen and Kristiansen 2004; Overa 2006; Amoako and Lyon 2014).

In this book, the author defines networks as the relationships that link actors with the external environment. Relationships are defined as the connections between actors and the external world and are broadly categorised as personal relationships (strong ties) and working relationships (weak ties) (Granovetter 1973). Personal relationships refer to pre-existing ties such as family and friends while working relationships refer to ties with business partners and acquaintances.

This chapter aims to draw on the institutional logic approach to investigate the 'socially constructed assumptions, values, and beliefs' by which entrepreneurs in Africa provide meaning to their networking activities (see Thornton et al. 2012). Specifically, this chapter focuses on the societal-level logics of state and indigenous cultural institutions that influence entrepreneurs' decisions about trust development in entrepreneurial relationships in Africa (see Chap. 2 for a detailed discussion of the institutional logics approach). The key questions to be answered are: 'What are the forms of entrepreneurial networks and relationships in Africa?' and 'How do logics of cultural institutions influence the development and management of entrepreneurial relationships in Africa?'

To answer these questions, this chapter draws on the literature and empirical evidence (see Chap. 1—the introductory chapter for details of methodology) to highlight the forms of entrepreneurial relationships that allow trust to develop and how indigenous institutions running side by side with state and market institutions shape the development and management of entrepreneurial relationships. This chapter shows that entrepreneurial relationships in Africa comprise of ties, with personal relationships relating to family/kinship and friendships, and working relationships with customers, suppliers, and enterprise facilitators. However, often entrepreneurial working relationships are personalised and hence there is an overlap between personal and working relationships. Yet, entrepreneurial relationships and trust development are influenced by logics of the weak state/market and indigenous institutions and these are legal/court systems and support institutions, oral contracts, traditional justice systems, trade associations, religion, norms of punctuality, and gift giving. Figure 5.1 presents a framework that summarises the discussions and the rest of the chapter will explore the model in more detail.

This chapter contributes to our knowledge in three main ways. First, it presents a framework to show the forms of entrepreneurial relationships and institutions that allow trust and cooperation to develop in weak institutional environments. Second, it offers an understanding of the processes through which entrepreneurs develop entrepreneurial relationships with customers, suppliers, and facilitators in the context of weak institutions. Third, it shows how the logics of African cultural-specific institutions shape the development of trust and cooperation and the management of entrepreneurial relationships. Understanding these logics is important due to their potential to give rise to differences in explanations and attributions for African entrepreneurial behaviour within relationships.

The rest of the chapter is organised in the following manner. The next section discusses the forms of networks and relationships that allow trust to develop. Then we discuss how culture-specific institutions shape the development of trust and management of entrepreneurial relationships in the context of weak institutions. The final section concludes the chapter.

5.2   Entrepreneurial Networks and Relationships in Africa

Recently, scholars regard entrepreneurship as a process that is embedded in networks, places, and communities that socially shape resources and opportunities (McKeever et al. 2014). The network approach is significant because it reasons that entrepreneurs as individuals neither exist nor operate in a vacuum, but instead other actors influence entrepreneurs in their social and business networks (Granovetter 1973;

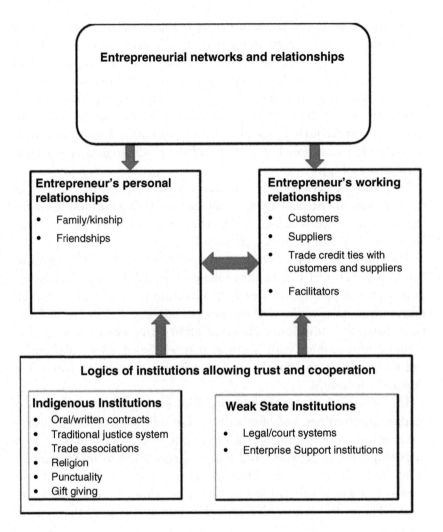

Fig. 5.1 Entrepreneurial relationships and institutions in Africa. (Source: Author's own research)

Aldrich and Zimmer 1986; Klyver et al. 2008). Networks extend the potential resource base of the entrepreneur (Aldrich and Zimmer 1986; Johannisson et al. 2002; Shaw 2006), and enhance the survival of the venture (Bruderl and Preisendorfer 1998). Thus, networks and relationships underpinned by trust are important to the entrepreneurial process (Casson and Della Giusta 2007; Burns 2016). This approach refutes the economic perspective that regards the firm is an atomistic actor governed by rational choice decision makers (Thorelli 1986; Johannisson 1995). It also rejects the psychological approach to entrepreneurship that focuses attention on the 'heroic entrepreneur' whose ingenuity enables them to mobilise resources to innovate and create value without recourse to social relations (see Chap. 2 for explanations of the economic rational approach and the psychological approach to entrepreneurship).

Even though networks are important for businesses operating in all markets, they are particularly essential for firms doing business in emerging economy contexts such as Africa where there are weak state and market institutions (Meyer et al. 2009).

The empirical study shows that entrepreneurs in Africa rely on different types of personal and working relationships. While personal relationships describe personal ties with family/kinship and friends, working relationships relate to ties with customers, suppliers, and enterprise facilitators (support institutions). However, often entrepreneurs develop close personal relationships with business partners based on family/kinship and friendship norms and these relationships may resemble family/kinship and friendships.

The personal and working relationships enable the identification of market opportunities, and offer access to critical resources such as market information, informal finance including trade credit, diverse skills, local knowledge, larger networks and markets, reputation, contract enforcement, and collective action. Thus, the relationships are fundamental to operating a successful business in Africa as, without them, it is nearly impossible to do business due to higher transaction costs that may be incurred.

The discussion in this chapter focuses on the personal and working relationships of entrepreneurs and the institutional logics that underpin trust development, and the management and governance of these relationships. The logics may be specific to a relationship, market, or industry. The next section analyses personal and working relationships developed and used by African entrepreneurs.

5.2.1 Personal Relationships

Entrepreneurs leverage ties in their personal as well as professional lives to access resources (Kregar and Antončič 2016). Personal relationships describe pre-existing ties with a strong degree of trust and emotional closeness with family/kinship and friends.

Family/Kinship/Friendship

In Africa, family/kinship, ethnic ties, and friendships are important in developing and managing entrepreneurial relationships. The empirical study shows that family values may promote honesty, diligence, and caring for one another, and entrepreneurs often rely on family members in the start-up process and to identify and build relationships with businesses. Family members also provide advice, market information, start-up capital, financial support, and help to identify business opportunities and potential business partners and employees.

On some occasions, family members and elders may mediate in resolving disputes between entrepreneurs and their business partners and in so doing assist in the enforcement of commercial agreements between partners. Some family members may also serve as employees, providing cheap labour, while others may become trusted business partners. Due to these benefits, many entrepreneurs regard working with family members as important. However, engaging family members in an African business divides opinions. To some entrepreneurs, family members remain the most trusted people who can be reliable and trustworthy employees or partners, and by employing them one can assist the family and improve the family's economy. Others contest that family members may take advantage as employees or business partners due to cultural logics of communalism and obligations inherent in the family/kinship system. Some entrepreneurs cite instances when family members misappropriated money in businesses and refused to pay money back when offered loans. Previous studies show the enabling and constraining nature of the African family system on entrepreneurship. As stated in this chapter and in Chap. 4, while the African family may offer great support to entrepreneurs, excessive demands from family members may pose serious liquidity challenges and, in extreme cases, lead to the collapse of micro and smaller businesses (Kuada 2015).

In managing entrepreneurial relationships, most entrepreneurs draw on ties embedded in family/kinship to promote trust building and cooperation between them and their trading partners within the domestic markets and in markets across borders. For example, entrepreneurs exporting cola nuts (a local stimulant) from Ghana draw on trust built originally between Hausa emigrants in Ghana and their kinsfolk in northern Nigeria (Amoako and Lyon 2014).

Interestingly, norms of reciprocity and obligations inherent in the family/kinship system allow entrepreneurs to talk and work with business partners as 'family members' (Amoako and Matlay 2015). Generally, entrepreneurs refer to close working business partners (who are not necessarily family members) as mothers, sisters, fathers, brothers or family members.

Friendships are also important in starting, managing, and growing businesses in Africa. Friendships and professional ties with contacts during education in schools, colleges, and universities, and contacts developed at conferences, seminars, workshops, meetings, social events, and trade fairs, and in the exchange of business cards (see Aldrich et al. 1987) may provide resources including ideas, information, and start-up capital. As a result, the friendship ties of Africans are also important in enhancing access to resources for entrepreneurs and smaller businesses.

Nevertheless, in spite of the benefits of family/kinship and friendship ties in promoting business relationships, personal ties may also constrain the building of entrepreneurial relationships. For example, in some African cultures, particularly those dominated by Islamic cultural logics, it is culturally unacceptable for women to sit with men who are not their husbands. In these cultures, it is challenging for married female entrepreneurs to spend time, communicate with, and build sustainable relationships with male business partners. Furthermore, patriarchal African cultures stereotype women based on domestic roles that may confine them to household chores and that may constrain their involvement in developing businesses or business relationships. In such cultures, female entrepreneurs are often either divorced or single because society may regard them as outcasts (Amoako and Matlay 2015).

Additionally, family/kinship and friendship norms may also constrain competitiveness in entrepreneurial relationships due to cultural-specific norms that render it morally wrong to abandon a 'brother' or 'sister' even though the business relationship may not be very beneficial. African family/kinship norms may also encourage family members to ignore rules in organisations or terms in contracts and may constrain trust building and enterprise development. Family/kinship and friendship may sometimes also pose immense challenges to some African entrepreneurs and SMEs. Amoako and Lyon (2014) refer to these paradoxical norms as 'the paradox of the family', see Chaps. 4 and 6 for details. However, the personal trust in family/kinship and friendships is critical for entrepreneurship due to lack of institutional trust.

5.2.2   Entrepreneurial Working Relationships

The entrepreneurial relationship management process starts with the entrepreneur (as an actor) building relationships with potential customers and suppliers and other key stakeholders (Shane 2003; Welter and Smallbone 2011), and these relationships are critically important for all firms irrespective of size (Morrissey and Pittaway 2004). In this subsection, the author examines entrepreneurial relationship development processes in Africa.

Customer Relationships

Entrepreneurs in Africa develop relationships with key customers in both domestic and international markets. Developing and managing key customer relationships is critical for the success of businesses (Hollensen 2015; Berry 1995; McKenna 1991). Customer relationship management (CRM) approaches focus on attracting, maintaining, and enhancing customer relationships (Berry 1995; McKenna 1991). The process includes attracting, developing, and building sustainable relationships with the most important customers to enhance superior, mutual, value creation. The long-term business-to-business (B2B) relationships involve repeated exchanges, cooperation, and collaboration that helps to reduce transaction costs for the partners involved (Berry 1995; Hollensen 2015; Parvatiyar and Sheth 2001).

The empirical study shows that African entrepreneurs attract and develop new customer (B2B) relationships through three main approaches. These approaches are networking and referrals, market research, and promotions. Yet, these three approaches are not mutually exclusive and entrepreneurs may deploy a number of them at the same time.

In the first approach, entrepreneurs rely on networking and referrals through personal and working relationships. African entrepreneurs ask for referrals from family members and friends as well as colleagues in trade associations, customers, and suppliers. Trade associations and state enterprise support organisations, non-governmental organisations (NGOs), and donor organisations may provide market information, organise training, and hold trade fairs that may open up new market opportunities in both domestic and international markets. Some entrepreneurs also attend seminars and workshops organised by these enterprise support institutions during which they talk about their businesses, products, and services and attempt to use the opportunity to identify and link up with potential customers. Satisfied customers and suppliers also serve as referrals for other businesses and entrepreneurs.

In the second approach, entrepreneurs prospect for business by researching and contacting potential customers. A significant number use information communication technologies (ICTs), mainly mobile phones, to call and send text messages to potential partners. Others search the internet and social media particularly Facebook, WhatsApp, Instagram, and LinkedIn to identify suitable business partners who may need or like their products and services. While all entrepreneurs may use networking and referrals, the use of the internet and social media is particularly popular among the well-educated and mostly younger generation of entrepreneurs. Apart from mobile phones, the internet, and social media, some entrepreneurs send emails to potential customers. Thus social media and ICTs in general enable entrepreneurs owning and managing SMEs to provide basic information about products and services to customers (Parida et al. 2009). Conversely, social media and ICTs also allow customers to manage relationships with entrepreneurs and this can be detrimental. For example, negative customer reviews can adversely affect the brand image and reputation of a business (see Gensler et al. 2013). Apart from social media and ICTs, a significant number of entrepreneurs use the traditional market research methods by visiting potential customers in their workplaces and in open markets to show samples/pictures of products/services and to solicit for business.

The third option used to attract new customers and suppliers is promotions. Entrepreneurs use social media including Instagram, Facebook, WhatsApp and LinkedIn to promote products and services. They may also develop websites to promote products and services to customers and suppliers who may use the details on the websites to contact them. Entrepreneurs may also use local FM radio stations that are common in most African countries to promote products and services. Others may use public announcement systems in street promotions and in open markets in towns and cities. However, start-ups and micro enterprises rarely use advertising on local TV and radio stations due to the high costs involved even though a growing number of medium enterprises may use these media. Figure 5.2 summarises entrepreneurial customer attraction strategies in Africa.

In international trade, entrepreneurs often rely on networking with partners in foreign markets to distribute their products. For example, small-scale food exporters in West Africa rely mainly on customers who are agents embedded in the landlord (*efiewura*) system (see Chap. 4) to successfully trade across the West African region (Lyon and Porter 2009; Amoako and Lyon 2014). However, a minority of small-scale entrepreneurs may rely on family/kinship ties that may cut across national borders.

Supplier Relationships

Supplier relationships are very important to entrepreneurs and all firms including those in Africa. In order for entrepreneurs and firms to acquire materials and services from suppliers (Scully and Fawcett 1994), they often spend over 50% of turnover on supplies. Hence, managing supplier

Entrepreneurial Customer Attraction Strategies		
Networking and referrals	Prospecting for business	Promotions
Personal relationships	*ICT Prospects*	*Web Presence*
Family/Kinship	Internet	Advertising
Friends	Telephone calls	Social media
Working Relationships	Text messages	Local radio
Customers	Emails	Local TV
Suppliers		Trade fairs
Trade Associations	*Visits to:*	Public announcements
NGOs	Markets and businesses	
Donors		
State support Institutions		

Fig. 5.2 Entrepreneurial customer attraction strategies. (Source: Author's own research)

relationships is critically important for the competitiveness of all firms. However, it is more important to entrepreneurs owning and managing SMEs due to the lack of resources (Morrissey and Pittaway 2004; Sako and Helper 1998).

African entrepreneurs develop new supplier relationships through networking and referrals from family/kinship, friends, NGOs, donors, trade associations, customers, and suppliers. Entrepreneurs often pitch their businesses, products, and services to prospective suppliers through conversations and telephone calls. They may also search on the internet, websites, and social media such as Facebook, WhatsApp, Instagram, and LinkedIn to identify and contact suitable suppliers. Entrepreneurs often visit workplaces of potential partners to develop supplier relationships. Conversely, most suppliers contact entrepreneurs to promote their products and services.

Building long-term relationships with suppliers is important as it allows access to reliable and regular supplies and at times trade credit.

Entrepreneurs involved in agriculture, manufacturing, and services rely on suppliers for raw materials and other inputs they use. Agricultural produce supplied to entrepreneurs includes pineapples, mangoes, vegetables, oranges, cashew nuts, cola nuts, maize, spices, poultry, egg, meat, and other fruits. Some of the raw materials supplied to entrepreneurs in the manufacturing sector include raw gold, shea nuts, spices, fruit, glass, timber, and chemicals. Supplies to entrepreneurs in the services sector—such as engineering, consultancy, and financial services—include spare parts, stationery, computers, printers, telephones, fax machines, and other ICTs. Trust and trade credit underpins long-term customer and supplier relationships.

Trade Credit Relationships with Customers and Suppliers

While bank financing could be the primary source of credit in advanced economies followed by trade credit (Wilson 2014), trade credit remains the most important source of financing for African entrepreneurs due to weak institutions and lack of access to formal forms of finance (Bruton et al. 2010; Mitra and Sagagi 2013).

Trade credit underpins most economic exchanges in domestic and cross-border exchanges in Africa, hence in some sectors it is important to provide and accept trade credit in order to run a successful business in Africa. This is because generally, there is a lack of bank finance and, when available, the higher cost of bank loans make them less useful so entrepreneurs strategically respond to this constraint by growing their businesses through the offer and acceptance of trade credit to trustworthy customers and from suppliers. Trade credit ranges from cash advances for goods, cash loans, and capital investment in projects (Amoako 2012). The logics of trade credit allow entrepreneurs to provide goods and services to trusted customers and receive supplies from suppliers if they are deemed trustworthy. Within trade credit relationships, entrepreneurs may receive cash transfers even before they supply the goods. This happens when demand for particular products increases in markets. Similarly, entrepreneurs extend trade credit to customers and suppliers in domestic and foreign markets. For that reason, entrepreneurs who refuse to offer trade credit may lose customers or suppliers to competitors who are prepared to offer it. Trade credit enables entrepreneurs selling to increase cash flow while those buying can secure reliable supplies and, in so doing, may enhance SME profitability (Martínez-Sola et al. 2014) and growth.

Yet, sometimes entrepreneurs encounter dishonest trading partners who default and renege on trade credit agreements in both domestic and international markets. In these circumstances, entrepreneurs rarely resort to the courts given the costs and challenges with the legal/court systems. Instead they draw on logics of indigenous cultural institutions, notably trade associations, family/kinship, and religious and community leaders/chiefs to enforce trade credit contracts. Chapters 6, 7, and 8 will discuss this in more detail. Case 5.1 shows how a young African social entrepreneur develops and manages her relationships with suppliers.

Case 5.1 Developing and Managing Entrepreneurial Relationships in Africa

Sally is from the Gambia and she completed her PhD in September 2018 in the UK. She owns 18 Forever, a social enterprise that aims to create employment opportunities for artisans in Africa. She explains that in most African countries there are many artisans with skills but who are unemployed and her company aims to enhance their employment opportunities. Currently, the company employs six people and manufactures in the Gambia, Nigeria, and Kenya. Manufacturing in each market focuses on particular products using African prints: dresses and jackets in the Gambia, handbags and clothing bags in Nigeria, and skirts and kimonos in Kenya. The products are sold online mainly to customers in the UK.

To develop entrepreneurial relationships, she needed to identify partners and Sally used referrals and undertook market research by walking through deprived neighbourhoods to identify artisans who she could work with. In the Gambia, she visited the local markets and neighbourhoods and talked to artisans before choosing her current partner. In the particular case of Kenya, she discussed her search for partners with a friend who she met during a conference in Portsmouth, UK in 2015. The friend knew a lady artisan in Kenya who was highly skilled but not making much money to support herself and her two children and he recommended her to Sally. When her friend returned to Kenya, he introduced the artisan to Sally who then spoke to her and asked for images of her products. After receiving the images, she was impressed and proceeded to place her first order for six products. She received the products through her friend and with the exception of one product, she was satisfied. She provided feedback on her concerns about the one product that was defective and then offered the artisan an application form to complete and a contract. Similarly, Sally identified an artisan in Nigeria based on a referral from her sister who personally knew the artisan.

To develop and manage the relationships, Sally collected a lot of information about the artisan partners which has enabled her to know details of where they live and work and they have been incredibly good partners. As a result of the cordial relationships, the artisans refer to Sally as a sister, as practised in Kenya and Nigeria. To sustain the relationships, Sally also gives gifts to her partners particularly at Christmas and when she pays for supplies she often adds a little for them to buy small gifts for their children. Sally explained that 'It is how I was raised and in the Gambia that is a cultural way of doing business and when you buy in the market you will be given something more and that is our culture'. Sally has developed WhatsApp groups for her partners in Kenya, the Gambia, and Nigeria and communicates regularly with them.

Facilitator Relationships

In addition to customers and suppliers, there are a number of state bodies charged with enterprise support in the various African countries. State-backed organisations provide services including information on markets, products, management training, financing, networking, and organising of trade fairs to a limited number of entrepreneurs and smaller businesses that operate in the formal sector and have registered with them. The limited scope of the services provided may originate from the limited resources allocated by governments.

Apart from state institutions, African entrepreneurs develop relationships with other organisations ranging from NGOs, donors, and other international bodies to private sector organisations. However, the scope of the services provided by these institutions also raises concerns due to lack of support to the many small firms in the informal sector that contributes about 55% of Africa's gross domestic product (GDP) and 80% of the labour force (Buruku 2015).

In addition, there are a number of agencies from countries such as the United States, Germany, the UK, Denmark, Japan, Sweden, France, the Netherlands, Canada, and China that support enterprise development activities in a number of countries in Africa. The services include managerial training, networking, and small grants, and information on international market opportunities, international standards, and environmental issues. Nevertheless, critics argue that most of the services provided serve the interest of Western or donor institutions as the services primarily target the formal sector (Hearn 2007).

Recently, there has been increased interest in investment banks and private sector organisations supporting entrepreneurship in Africa. For example, the European Investment Bank (EIB) and the African Development Bank (AfDB) in partnership with the European Commission launched the Boost Africa Initiative in 2016 to provide investment funds, technical assistance, and an innovation and information lab to foster an entrepreneurial ecosystem on the continent. The project is unique due to its emphasis on supporting ventures that are usually too small, too risky and too time consuming. The project also includes a sizeable technical assistance package (EIB 2016).

Apart from international agencies, there are a number of private initiatives such as Afrilabs that provides a network of innovation centres across a number of African cities with the aim of raising successful entrepreneurs who will create jobs. Others include Funds 4 Africa which is a funding research site that provides opportunities for entrepreneurs to attract and link up with investors in different entrepreneurial projects.

In spite of these support initiatives, there is a wide gap in the institutional support environment in many countries and many industry- and trade-based associations have sprung up to fill the gap by providing the support services needed for entrepreneurs. Further on in this chapter and subsequent chapters, there will be discussions on the unique role of trade associations in facilitating entrepreneurial relationships.

5.3 Indigenous Institutions Shaping the Development and Management of Entrepreneurial Relationships in Africa

In order to understand the process of managing entrepreneurial relationships in Africa, it is important to emphasise that entrepreneurs and their firms are embedded actors in institutional environments (see Granovetter 1973 and Chaps. 2 and 4). Furthermore, the institutional logics approach focuses attention on how cultural dimensions both enable and constrain social action (Thornton and Ocasio 2008). The discussions in this section therefore highlights how entrepreneurs as actors use cultural logics to interpret and make sense of the world while the logics offer resources for relationship building and decision making (Vickers et al. 2017). Figure 5.1 focuses attention on the weak legal and enterprise support institutions, family/kinship and friendships, oral contracts, traditional justice systems, trade associations, religion, punctuality, and gift giving. It is equally important to highlight that these norms are not exhaustive as Africa is vast with a rich and diverse culture. Hence other cultural logics may pertain to particular countries, industries, sectors, and markets and there is a need for understanding those that are critical for doing business in each context. The discussions in this section focus on the key common norms that cut across cultures and are critically important in developing and managing entrepreneurial relationships. These norms are not mutually exclusive as entrepreneurs may deploy a number of them simultaneously depending on the nature of specific relationships, associations, and/or the industry, sector, and market.

5.3.1 Weak Legal and Enterprise Support Systems

In managing relationships, entrepreneurs draw on the logics of weak legal systems and state support institutions in African economies. Legal systems influence relationship development and management due to the impact on contract enforcement (North 1990). However, as stated in Chap. 4, generally, entrepreneurs from most African countries rarely engage with the legal system due to perceptions of it being weak, corrupt and unable to support contract enforcement for smaller businesses (Bruton et al. 2010; Amoako and Lyon 2014). Furthermore, there is limited enterprise support from the state and most entrepreneurs rely on trust in indigenous institutions to develop personalised relationships that enable them to access needed resources (Sakarya et al. 2007).

5.3.2   Oral Contracts

African entrepreneurs rarely use written, legally binding contracts that is the norm in developed countries. Traditionally, oral contracts via face-to-face verbal conversations, telephone calls, and messages through mobile phones and social media underpin entrepreneurial relationships with customers and suppliers in domestic and regional African markets. Hence, entrepreneurs usually distribute goods and provide services to customers and/or receive goods and services from suppliers based on oral contracts. However, it is important to note that, in most cases, entrepreneurs make records of the goods/services supplied or received on invoices, notebooks, and sheets of paper.

In contexts where there may be a lack of prior knowledge in domestic or regional markets, face-to-face oral contracts are agreed in the presence of trade association members, or two or three other people, who serve as witnesses (Amoako and Matlay 2015).

The use of oral contracts is widespread for a number of reasons. First, such contracts are simple and efficient, as they do not involve time searching for lawyers who may often charge huge amounts of money. Second, some of the entrepreneurs engaged in micro and small businesses are illiterates who are unable to read, write, or understand written contracts. Third, trust is the basis of economic exchange among smaller businesses, hence some partners even become suspicious if entrepreneurs insist on written contracts.

Oral contacts are based on trust and there are expectations that customers and suppliers will honour their obligations by, for example, supplying the agreed quantity and quality of goods. While oral agreements may not be enforceable within the legal systems of African countries, in the overwhelming majority of cases, the exchange partners honour their obligations. This corroborate the importance of social norms, trust, and informal collaborations in contexts such as Africa where formal institutions that enforce contracts are less developed (Welter and Smallbone 2006; Bruton et al. 2010), and traditionally informality remains the norm for economic exchanges.

In spite of the widespread use of oral contracts, some entrepreneurs engaged in international trade with partners outside of Africa rely on a memorandum of understanding (MOU) while a few others utilise written contracts in relationships. Furthermore, entrepreneurs who develop relationships with enterprise facilitators such as donors and private institutions often have to sign contracts in order to benefit from the services offered by these institutions.

Interestingly, in most cases the entrepreneurs who benefit from these services have worked, lived, or travelled in Western countries or are well educated or have an understanding of Western business culture.

The effectiveness of the norms of oral contracts is embedded in the traditional African justice system that enhances conflict resolution across African societies.

5.3.3   Traditional Justice System

Entrepreneurs rely mostly on the traditional justice system which runs parallel to the formal justice systems in repairing trust and resolving conflict (Tillmar and Lindkvist 2007; Amoako and Lyon 2014). The legal/court systems of African states were imposed by colonial authorities and have, in the main, been culturally incongruent (Myers 1992) and less useful for entrepreneurship development. In contrast, traditional courts draw on the communal nature of African societies to seek the truth, restore social harmony, punish perpetrators, and compensate victims. This is contrary to Western conflict resolution imposed by the existing formal legal and court systems that draw on individualism, and are mainly retributive, adversarial, and based on a winner-loser approach (Myers 1992; Ingelaere 2008). In the context of SMEs, comparatively, the traditional conflict resolution system remains relatively efficient and more enterprise friendly than the court system because it is informal and simple, cost effective, involves quicker processes that saves time, and is less corrupt.

It is not surprising that the traditional African justice system is embedded in a number of cultural institutions that facilitate entrepreneurship including those of family/kinship, trade associations, and religion and these are important in resolving conflicts and disputes between entrepreneurs and their trading partners.

5.3.4   Trade Associations

Trade associations are very important in managing entrepreneurial relationships in Africa and the overwhelming majority of African entrepreneurs are members of associations. Trade associations often make the rules, mediate in disputes, and enforce contracts between entrepreneurs and their exchange partners. While the conflict resolution approaches and structures used by trade associations are often shaped by the traditional African justice systems, the structures of many trade associations are a hybrid of Western and religious norms and values. For example, in Nigeria, small entrepreneurs in the open markets across the country prefer to report defaulters to the association rather than to the courts. The trade associations use the traditional court processes to resolve the conflicts. The processes are flexible, fair, less time consuming and usually free. Hence, they function as parallel institutions to the courts and fill the void left by the weak and inaccessible legal institutions. In this way, trade associations provide 'parallel institutional' trust. Trade associations are therefore critical for the survival of smaller businesses (see Chap. 4 for more information on the nature of the associations and Chap. 6 on how trade associations enhance trust development in entrepreneurial relationships in Africa).

5.3.5 Religion

Religious norms shape the nature of entrepreneurial networks and trust-building processes (Drakopoulou Dodd and Gotsis 2007; Dietz et al. 2010; Dana 2010). Among African entrepreneurs, it is evident that shared religious beliefs foster relationship building. This confirms previous studies showing how coreligionists build strong personal ties, friendships, and trust with fellow worshippers (Drakopoulou Dodd and Gotsis 2007; Dana 2010), and depend on fellow believers for credit and information (Dana 2006; Dana and Dana 2008; Galbraith 2007). However, the majority of entrepreneurs build business relationships with exchange partners irrespective of religious background.

Additionally, entrepreneurs sometimes rely on religious leaders and logics of religion to resolve disputes with business partners. Some entrepreneurs rely on ministers of religion—pastors, imams, and clerics—and traditional religious leaders instead of the courts in resolving disputes and to enforce agreements between entrepreneurs and their partners. Nonetheless, there are fake religious leaders who may deceive entrepreneurs if they are followers based on claims of having links to the spirits and receiving 'divine' messages in order to defraud them (De Witte 2013).

In desperate circumstances, some entrepreneurs may draw on religious beliefs to invoke curses from God, Allah, and/or the smaller traditional deities and gods to sanction partners who refuse to abide by contractual obligations (Amoako and Matlay 2015). Yet, it is not clear whether the threat of these types of sanctions is effective in relationships with partners who do not share common religious values and norms. Additionally, norms of superstition and fatalism originating from Christianity, Islam, and Animists belief systems may also inform the decision of entrepreneurs to accept vulnerability and rebuild trust after apparent violations by business partners, and this will be explored in more detail in Chap. 7. Another indigenous institution used to develop and manage entrepreneurial relationships with key partners is gift giving.

5.3.6   Gift Giving

Gift giving is an important part of African culture that fosters peaceful coexistence and harmony and is legitimate (Yanga and Amoako 2013; Ayittey 1991; Kenyatta 1965). Entrepreneurs offer gifts to and/or receive gifts from business partners. The gifts include small amounts of cash, food items, toiletries, clothing, jewellery and so on. Even though entrepreneurs may offer gifts to business partners or receive gifts from partners throughout the year, gifts are particularly given or received during celebrations, mostly on religious holidays such as Eid al-Fitr, Eid al-Adha, Christmas, and New Year. The gifts serve as acts of appreciation and may help to gain favours; they may also help build and cement relationships through indebtedness, reciprocity, and control. Even though there is a consensus among entrepreneurs on gift giving in entrepreneurial relationships, there is lack of agreement on whether gift giving to public officials enhances bribery and corruption in Africa. The contrasting views of entrepreneurs, however, reflect a bigger debate on the ethics of gift giving and its role in the perpetuation of corruption among state officials in Africa (see Chaps. 4 and 6).

Case 5.2 Gift Giving and Entrepreneurial Relationship Management in Africa
Mary (anonymised) is the owner/manager of a small-scale food exporting business based in Douala in Cameroon. She exports most of her foodstuffs to neighbouring Equatorial Guinea and Nigeria. She explained that trust underpins her business with key customers and suppliers and she offers trade credit to those she trusts. She emphasises that 'I know their place, I know where they live, I know everything about them, I don't give trade credit to people I don't know'. Knowing her trade credit partners enables her to trace them in case of default. In terms of managing key relationships, she communicates regularly on her mobile phone with her partners and also occasionally offers gifts to and receives gifts from them. She offers gifts in appreciation to customers who have been faithful and to those who have worked with her for a long time. She explains that 'appreciating people is part of our culture, it is cultural, so there is nothing wrong with it'. Mary may offer gifts to her trading partners at any time of the

year, nonetheless she give the gifts particularly during festive occasions like Christmas or during the Islamic festivals of Id el Maulud or Id el Fitri and the gifts range from food items, chicken, small amounts of cash to toiletries. She disclosed that her Christian faith provides her with values and her relationship development is based on shared values and beliefs in her business, and yet, she does business with partners irrespective of their religious beliefs. Mary is a member of the local food exporters association.

5.4   Conclusion

This chapter sets out to examine the forms of relationships African entrepreneurs develop and how they manage these relationships in the context of weak formal institutions. This chapter shows that a significant number of entrepreneurs utilise personal relationships with family/kinship and friendship in order to access resources such as information, capital, customers, and markets. African entrepreneurs also develop and use personal relationships with customers and suppliers who may not necessarily be family members, kinsfolk or friends by drawing on norms of reciprocity and mutual obligations of family/kinship and friendship in their relationships. As a result, personalised trust helps to reduce opportunism and enhance economic exchanges (Granovetter 1973; Berry 1997; Johannisson et al. 2002). Relationships with state and non-state enterprise facilitators and intermediaries also remain important despite the limited number of entrepreneurs supported. Apart from trade associations that cater for entrepreneurs in both informal and formal sectors, the services and support from facilitators are often limited to entrepreneurs operating in the formal sector while those in the informal sector that contribute about 55% of the GDP of African countries are ignored (Buruku 2015).

To develop and manage relationships with customers and suppliers in domestic and African markets, entrepreneurs draw on logics of indigenous cultural institutions and norms. These are logics of oral contracts, traditional justice systems, trade credit, family/kinship and friendship, religion, trade associations and gift giving. These logics enable entrepreneurs to develop personalised relationships with customers, suppliers, and some facilitators in domestic markets and in markets across the continent.

While these indigenous institutions are embedded in African societies, some of the institutions such as trade associations may be a hybrid of Western norms. However, in relationships with partners outside of Africa, entrepreneurs have to rely on logics of Western business institutions including memorandum of understanding and written contracts. This chapter confirms that in the context of weak institutions, entrepreneurs draw on socio-cultural institutions and norms to build relationships (Lyon 2005; Welter and Smallbone 2006; Tillmar and Lindkvist 2007). Furthermore, it highlights how entrepreneurs operate in the context of weak formal institutions by relying on indigenous institutions that substitute for state and market institutions (Estrin and Pervezer 2011) and yet very little is known about these indigenous institutions.

This chapter contributes to the literature in three ways. First, it presents frameworks to show the forms of entrepreneurial relationships and institutions that allow trust to develop in entrepreneurial relationships in weak institutional environments. Second, it describes the processes through which entrepreneurs develop entrepreneurial relationships with customers, suppliers, and facilitators in the context of weak institutions. Third, it presents the debates, contradictions, and misunderstandings surrounding some of the socio-cultural institutions and norms that provide the logics that facilitate entrepreneurial trust development and the management of entrepreneurial relationships in Africa. As a result, it contributes to an understanding of the complex processes of developing and managing sustainable entrepreneurial relationships with customers, suppliers, and enterprise facilitators in Africa.

The next part, comprising Chaps. 6, 7 and 8, will examine the development of trust, trust violations, and trust repair in an African context.

References

Aarstard, J., I.B. Pettersen, and K.E. Henriksen. 2016. Entrepreneurial experience and access to critical resources: A learning perspective. *Baltic Journal of Management* 11 (1): 89–107.

Accenture. 2010. Africa: The new frontier for growth. Online access on 13 Feb 2012. http://nstore.accenture.com/pdf/Accenture_Africa_The_New_Frontier_for_Growth.pdf.

Aldrich, H., and C. Zimmer. 1986. Entrepreneurship through social networks. In *The art and science of entrepreneurship*, ed. D.L. Sexton and R.W. Smilor, 3–23. Cambridge: Ballinger Publishing Company.

Aldrich, H., B. Rosen, and W. Woodward. 1987. The impact of social networks on business foundings and profit: A longitudinal study. In *Frontiers of entrepreneurship research*, ed. N.S. Churchill, J.A. Hornaday, B.A. Kerchhoff, O.J. Kranser, and K.H. Vesper, 54–168. Babson Park: Center for Entrepreneurial Studies.

Amoako, I. O. 2012. Trust in exporting relationships: The case of SMEs in Ghana. Published PhD thesis. Centre for enterprise and economic development research (CEEDR), Middlesex University, London. http://eprints.mdx. ac.uk/12419.

Amoako, I.O., and F. Lyon. 2014. We don't deal with courts: Cooperation and alternative institutions shaping exporting relationships of SMEs in Ghana. *International Small Business Journal* 32 (2): 117–139.

Amoako, I.O., and H. Matlay. 2015. Norms and trust-shaping relationships among food-exporting SMEs in Ghana. *International Journal of Entrepreneurship & Innovation* 16 (2): 123–124.

Ayittey, G. 1991. *Indigenous African institutions*. New York: Transnational Publishers.

BBC News. 2018. May in Africa: UK Prime Minister's mission to woo continent after Brexit. *BBC News*, London. August 28. http://www.bbc.co.uk/news/world-africa-45298656.

Berry, L.L. 1995. Relationship marketing of services growing interest, emerging perspectives. *Journal of the Academy of Marketing Science* 23: 236–245.

Berry, A. 1997. *SME competitiveness: The power of networking and subcontracting*, 1–36. Washington, DC: InterAmerican Development Bank.

Biggs, T., and M.K. Shah. 2006. African SMES, networks, and manufacturing performance. *Journal of Banking and Finance* 30 (11): 2931–3256.

Birley, S. 1985. The role of networks in the entrepreneurial process. *Journal of Business Venturing* 1: 107–117.

Bruderl, J., and P. Preisendorfer. 1998. Network support and the success of newly founded businesses. *Small Business Economics* 10: 213–225.

Bruton, G.D., D. Ahlstrom, and H.-L. Li. 2010. Institutional theory and entrepreneurship: Where are we now and where do we need to move in the future? *Entrepreneurship Theory and Practice* 34 (3): 421–440.

Buame, S.K. 1996. *Entrepreneurship: A contextual perspective, discourses and praxis of entrepreneurial activities within the institutional context of Ghana*. Lund: Lund University Press.

Burns, P. 2016. *Entrepreneurship and small business, tart-up, growth and maturity.* 4th ed. London: Palgrave Macmillan.

Buruku, B. 2015. *Perspectives, how to support youth entrepreneurship in Africa,* General Electric (GE) reports. Boston: African Center for Economic Transformation.

Casson, M., and M. Della Giusta. 2007. Entrepreneurship and social capital. *International Small Business Journal* 25 (3): 220–244.

Curran, J. Blackburn R.A. and Kitching J. 1995 Small businesses, networking and networks: A literature review, policy survey and research agenda. Kingston upon Thames: Kingston University, UK/Small Business Research Centre.

Dana, L.P. 2006. A historical study of the traditional livestock merchants of Alsace. *British Food Journal* 108 (7): 586–598.

———. 2010. Introduction: Religion as an explanatory variable for entrepreneurship. In *Entrepreneurship and religion,* ed. L.P. Dana, 1–24. Cheltenham: Edward Elgar Publishing Ltd.

Dana, L.P., and T.E. Dana. 2008. Ethnicity and entrepreneurship in Morocco: A photoethnographic study. *International Journal of Business and Globalisation* 2 (3): 209–226.

De Witte, M. 2013. The electric touch machine miracle scam: Body, technology, and the (dis) authentication of the pentecostal supernatural. In *Ex-Machina: Religion, technology, and the things in between,* ed. Stolow J. Deus, 61–82. New York: Fordham University Press.

Delloitte. 2014. *The Delloitte consumer review Africa: A 21st century view.* London.

Dietz, G., N. Gillespie, and G.T. Chao. 2010. Unravelling the complexities of trust and culture. In *Organizational trust: A cultural perspective,* ed. M.N.K. Saunders, D. Skinner, G. Dietz, N. Gillespie, and R.J. Lewicki. Cambridge: Cambridge University Press.

Drakopoulou Dodd, S., and G. Gotsis. 2007. The interrelationships between entrepreneurship and religion. *International Journal of Entrepreneurship and Innovation* 8 (2): 93–104.

Estrin, S., and M. Pervezer. 2011. The role of informal institutions in corporate governance: Brazil, Russia, India, and China compared. *Asia Pacific Journal of Management* 28 (1): 41–67.

European Investment Bank. 2016. *Launch of Boost African initiative, a new integrated approach to boost young innovative entrepreneurs across Africa.* Luxembourg.

Galbraith, C.G. 2007. The impact of ethnic-religious identification on buyer-seller behaviour: A study of two enclaves. *International Journal of Business and Globalisation* 1 (1): 20–33.

Gensler, Sonja, Franziska Völckner, Yuping Liu-Thompkins, and Caroline Wiertz. 2013. Managing brands in the social media environment. *Journal of Interactive Marketing* 27 (4): 242–256.

George, G., J.N.O. Khayesi, and M.R.T. Haas. 2016. Bringing Africa in: Promising directions for management research. *Academy of Management Journal* 59 (2): 377–393.

Georgiou, C., S. Drakopoulou-Dodd, C. Andriopoulos, and M. Gotsi. 2011. Exploring the potential impact of colonialism on national patterns of entrepreneurial networking. *International Small Business Journal*. https://doi.org/10.1177/0266242611404261.

Granovetter, M.S. 1973. The strength of weak ties. *American Journal of Sociology* 6: 1360–1380.

Hearn, J. 2007. African NGOs: The new compradors? *Development and Change* 38 (6): 1095–1110.

Hollensen, S. 2015. *Marketing management – A relationship approach*. 3rd ed. Harlow: Financial Times/Prentice Hall.

Ingelaere, Bert. 2008. The Gacaca courts in Rwanda. In *Traditional justice and reconciliation after violent conflict: Learning from African experiences*, ed. Luc Huyse and Mark Salter. Stockholm: International IDEA.

Jenssen, J.I., and S. Kristiansen. 2004. Sub-cultures and entrepreneurship: The value of social capital in Tanzanian business. *Journal of Entrepreneurship* 13: 1.

Johannisson, Bengt. 1995. Paradigms and entrepreneurial networks – Some methodological challenges. *Entrepreneurship & regional development* 7 (3): 215–232.

Johannisson, B., M. Ramı́rez-Pasillas, and G. Karlsson. 2002. The institutional embeddedness of local inter-firm networks: A leverage for business creation. *Entrepreneurship and Regional Development* 14: 297–313.

Kale, P., and H. Singh. 2007. Building firm capabilities through learning: The role of the alliance learning process in alliance capability and firm level alliance success. *Strategic Management Journal* 28 (10): 981–1000.

Kenyatta, J. 1965. *Facing Mount Kenya: The tribal life of the Gikuyu*, 253–258. New York: Vintage Books.

Klyver, K., K. Hindle, and D. Meyer. 2008. Influence of social network structure on entrepreneurship participation—A study of 20 national cultures. *International Entrepreneurship and Management Journal* 4: 331–347. https://doi.org/10.1007/s11365-007-0053-0.

Kregar, T. B., and Boštjan Antončič, B. 2016. The relationship between the entrepreneur's personal network multiplexity and firm growth. Economic Research-Ekonomska Istraživanja 29(1), 1126–1135, https://doi.org/10.1080/1331677X.2016.1211947.

Kuada, J. 2015. Entrepreneurship in Africa—A classifactory framework and a research agenda. *African Journal of Economic and Management Studies* 6 (2): 148–163.

Lyon, F. 2005. Managing co-operation: Trust and power in Ghanaian associations. *Organization Studies* 27 (1): 31–52.

Lyon, F., and G. Porter. 2009. Market institutions, trust and norms: Exploring moral economies in Nigerian food systems. *Cambridge Journal of Economics* 33 (5): 903–920.

Mambula, C.J. 2008. Effects of factors influencing capital formation and financial management on the performance and growth of small manufacturing firms in Senegal: Recommendations for policy. *International Journal of Entrepreneurship* 12 (4): 92–106.

Martínez-Sola, C., P. García-Teruel, and P. Martínez-Solano. 2014. Trade credit and SME profitability. *Small Business Economics* 42: 561–577. https://doi.org/10.1007/s11187013-9491-y.

McKeever, E., S. Jack, and A. Anderson. 2014. Embedded entrepreneurship in the creative re-construction of place. *Journal of Business Venturing* 30 (1): 50–65.

McKenna, R. 1991. *Relationship marketing: Successful strategies for the age of the customers*. Reading: Addison-Wesley.

Meyer, K.E., S. Estrin, S. Bhaumik, and M.W. Peng. 2009. Institutions, resources, and entry strategies in emerging economies. *Strategic Management Journal* 30 (1): 61–80.

Mitra, J., and M. Sagagi. 2013. Special issue: The changing dynamics of entrepreneurial Africa. *Entrepreneurship and Innovation* 4 (14): 211–218.

Morrissey, B., and L. Pittaway. 2004. A study of procurement behaviour in small firms. *Journal of Small\Business and Enterprise Development* 11 (2): 254–262.

Myers, Samuel L. 1992. Crime, entrepreneurship, and labor force withdrawal. *Contemporary Economic Policy* 10 (2): 84–97.

North, D.C. 1990. *Institutions, institutional change and economic performance*. Cambridge: Cambridge University Press.

Overa, R. 2006. Networks, distance, and trust: Telecommunications development and changing trading practices in Ghana. *World Development* 34 (7): 1301–1315.

Parida, V., M. Westerberg, and H. Ylinenpaa. 2009. How do small firms use ICT for business purposes? A study of Swedish technology-based firms. *Journal of Electronic Business* 7 (5): 536–551.

Parvatiyar, Atul, and Jagdish Sheth. 2001. Customer relationship management: Emerging practice, process and discipline. *Journal of Economic and Social Research* 3 (2): 1–34.

Peng, M.W., D.Y.L. Wang, and J. Yi. 2008. An institution-based view of international business strategy: A focus on emerging economies. *Journal of International Business Studies* 39: 920–936.

Sakarya, S., M. Eckman, and K.H. Hyllegard. 2007. Market selection for international expansion: Assessing opportunities in emerging markets. *International Marketing Review* 24 (2): 208–238.

Sako, M., and S. Helper. 1998. Determinants of trust in supply relations: Evidence from the automotive industry in Japan and the United States. *Journal of Economic Behaviour and Organisation* 34: 387–417.

Scully, J.I., and S.E. Fawcett. 1994. International procurement strategies: Challenges and opportunities for the small firm. *Production and Inventory Management Journal* 35 (2): 39–46.

Shane, S. 2003. *A general theory of entrepreneurship*. Northampton: Edward Elgar.

Shaw, E. 2006. Small firm networking. *International Small Business Journal* 24 (1): 5–29.

Sorensen, O.J. 2003. Barriers to and opportunities for innovation in developing countries: The case of Ghana. In *Putting African first: The making of African innovation systems*, ed. M. Muchie, P. Gammeltoft, and B.A. Lundval, 287–304. Aalborg: Aalborg University Press.

Street, C.T., and A.F. Cameron. 2007. External relationships and the small business: A review of small business alliance and network research. *Journal of Small Business Research* 45 (20): 239–266.

Tesfom, G., C.H.M. Lutz, and P.N. Ghauri. 2004. Comparing export marketing channels: Developed versus developing countries. *International Marketing Review* 21 (4–5): 409–442.

Thorelli, H.B. 1986. Networks: Between markets and hierarchies. *Strategic Management Journal* 7: 37–51.

Thornton, P.H., and W. Ocasio. 2008. Institutional logics. In *The Sage handbook of organizational institutionalism*, ed. R. Greenwood, C. Oliver, R. Suddaby, and K. Sahlin Andersson. London: Sage.

Thornton, Patricia H., William Ocasio, and Michael Lounsbury. 2012. *The institutional logics perspective: A new approach to culture, structure and processes*. Oxford: Oxford University Press.

Tillmar, M. 2006. Swedish tribalism and Tanzanian entrepreneurship: Preconditions for trust formation. *Entrepreneurship and Regional Development* 18 (2): 91–108.

Tillmar, M., and L. Lindkvist. 2007. Cooperation against all odds, finding reasons for trust where formal institutions fail. *International Sociology* 22 (3): 343–366.

Vickers, I., F. Lyon, L. Sepulveda, and C. McMullin. 2017. Public service innovation and multiple institutional logics: The case of hybrid social enterprises providers of health and wellbeing. *Social Policy* 48: 1755–1768.

Welter, F., and D. Smallbone. 2006. Exploring the role of trust in entrepreneurial activity. *Entrepreneurship Theory and Practice* 30 (4): 465–475.

Welter, F., and F. Smallbone. 2011. Institutional perspectives on entrepreneurial behaviour in challenging environments. *Journal of Small Business Management* 49 (1): 107–125.

Wilson, N. 2014. *Trade credit in the UK economy (1998–2012): An exploratory analysis of company accounts*. Leeds: Leeds University Business School/Credit Management Research Centre Working Paper.

Witt, P. 2007. Entrepreneurs' networks and the success of start-ups. *Entrepreneurship and Regional Development* 16 (5): 391–412. https://doi.org/10.1080/08985620420000188423.

World Economic Forum. 2015. Why SMEs are key to growth in Africa. https://www.weforum.org/agenda/2015/08/why-smes-are-key-to-growth-in-africa/.

Yanga, M.L., and I.O. Amoako. 2013. Legitimizing dishonesty in organizations: A survey of managers in four sub-Sahara African countries. In *(Dis)Honesty in management*, Advanced series in management, ed. Tiia Vissak and Maaja Vadi, vol. 10, 243–268. Bingley: Emerald Group Publishing.

Zaheer, A., and D. Kamal. 2011. Creating trust in piranha-infested waters: The confluence of buyer, supplier and host country contexts. *Journal of International Business Studies* 42: 48–55.

Part III

Trust in African Entrepreneurial Relationships

6

Trust Development in Entrepreneurial Relationships in an African Context

6.1 Introduction

Entrepreneurs owning and managing small and medium-sized enterprises (SMEs) do not normally have extensive resources at their disposal and this is especially the case in emerging economy contexts such as Africa where there is limited support from the state (Quartey et al. 2017; Etebefia and Akinkumi 2013). One promising means of ensuring access to resources is establishing cooperation in relationships with partners to bundle and create new and unique set of resources that can enhance the performance of both partners (Fink and Kessler 2010; Tesfom et al. 2004). However, entering into cooperative relationships entails risks as the performance of cooperating businesses becomes dependent on the future behaviour of the partner. In these relationships, mutual trust becomes an important coordinating mechanism that shapes the structure and performances of organisations (Vanneste 2016). As a coordination and control mechanism, trust reduces uncertainty by serving as a glue that holds relationships together and offering incentives for long-term cooperation (Altinay et al. 2014; Nooteboom et al. 1997; Deutsch et al. 2011).

© The Author(s) 2019
I. O. Amoako, *Trust, Institutions and Managing Entrepreneurial Relationships in Africa*,
Palgrave Studies of Entrepreneurship in Africa,
https://doi.org/10.1007/978-3-319-98395-0_6

Yet, trust is a very complex concept with diverse disciplines studying it based on divergent assumptions (Möllering 2006). The various disciplines often emphasise different elements of trust while paying less attention to the other equally important aspects. For example, psychology adopts behavioural approaches to trust. This approach focuses on internal cognitions of trustors and trustees, and observable choices of the trustor in interpersonal contexts based on rational expectation by referring to events produced by persons and impersonal agents (Lewicki et al. 2006), and thereby paying less attention to context. Similarly, mainstream economics focuses on the rational choice perspective and emphasises that rational actors are able to calculate and evaluate available alternatives and choose the best solution that optimises the decision maker's utilities (Misztal 1996). Based on this approach, trust is regarded as based on reason, conscious and calculated (e.g. Gambetta 1988), and hence this perspective pays little attention to context. In contrast, the sociological approach focuses on institutions and social relations. Thus, this approach emphasises the role of culture cognition, norms, values, beliefs, and habits and routines (Zucker 1986; Möllering 2006). However, it underestimates the role of the trustor and trustee. Based on the above three perspectives, academics have regarded trust as an attribute based on internal cognitions including rational choice (Gambetta 1988), trust as routine and taken for granted (Zucker 1986), and trust as a reflexive process (Möllering 2006).

Due to the differences in theoretical approaches, there is no agreed definition of trust in the literature. However, Zucker (1986, 54) defines trust as 'a set of expectations shared by all those involved in an exchange'. Zucker's definition suggests that trust is both a state of mind developed by an individual through interaction with others and a reliance based on institutions (Bachmann and Inkpen 2011). Rousseau et al. (1998, 395) define trust as 'a psychological state comprising the intention to accept vulnerability based upon positive expectations of the behaviour of another'. This definition recognises the cognitive rational and sociological habitual views of trust. The author draws on Zucker's (1986) and Rousseau et al.'s (1998) definitions to develop a working definition of trust as; 'a set of positive expectations that is shared by parties in an exchange that things and people will not fail them in spite of the possibility of being let down'. Section 6.2 explains the basis of this working definition.

Personal trust, organisational trust and institutional trust are further forms of trust. The integrity, ability and benevolence of the trustee forms the basis of the development of personal trust (Mayer et al. 1995). However, the development of organisational trust depends on trust in leaders or others in the organisation as well as on the reputations and brands (Zaheer et al. 1998), and institutional trust is based in and on institutions (Zucker 1986; Möllering 2006): see Chap. 3 for more details on the forms of trust.

The discussions in this chapter focus on trust development in entrepreneurial relationships in Africa, where there has been very little research on trust development. Even though during the past two decades there has been significant theoretical progress in trust research, there is a dominance of studies on trust development that draws mostly on Western institutional contexts where models, concepts, and measures emphasise the importance of trust based on psychological approaches and strong state and market institutions and legal contracts (see Mayer et al. 1995; Zaheer et al. 1998). Compared to Western contexts, researchers have not given much attention to trust development in emerging economy contexts where state and market institutions are weak. In emerging economy contexts, there are weak legal systems, weak contract enforcement, and hence limited institutional trust. Yet, emerging economies such as China, India, the Philippines, Brazil, Ethiopia, Rwanda, and Ghana have witnessed increased entrepreneurship and rapid economic growth (PWc 2017). In these economies, entrepreneurs develop trust in less formal (parallel) institutions such as networks, trade associations, and religions. Hence, informal cultural institutions provide the basis of trust (see Amoako and Lyon 2014; Welter et al. 2005, Wu et al. 2014). However, there is little knowledge about how the logics of informal cultural institutions shape trust development processes in entrepreneurial relationships in emerging economies including Africa (Wu et al. 2014; Amoako and Lyon 2014; Li 2016).

Another major limitation relating to discussions on SMEs interorganisational trust development in African and Ghanaian contexts relates to limited knowledge about how trust is developed. While in larger organisations, personal trust enhances interorganisational trust through the attitudes, characteristics, and actions of boundary spanners (Zaheer et al. 1998; Vanneste 2016), in SMEs in Ghanaian and African contexts, the distinction between interorganisational trust and interpersonal trust is more complex and unclear. This is due to the smaller sizes of SMEs and also to the high power distance in African cultures, as a result of which entrepreneurs owning and managing smaller businesses remain key decision makers and key boundary spanners for their organisations (Kuada and Thomsen 2005). Consequently, it is difficult to differentiate between trust in partner SMEs and trust in entrepreneurs who own and manage those businesses (Amoako 2012). As a result, interorganisational trust in entrepreneurial relationships with SMEs tends to be more personal. The entrepreneurs (trustees) owning and managing SMEs base trustworthiness in these firms on the characteristics, behaviour, actions, and interactions with partner entrepreneurs (Zucker 1986; Mayer et al. 1995; Möllering 2006). This may differ in larger organisational contexts where the number of employees is higher and a number of managers engage in decision making. It may also differ in other economies and contexts where there is less power distance and SMEs may have larger numbers of employees (Rousseau et al. 1998). Yet, the literature has not paid much attention to these differences.

This chapter aims to address these gaps by examining how state and market institutions as well as cultural institutions influence the processes of trust development in Ghana. It also explores how entrepreneurs owning and managing SMEs develop personal/organisational trust in entrepreneurial relationships. Given that Africa is a vast continent that has many national and distinct institutions, cultures, and sub-cultures, the current discussions and analysis of trust development in this chapter will be based on the literature and an empirical study in Ghana (see Chap. 1 for details on methodology). This approach aims to enhance an in-depth understanding of how entrepreneurs draw on logics of societal institutional orders such as weak legal systems, and cultural institutional orders such as family/kinship, trade associations, and religion in trust development processes in an African context.

The literature suggests that actors use institutional logics to interpret and make sense of the world although not always consciously to support networking and trusting behaviour, while at the same time actors' networking and trusting practices and behaviour can both reinforce and challenge the assumptions, values, beliefs, and rules considered appropriate in a particular sphere of social life (see Besharov and Smith 2014). Hence, institutional logics offer strategic resources that connect organisations' strategy and decision making (see Durand et al. 2013). Throughout this book, the author argues that entrepreneurs in Africa as actors use logics to interpret and make sense of the contexts, not always consciously, to support networking and trusting behaviour, while at the same time actors' networking and trusting practices and behaviour can both reinforce and challenge the assumptions, values, beliefs, and rules considered appropriate in a particular sphere of social life (see Chap. 1). In this Part III (covering Chaps. 6, 7 and 8), the author examines how societal-level logics of state and indigenous cultural institutions and norms underpin entrepreneur's decisions to develop trust, interpret trust violations, and repair trust.

The investigations and discussions in this chapter focus on the following questions: (1) 'What are the institutions that shape trust development?' (2) 'How do entrepreneurs perceive trustworthiness and what are the forms of trust developed?' (3) 'What are the outcomes of interorganisational trust?'

The empirical study discussed in this chapter shows that while some of the stages and processes of trust development in SME interorganisational relationships may be similar to existing processes outlined in the literature, there are notable differences. While confirming that entrepreneurs' trusting behaviour depends on the trustworthiness of trustees, the entrepreneur's propensity to trust, and interactions in networks and relationships as outlined in Chap. 3, the trust development processes are embedded in logics of weak state and market institutions, and indigenous cultural institutions in Ghana, thus, showing the importance of context in trust development. Furthermore, in the context of SMEs operating in Ghana, entrepreneurs develop personal/organisational trust and parallel institutional trust instead of personal, organisational, and institutional trust found in the literature. The forms of trust enable access to resources. The framework (Fig. 6.1) summarises the findings of this chapter and the rest of the chapter discusses the framework in detail.

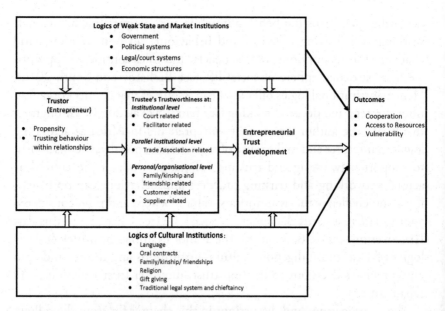

Fig. 6.1 Entrepreneurial trust development in weak institutional contexts. (Source: Own research)

This chapter contributes to the literature by first, presenting a framework that visualises a holistic approach to trust development in SME interorganisational relationships in an emerging economy (and African) context based on the entrepreneur (trustor), his or her trading partner (trustee), their relationship, and the external cultural norms that shape the trust processes within relationships. Second, reconceptualising the role of state and market institutions and identifying cultural-specific institutions that provide the logics that enhance trust development in entrepreneurial relationships in an African context. Third, showing how personal/interorganisational trust comingles in the SME context due to the dominant role of the entrepreneur who as an actor develops trust in relationships to mitigate institutional weaknesses in Ghana. Fourth showing how as actors entrepreneurs do not necessarily yield to formal institutional constraints but respond by relying on alternative indigenous institutions.

The rest of this chapter is structured as follows. Section 6.2 analyses the contexts focusing on the logics of institutions and relationships that shape trust development in Ghana. Section 6.3 discusses the entrepreneur as an actor—propensity to trust and trusting behviour. Section 6.4 examines trustee's trustworthiness and forms of trust developed in entrepreneurial relationships. Section 6.5 describes trust outcomes and Sect. 6.6 concludes the chapter.

6.2 Ghana: Logics of State, Market and Cultural Institutions Shaping Trust Development

Like some African countries, the British colonial administration created Ghana. Ghana is located on the Atlantic Coast of West Africa and shares borders with Togo to the east, Cote D'Ivoire to the west, and Burkina Faso to the north, and currently has a population of about 29.6 million (Ghanaian Times 2018).

6.2.1 Logics of Government, Political, Legal, and Economic Institutions

During the immediate years after independence in 1957, the state adopted protectionist trade policies and institutions dominated by state-owned enterprises. Based on this ideology, state institutions and the public sector received priority while the domestic indigenous sector and entrepreneurial class were regarded as a threat to the political system and was not encouraged (Kayanula and Quartey 2000). State-led development persisted until 1983 by which time the economy had nearly collapsed (Nowak et al. 1996). The country also experienced political turmoil from military takeovers between 1966 and 1982. During this era and beyond, the military and political system often accused entrepreneurs of *kalabule* or profiteering and the harassment, interference, bureaucracy, and corruption from the military and government officials constrained the growth of entrepreneurship and SMEs (see Buame 1996; Ninsin 1989). Nonetheless, since 1992, Ghana has practised multi-party democracy characterised by freedom of speech and a vibrant press. As a result, the country enjoys high levels of social capital.

Between 1970 and 1985, some attempts were made to stimulate entrepreneurship through a number of policies and the establishment of state institutions. For example, in 1970 the government enacted the Ghanaian Business Promotion Act (Act 334) to facilitate entrepreneurship and small business development (Ninsin 1989). Furthermore, in 1985 the government established the National Board for Small Scale Industry (NBSSI) based on Act 434 of 1981 to serve as the government institution responsible for the promotion and development of micro and small enterprises (MSEs) primarily in the informal sector. However, the policies are scattered around several government ministries and institutions that rarely interact with each other.

Nonetheless, since the year 2000, there has been a number of initiatives to address these constraints. For example, in 2017 the government launched the Ministry of Business Development to champion entrepreneurship in Ghana. The flagship programme of this ministry is the National Entrepreneurship and Innovation Plan (NEIP). NEIP has an initial seed capital of $10 million that will be increased to $100 million through private sector development partners. The capacity-building project aims to equip the youth with entrepreneurial skills and to enhance start-ups, business growth, and economic development.

British Common Law underpins the legal/court systems in Ghana and yet traditionally Ghana's legal/court system does not pay much attention to private sector and enterprise development. Primarily, the laws and regulations enacted by formal institutions are not targeted at entrepreneurship and so the system is expensive, time consuming, and corrupt all of which constrain institutional trust and this will be explored further in Sect. 6.4.1.

Nonetheless, Ghana is one of the African countries that has achieved remarkable economic growth since 2000. Currently, Ghana is a lower middle-income country with gross domestic product (GDP) per capita of US $ 1632 (GSS 2018). In 2018, Ghana was one of the world's fastest-growing economies with projected growth between 8.3% and 8.9% (New York Times 2018). However, interest rates and inflation still remain relatively high at 20% and 10.6% year on year in 2018 (Trading Economics 2018), so the cost of finance for entrepreneurship still remains very high.

Yet, many businesses have sprung up, and as in most Africa countries, the majority of businesses (62%) are SMEs operating in the informal sector that is composed of unregistered firms offering wage employment in unregulated and unprotected jobs. Informal businesses used to employ over 90% of the total workforce (World Bank 2004; GSS 2010). The Ghana Statistical Service defines an informal business as a business that does not have professionals keeping its accounting records (GSS 2016) and therefore mostly operating outside the tax net. Yet, this definition is contestable as the overwhelming majority of businesses in the sector operating in the open markets and in the streets pay various forms of taxes to local government tax officials. SMEs dominate the three main sectors of the economy: agriculture (19.5%), manufacturing (24%), and services (56.4%) (CIA World Factbook 2016). Therefore, Ghanaians respect entrepreneurs and regard starting and managing an SME as a good career choice in the country.

However, there is no single definition of SMEs in Ghana (Teal 2002). Hence, for practical application, this study adopts the definition of SMEs from the Ministry of Local Government based on the number of people employed: micro having 1 to 5 employees, small having 6 to 29, medium having 30 to 100, and large more than 100. The analysis of trust development, trust violations, and trust repair in Part III of this book therefore focuses on the businesses employing 100 or fewer people and operating in agricultural, services, and manufacturing sectors of the economy.

6.2.2   Logics of Cultural Institutions Shaping Trust Development

In domestic and West African markets, entrepreneurs refer to logics of cultural-specific norms and indigenous institutions in entrepreneurial relationships with customers, suppliers, and facilitators showing how personal/organisational trust and relationships are embedded in existing social structures. The logics of language, oral contracts, family/kinship and friendships, religion, punctuality, gift giving, and chieftaincy underpin trust development and the management of relationships.

6.2.3   Logics of Language Shaping Personal/ Organisational Trust

One of the key influences on personal/organisational trust is language and yet researchers have paid very little attention to how different languages conceptualise trust (Lyon et al. 2012). In Ghana, Akan/Twi which is spoken by nearly half (47.5%) of the population (GSS 2010), conceptualises trust as *gyedie, ahotosoo*, or *twere*. *Gyedie* means 'belief or faith', *ahotosoo* means 'reliability and dependability', and *twere* (a verb) literally means 'to lean on' (Amoako 2012). Entrepreneurs often lean on relationships with key partners to grow their businesses. Whilst *gyedie* (faith or belief) describes the psychological state of the actor (trustor), *ahotosoo* (reliability or dependability) is similar to both ability and integrity of exchange partners (Mayer et al. 1995). Leanability (*twere* or to lean on) suggests that the entrepreneur expects the partner (trustee) to willingly support the entrepreneur (trustor) and so highlights the norms and expectations to be fulfilled by the trustee. However, *twere* (to lean on) has received less attention in the literature. 'Leanability' as a trust expectation, suggests stronger elements of obligation between relationship partners. This could be related to the norms of the Akan and African family systems that oblige members to remain loyal to and support each other. Hence, trust in the Akan context of Ghana may often be based on stronger expectations and obligations than in Western cultures where there are less obligations in the family system (Amoako 2012).

Therefore, in this book, the meaning of trust in Akan/Twi (*gyedie, ahotosoo,* and *twere*) which emphasises the trustor's faith or belief, reliability, expectations, and vulnerability provides a working definition. As stated in Sect. 6.1, the author defines trust as; 'a set of positive expectations that is shared by parties in an exchange that things and people will not fail them in spite of the possibility of being let down'. This definition focuses on personal/organisational trust and institutional trust. These forms of trust are embedded in oral contracts; a key, culturally specific institution that facilitates entrepreneurial relationship development.

6.2.4   Logics of Oral Contracts Shaping Personal/ Organisational Trust Development

Entrepreneurs trading in Ghana and in other African countries rely on personal/organisational trust based on oral contracts. This is contrary to advanced economies where entrepreneurs rely mainly on institutional trust based on written contracts and less on personalised trust (Welter and Smallbone 2006; Welter et al. 2005). Amoako (2012) defines a written contract as 'a written agreement between exchange partners prepared by a lawyer with clauses that ensure that exchange partners are accountable and liable in case of non-compliance'.

Entrepreneurs use oral contracts within entrepreneurial customer and supplier relationships during face-to-face meetings and telephone conversations. However, occasionally, they may write agreements on pieces of paper in the presence of other traders or family members and friends who may serve as witnesses. Entrepreneurs use trust in personal relationships and social norms to enforce these oral contracts and sanction defaulters. These measures are relatively effective as, in most relationships, partners do not renege on their obligations.

Nevertheless, a few entrepreneurs rely on a memorandum of understanding (MOU) and even fewer on written contracts in their relationships, particularly in international markets. These entrepreneurs are mostly exporting to Western countries and other markets outside of Africa. That said, it is important to emphasise that the entrepreneurs using contracts understand that personal relationships based on trust remain very important as day-to-day relationship management depends a lot on personal trust. This is understandable since covering all expectations in a contract is practically impossible (Arrow 1974).

Ghanaian entrepreneurs' reliance on personal trust could be attributed to the relatively weak enforcement and sanctioning mechanisms imposed by legal systems (Amoako and Lyon 2014). However, it is also important to emphasise that norms of contracts were also part of the colonial institutions exported by the British colonial administration that are yet to be assimilated into the social and business norms of smaller businesses which have historically relied on trust in personal networks to do business.

6.2.5   Logics of Family/Kinship and Friendship Shaping Personal/Organisational Trust Development

The British carved out Ghana without recourse to ethnic affinity even though kinship ties underpin the socio-cultural structures of all ethnic groups. Ghana is a multiethnic and multicultural country. There are about 92 different ethnic groups usually classified into a few larger groups: Akan (47.5%), Mole Dagbani (16.6%), Ewe (13.9%), Ga Adangbe (7.4%), Geme (Gurma) (5.7%), Guan (3.7%), Grusi (2.5%), Mande Busanga (1.1%), and others (1.4%) (Ghana Statistical Service 2010). These different ethnic groups are, in most instances, mixed and scattered in the 10 regions in the country and with the exception of a few ethnic conflicts in the north of the country, the various groups coexist peacefully.

Within the ethnic groups, individuals have a close network of ties through family members, extended family members, community, tribe, and/or ethnicity (Gambetta 1988). The extended family develops the norms, values, and behaviour that society regards as acceptable. Individuals, as a result, have extended rights as well as extended obligations (Acquaah 2008; Amoako and Lyon 2014).

In the context of entrepreneurship, the literature posits that norms of family/kinship/friendship emphasise loyalty based on emotion, caring, and sharing and as a result can enhance the competitiveness of a business through decision making, strategic planning, and motivating family members and employees to work harder. A family can particularly bring clear values, beliefs, and a focused direction into the business (Burns 2016; Tokarczyk et al. 2007; Aronoff and Ward 2000). Family norms can further enhance SME internationalisation based on trust in family ties (Oviatt and McDougall 2005). Nevertheless, family values can also bring a lack of professionalism, nepotism instead of meritocracy, rigidity, and family conflict into the workplace (Schulze et al. 2001; Miller et al. 2009; Burns 2016).

In Ghana, family networks may provide access to suppliers, customers, and start-up capital and may also allow entrepreneurs to hire less-qualified family members—and yet the hiring of unqualified family members may hamper innovation (Robson and Obeng 2008). The empirical study reveals that norms of family also enable entrepreneurs to develop trust in relationships with customers, suppliers, and facilitators. Furthermore, trust development processes in entrepreneurial relationships draw on logics of family/kinship such as reciprocity, caring, and support of members to help cement relationships. Again, entrepreneurs' trust propensity is influenced by norms of family that lead to the development of positive attitudes towards partners they regard or who regard them as family members rather than business partners. Interestingly, the norms of the Akan family system make it morally wrong to abandon a 'brother', 'sister', or family member. This may explain why, on some occasions, some entrepreneurs are stuck in relationships that may not be very beneficial. In such cases, they need repeated evidence of untrustworthy behaviour to change their initial trust levels (Bachmann and Zaheer 2013).

Entrepreneurs also draw on the logics of family to enforce contract agreements within entrepreneurial relationships in the midst of weak and corrupt legal systems (Amoako 2012). The contract enforcement process involves the use of the traditional judiciary system that initially starts with family elders and can be escalated to the chief, paramount chief, or king only if the elders fail to find a solution (Myers 1992; Osei-Hwedie and Rankopo 2012).

Yet, the logics of family may constrain the development of entrepreneurship by limiting the ability of married females to independently establish and manage their own businesses. For those who manage to do so, the development of trust in entrepreneurial relationships is often constrained due to norms of family that disallow females to 'sit' and have conversations or establish close relationships with men who are not their husbands (Amoako and Matlay 2015). This is customarily common in some parts of the north of the country where Islam deeply influences family norms. Amoako and Lyon (2014) have dubbed the contradictory roles of family/kinship as 'the paradox of the family'. Throughout Africa, patriarchal family/kinship systems in most cultures constrain women's businesses (see Chap. 4).

6.2.6   Logics of Religion Shaping Personal/ Organisational Trust Development

Logics of religion shape the psychological state, the entrepreneurial networks (Vinten 2000; Drakopoulou Dodd and Gotsis 2007; Dana 2010), and the trust building of entrepreneurs (Amoako and Matlay 2015). Nevertheless, the relationship between religion and entrepreneurship remains complex (Drakopoulou Dodd and Seaman 1998).

Religion is a very important cultural factor in Ghana. The population is composed of about 71.2% Christians, 17.6% Muslims, and about 5.2% Animists and those not affiliated to any religion is 5.3% (Ghana Statistical Service 2010). Islam remains the dominant religion in some parts of the northern regions of the country whilst Christianity is the dominant religion in the south of the country. This is due to historical influences based on trading links with Arabs and Europeans. While Arabs (Muslim) merchants focused their activities in the north, European merchants (mostly Christians) settled in the south (coast) of the country during the colonial era.

Religious norms of fairness, reciprocity, and 'brotherliness' all promote trust building between partners in Ghana and in West African markets (Amoako and Lyon 2014; Amoako and Matlay 2015). Religion also promotes trust development in the entrepreneurial relationships of Ghanaian internationally trading SMEs based on shared beliefs, values, and faith. Entrepreneurs often refer to God-fearing people as being trustworthy as those partners often abide by contract agreements. Hence, religious norms influence entrepreneurs' trust propensity by leading to the development of more positive attitudes and higher disposition to trust which make them less suspicious of partners (Bachmann and Zaheer 2013), particularly those who share their religion. Logics of religion facilitate advancing trade credit to partners, especially fellow believers. Logics of religion also facilitate enforcement of agreements and in cases of default, entrepreneurs may resort to mediation through prayer, religious leaders (pastors, imams, akomfoo, and deities) to enforce trade agreements (Amoako 2012). Furthermore, logics of superstition and fatalism from Christianity, Islam, and traditional African religions may all enhance trust development and conflict resolution due to their inherent moral beliefs that restrain followers from opportunism. However, entrepreneurs may also invoke God, Allah, or traditional gods to sanction (curse) customers, suppliers and facilitators who refuse to fulfil their contractual obligations in relationships. The use of logics of religion shows how actors may internalise norms and thereby behave morally to avoid guilt and shame in economic exchanges (Platteau 1994). However, due to logics of fatalism, at times entrepreneurs who hold fatalistic beliefs accept vulnerability in their relationships (Amoako and Matlay 2015). Furthermore, fake religious leaders may violate trust and exploit entrepreneurs (see Chaps. 4 and 5). However, religion has less impact on entrepreneurial relationships in international markets.

6.2.7   Logics of Gift Giving Shaping Personal/ Organisational Trust Development

The practice of giving gifts to business partners is a norm in the development of trust and management of entrepreneurial relationships in Africa (see Chaps. 4 and 5 and Yanga and Amoako 2013). Gift giving enhances favours, obligations, and reciprocity among African communities and thereby fosters peaceful coexistence (Kenyatta 1965). Without exception, Ghanaian entrepreneurs sometimes offer gifts to and/or receive gifts from their business partners. The gifts include small amounts of cash, food items, toiletries, clothing, jewellery, and many other items. As stated in Chap. 5, even though gifts may be given to business partners throughout the year, they may be particularly given during festive occasions such as Eid al-Fitr, Eid al-Adha (Islamic holidays), Christmas, and New Year. Entrepreneurs also at times offer gifts to other stakeholders such as family members of their trading partners, traditional chiefs, religious leaders, community leaders, and officials in state institutions. In her study of trust development among yam and cassava traders in Ghana, Lassen (2016) confirms that gift giving is an integral part of cementing trading relationships in Ghana.

Yet, some Ghanaian entrepreneurs insist that gift giving to officials of state institutions is contentious since it can perpetuate corruption. As a result, they do business with government officials without giving gifts, while others concede that at times they offer gifts in order to obtain assistance from state officials, some of who may not perform their duties because they do not receive gifts. However, as stated in Chap. 4, the request for and giving of gifts to state officials raises ethical concerns relating to the perpetuation of corruption and needs to be examined thoroughly to enhance accountability of state officials in Ghana and other African countries.

6.2.8   Logics of Traditional Legal Systems and Chieftaincy Shaping Trade Associations and Parallel Institutional Trust Development

Trust in trade associations is partly due to the ability of trade associations to mediate in disputes between entrepreneurs and their trading partners in local and West African markets. The associations run parallel to state institutions and play a critical role in contract enforcement. However, most associations adopt conflict resolution structures from indigenous, traditional chieftaincy and justice systems. For example, among the food trading and exporting sectors with predominantly female entrepreneurs, in the Akan areas of Ghana, the leader of a trade association in the open markets often has the title of *ohemma*, which is the traditional chieftaincy title for the queen and is linked with the name of a particular commodity, such yam (*bayere*). Hence, the title of the leader of the yam trade association is *bayere hemma* (literally yam queen). Similarly, the title of the leader of the orange sellers association is known as *ankaa hemma* (literally orange queen). The *ohemma* has a secretary who, although acting like a spokesperson, also controls access to the queen. This role also reflects the role of the *okyeame*-traditional linguist, the spokesperson for the traditional chief. The use of the English word 'secretary' in the Twi/Akan language reflects the hybridisation of Western corporate and cooperative norms in Ghana. The powerful trade associations are those that have the endorsement of traditional rulers and local government officials and, as a result, have the backing of authorities at the grassroots level. In this way, norms of chieftaincy enable trade associations to serve as important institutions parallel to the courts, which are perceived to be corrupt, expensive, and a waste of time (Amoako and Lyon 2014; Amoako and Matlay 2015).

Similarly, the indigenous *efiewura* (landlord) system dominating the trade associations operating in the food export sector in Ghanaian and West African markets is embedded in industry-specific trade associations operating in the open markets in West African markets. Entrepreneurs trading in agricultural goods, particularly food, in West African markets often accompany their goods to export destinations and wait to collect their money from their customers (*efiewuranom*) when they have finished selling the produce.

Logics of traditional institutions such as chieftaincy, in various ways, help to reduce uncertainty and enhance entrepreneurship in Ghana and West Africa. However, norms of chieftaincy can also constrain entrepreneurship. For example, chiefs can prevent entrepreneurs from getting land when the ruler disagrees with what they want to do or feels threatened by the activities of the entrepreneur.

6.3   The Entrepreneur as Trustor: Propensity to Trust and Trusting Behaviour Within Relationships

Ghanaian entrepreneurs owning and managing internationally trading SMEs, as actors, play dominant roles in the development of interorganisational trust. Even though there are examples of other staff being involved in the process, the entrepreneur remains the key decision maker in trust development. Entrepreneurs' propensity or readiness to trust and expectations about the trustworthiness of partners in relationships shape their trusting behaviour and trust development in SME interorganisational relationships (Rotter 1967; Mayer et al. 1995; Tanis and Postmes 2005).

Apart from family/kinship and friendships, entrepreneurs rely on relationships with customers (who could be intermediaries or agents) and suppliers in local, West African, and international markets. Reciprocity and mutuality between organisations and between individuals in each organisation form the basis of these relationships (Zaheer et al. 1998; Vanneste 2016). However, there is a distinction between cross-cultural relationships with West African partners where there is evidence of personal trust based on oral contracts, social relationships, and other common norms related to doing business in the region, and those in intercontinental relationships outside of Africa where norms of contracts and memorandums of understanding are more common.

In local and West African markets, entrepreneurs embark on visits to business places and homes to meet employees, family members, and at times community leaders to reinforce their relationships. Entrepreneurs also use indigenous institutions such as gift giving and social events such as weddings and funerals to cement relationships. In distant local and West African regional markets, to be successful, entrepreneurs trading in agricultural produce rely on relationships with *efiewuranom* or commission agents in neighbouring countries such as Nigeria, Burkina Faso, Niger, and Mali. Entrepreneurs offer their goods on credit to the *efiewuranom* or agents who take delivery of the goods and sell them for a commission. The process can last from a few days to a few weeks. These agents serve as intermediaries who shrink the psychic distance between exporters and the markets of their choice. Personalised trust and parallel institutional trust in trade associations rather than formal contracts or memorandums of understanding underpin relationships within the traditional system. The relationships are often reinforced through common languages, religious beliefs, the sharing of information, and at times the provision of accommodation for the agents in distant, regional, West African markets (Amoako and Lyon 2014; Amoako and Matlay 2015).

In contrast, in intercontinental trade with customers abroad—mainly in the European Union, Asia, the United States, and Canada—entrepreneurs often rely on institutional trust in the form of written agreements, primarily memorandums of understanding and a few formal legal contracts. As a result, most entrepreneurs use written purchase orders when operating outside Africa. However, entrepreneurs encounter challenges in enforcing these contracts in Ghana since the courts lack jurisdiction in cases involving partners who do not reside in Ghana.

Apart from customers and suppliers, about half of the entrepreneurs operating in the formal sector collaborate with enterprise facilitators funded by the state or international donors. The various facilitators play diverse roles in assisting entrepreneurs to acquire skills in finance, market information, marketing, and networks. However, all the entrepreneurs belong to trade associations that can be conceptualised as forms of institutional-based trust with these less-formal institutions operating in parallel to the state institutions. The trade associations play a crucial role in trust development and in promoting international business through offering crucial services to entrepreneurs, as will be discussed later in this chapter.

6.4   Trustees' Trustworthiness and Forms of Trust Developed in Entrepreneurial Relationships

Trustworthiness refers to the behaviour and actions of trustees that will lead them to be more or less trusted by the trustor (Mayer et al. 1995; Rousseau et al. 1998). These actions and behaviour form the basis on which the trustor becomes willing to be vulnerable. In entrepreneurial relationships with SMEs in Ghana, the actions and behaviour of the partner entrepreneur forms the basis of trustworthiness. However, in relationships with larger organisations, the actions and behaviour of managers who serve as key boundary spanners determine trustworthiness even though there is evidence that the characteristics and reputation of the firm also count for some entrepreneurs (Zaheer et al. 1998; Gillespie and Dietz 2009). Similarly, the actions and behaviour of key boundary spanners and officials of state institutions also determine the trustworthiness of institutions (Mitchell 1999). Hence, entrepreneurs perceive trustworthiness at the institutional level, parallel institutional level, and personal/organisational level. While the literature suggests that entrepreneurs rely on personal trust, organisational trust, and institutional trust (see Chap. 3), in the empirical study, the evidence shows that Ghanaian entrepreneurs do not often differentiate between the entrepreneurs who own and manage partner SMEs and their firms, in terms of trustworthiness. As a result, personal trust and organisational trust are not distinct but rather form a mixture with each substituting for or complementing the other at different times within the working relationships of the entrepreneur.

6.4.1 Trustworthiness at the Institutional Level

Institutional trust refers to trust within and among institutions as well as the trust individuals have in those institutions (Möllering 2006). Institutional trust allows relationships to develop based on expectations that all parties will observe legal systems and common norms (Zucker 1986). However, entrepreneurs in Ghana have limited institutional trust in the courts and state-backed enterprise support institutions due to widespread allegations of bribery and corruption (Amoako 2012; Damoah et al. 2018).

Trustworthiness in institutions relates to the degree to which the behaviour of officials of enterprise support institutions is consistent with the rules, regulations, and objectives of those institutions (Mitchell 1999). The character, actions, and behaviour of officials and key boundary spanners shape the level of trust and the reputation of institutions (Mayer et al. 1995; Zaheer et al. 1998; Gillespie and Dietz 2009).

To entrepreneurs, honesty of officials remains the most important expectation that determines the trustworthiness of state and market institutions. Honest officials refer to those who are not corrupt and provide services to entrepreneurs without asking for bribes and favours. One of the key institutions whose officials and effectiveness influence institutional trust is the legal/court system in any country (Zucker 1986). Yet, Ghanaian internationally trading entrepreneurs generally do not use the courts due to widespread allegations of corruption by officials, delays due to long and cumbersome processes, and high costs. Similarly, perceptions of delays due to long processes and corruption prevent entrepreneurs from using the courts in West African markets. Entrepreneurs exporting to international markets also perceive the legal systems to be inaccessible and unaffordable (Amoako and Lyon 2014; Amoako 2012). Due to these barriers, there is lack of trust in the courts.

Furthermore, entrepreneurs link the lack of institutional trust to the level of limited support from state institutions that are meant to facilitate entrepreneurship. State institutions provide limited support to entrepreneurs in the formal sector regarding financial assistance from banks, market information, and training. However, those operating in the informal sector do not receive support from the government even though the sector employs over 90% of the total workforce (World Bank 2004; GSS 2010).

Previously there was distrust due to suspicion and harassment from both local and central government officials involved with the collection of taxes from entrepreneurs (Palmer 2004). Nevertheless, currently, due to government's emphasis on entrepreneurship, and the fight against corruption there seems to be an upsurge of trust in the prospects for entrepreneurship and small businesses in the country. For example, in 2017 the government passed a bill setting up the Office of the Special Prosecutor to combat corruption in the country. The Special Prosecutor has a mandate to investigate and prosecute cases of alleged corruption-related offenses involving political office holders, public officers, and their accomplices.

Some entrepreneurs operating in the formal sector develop trust in donor agencies and non-governmental organisations (NGOs) that support enterprise development in Ghana. These organisations include the British Council, the United States Agency for International Development (USAID), Danish International Development Agency (DANIDA), and Gesellschaft für Technische Zusammenarbeit (GTZ), and NGOs. Trustworthiness of these institutions relates to the actions and behaviour of officials of these organisations as well as the nature of the services provided to entrepreneurs. The services provided include training, finance, market information, and networking. While these institutions may not be corrupt, their services are mainly limited to highly educated entrepreneurs operating in the formal sector (Amoako 2012) and so entrepreneurs in the informal sector do not trust them.

In the midst of limited support and trust in state and market institutions, entrepreneurs in Ghana rely on trust in alternative indigenous institutions, such as trade associations, to develop parallel institutional trust in order to enhance their activities (Amoako and Lyon 2014).

6.4.2 Trustworthiness at the Parallel Institutional Level

The author defines parallel institutional trust as 'trust in local cultural institutions that run side-by-side [with] state institutions to facilitate entrepreneurship' (Amoako 2012). Notably, trade associations provide parallel institutional trust based on their stock of social capital and the selective incentives they provide to their members (Ville 2007; Reveley 2012). Hence, all the internationally trading entrepreneurs involved in this study are members of trade associations.

Two of the key expectations of trustworthiness in trade associations are honesty and reputation of the leaders, and the reputation of the association itself. Honest association leaders do not exploit business opportunities for themselves and do not indulge in corrupt practices, while the reputation of the association depends on the quality of services rendered to members and their trading partners. Trustworthiness of trade associations also relates to expectations about the delivery of a number of critical services in an industry. The expectations include regulation, conflict resolution, advocacy, legitimacy, networking, sharing market information, references for reputation and creditworthiness, skills development, and welfare. Through delivering these services, trade associations and their leaders provide the logics that enable the associations to function as bridges between entrepreneurs and their customers, suppliers, and intermediaries in local and distant West African markets and, in some instances, in international markets outside of West Africa. Table 6.1 summarises the role of trade associations in enhancing the development of parallel institutional trust.

As shown in Table 6.1, trade associations offer important services and are unique in defining norms, regulating industries, resolving conflicts, and offering many other critical services to entrepreneurs. These capabilities relate to the unique structures of associations that, in some cases, are a hybrid of the traditional chieftaincy model and Western corporate or cooperative management styles (Amoako and Lyon 2014). Yet, Ghana and other African states and international donor agencies rarely fund trade associations, and those that are funded are not encouraged to build on their existing indigenous practices but instead they are required to conform to imported Western norms which often may not be fit for purpose (Amoako and Lyon 2014).

Case 6.1 Trade Association Leader and Parallel Institutional Trust in Ghana

Obiri is an entrepreneur who exports about 70% of his fresh oranges to distant markets in Northern Ghana, Burkina Faso, and Niger. He founded his company in 1985 and operates from Techiman Market in the Brong Ahafo region of Ghana. He has not registered his company with the Registrar General, but instead he operates in the informal sector under the umbrella of a cooperative—the Orange and Fruit Sellers Association. Obiri is a founding member of the association and has served as the secretary and *okyeame* to the chairperson, the *ankaa hemma* (orange queen) for more than 20 years. As the secretary and *okyeame*, he serves as the spokesperson or linguist who in the traditional chieftaincy model serves as a gatekeeper to the traditional chief. Together with the chairperson, they transformed the association into a vibrant export network that works closely with entrepreneurs, trade associations and agents (*efiewuranom*) in distant markets in Northern Ghana and neighbouring countries in West Africa. Additionally, as the secretary he liaises with the *ohemma* to regulate prices in the local market and works with the local chiefs and government officials to provide advocacy and legitimacy to members. Obiri is also involved in the provision of market information, networking, references regarding reputation and creditworthiness of members, as well as welfare to needy members. One of his key roles is to help resolve conflicts among members of the association and between members and their customers and suppliers. Through these activities, Obiri and the *ohemma*, as leaders of the trade association provide parallel institutional trust that allows the orange and fruit sellers to operate across local, distant, and neighbouring West African markets without much support from state and market institutions.

Table 6.1 Trade associations and trust development in Ghanaian and West African markets

Trust expectation	Association activities underpinning trust expectation
Regulation	Controlling access to market spaces in local open markets
	Setting prices and controlling supplies to local open markets
Conflict resolution	Resolving and mediating in conflicts and disputes between members and between members and their trading partners
	Sanctioning members who may blatantly abuse general norms of the association and/or their obligations to trading partners

(continued)

Table 6.1 (continued)

Trust expectation	Association activities underpinning trust expectation
Advocacy	Representing members
	Liaising with traditional rulers, and national and local governments on matters such as taxes and market spaces
	Liaising with external bodies such as other associations and NGOs
Legitimacy	Ensuring the activities of businesses in the industry are lawful and socially acceptable
Networking	Organising meetings and functions that facilitate friendships, cooperation, and learning
Sharing market information	Providing information about market opportunities and risks
Reference for reputation and creditworthiness	Providing information about members' traceability and creditworthiness to potential customers in domestic and international markets
Skills development	Building the skills of members through training programmes on management, standards, and specifications
Welfare	Providing welfare to members through donations during ill health and other issues to help sustain the working capital of members
	Providing informal forms of insurance to members in extreme cases

Adapted from Amoako (2012)

6.4.3 Trustworthiness at the Personal/Organisational Level

As stated at the beginning of this section, trustworthiness at the personal/organisational level is linked mainly to the behaviour and actions of entrepreneurs and managers of partner firms that lead them to be more or less trusted by the entrepreneur (Mayer et al. 1995; Rousseau et al. 1998). Yet organisational factors like reputation can also form the basis of personal/organisational trust. Entrepreneurs base these behavioural dimensions more on rationality as they often calculate the risks involved in trusting. This study uncovers that, while the literature on buyer-supplier relationships refers to trust within buyer-supplier relationships (e.g. Smith et al. 1995), trustworthiness and trust expectations in customer relationships differ from those in supplier relationships. Hence, here, trust developments in the two entrepreneurial relationships are distinct and discussed separately.

6.4.4 Trustworthiness in Family/Kinship and Friendships

The logics of family/kinship and friendships underpin trust development in Ghana. Trustworthiness in family/kinship and friendship in entrepreneurship relates to the development of personalised relationships based on logics of family/kinship such as reciprocity, caring, and support of members to help cement relationships. The norms of the Akan family system make it morally wrong to abandon a 'brother', 'sister', or other family member. (See Sect. 6.2.5 for more details on family/kinship and friendship and trust development.)

6.4.5 Trustworthiness in Working Relationships

While, the literature refers to trust within buyer-supplier relationships (Smith et al. 1995), in this study, it is shown that trustworthiness and trust expectations in customer and supplier relationships are different: hence the two concepts are referred to as customer-related trust and supplier-related trust.

6.4.6 Trustworthiness in Customer Relationships

Honesty

To entrepreneurs in all the three sectors (agriculture, services and manufacturing), honesty is the most important attribute that determines trustworthiness of customers in domestic, West African, and international markets. Honesty is important since it is impossible for agreements and contracts to cover all expectations in any contract or agreement (Arrow 1974), as a result, entrepreneurs expect that customers will do what they have promised to do. An honest customer abides by his or her promises and tries not to take advantage of entrepreneurs or defraud them. Honesty also relates to customers keeping promises to pay for goods or services supplied on trade credit. The expectation that exchange partners will perform their role in the agreement describes honesty and it is similar to goodwill trust (Tillmar 2006; Nooteboom 1996; Fukuyama 1995) and integrity (Mayer et al. 1995).

Trade Credit

Entrepreneurs, irrespective of the markets in which they trade, recognise trade credit as a very important trust expectation in entrepreneurial relationships. This is understandable given the limited access to bank finance (Abor and Quartey 2010; Amoako and Matlay 2015) and higher costs of financial debt due to higher interest rates and inflation in Ghana. Trade credit also enhances entrepreneurs' strategies to boost accounts receivables and grow their businesses (Petersen and Rajan 1997). Yet, culturally specific norms of visits and payments guard trade credit relationships in Ghana. According to Amoako et al. (2018), in Ghana, the overwhelming majority of entrepreneurs develop trust in customers who make timely payments for goods already supplied. Often entrepreneurs 'start a little at a time' based on a number of transactions and a timely payments history based on a number of previous trade credit transactions and these often determine whether customers would benefit from a larger trade credit or not. Based on this approach, customers who have paid their previous trade credit as promised are seen to be trustworthy. Yet, the importance of timely payment varies from sector to sector. For example, in West African agriculture trade, entrepreneurs receive payment usually after the customer, who acts as an agent (*efiewura*), finishes selling the goods and takes commission, in a process that can last weeks. The difference in the sectors is due to differences in the norms governing the various sectors and markets.

Apart from timely payments, the vast majority of entrepreneurs assess the assets of partner entrepreneurs and organisations to ascertain their ability to fulfil payment obligations before trusting them. The ability to fulfil payment obligations relates closely to competence trust (Nooteboom 1996). In the assessment, entrepreneurs use the value of assets as a proxy for a partner's capacity to offer or to pay trade credit. Entrepreneurs therefore usually visit their partner's working place or home to collect information by assessing their assets such as equipment, machinery, and property. During these visits, entrepreneurs may talk to employees, family members, and at times members and leaders of the community to collect information on the reputation and therefore creditworthiness of their potential trade credit partners. Entrepreneurs rely on different types of information about the partner from the local community to evaluate the risks in trusting the partner company. It is also common practice for partners who request trade credit to be proactive and invite entrepreneurs to their business places and homes. The invitations to customers' and suppliers' homes and business places are very important because they enable entrepreneurs to locate their potential trade creditors in cases of default. In particular the invitations supposedly show the willingness of potential trade debtors to pay if they are offered trade credit, even though there are no guarantees that the trustee (debtor) will not relocate and 'disappear'. Gathering information about the assets of trading partners is very important in Ghana, and in Africa in general, since there is limited public information on the credit history of individuals and firms (Owusu Kwaning et al. 2015). However, occasionally entrepreneurs may take a greater risk by trusting strangers and extending trade credit to partners they do not know, based on gut feeling.

Reputation

Another important attribute that enhances customer trust is reputation (Weiwei 2007). Ghanaian entrepreneurs like supplying goods and services to entrepreneurs and companies who have a good reputation. These are entrepreneurs or firms that are honest and well established, and have been in business for a while so have a track record. Companies that have economies of scale, better cash flow, and are unlikely to be bankrupt are appealing and, not surprisingly, entrepreneurs in Ghana often perceive larger organisations to be more trustworthy compared to SMEs. Consequently, in general entrepreneurs prefer to trust and supply goods and services to reputable larger companies or medium companies than to work with micro and smaller businesses, and the perception that reputable firms are old and large compared to young and small firms has been confirmed by academics (Schwartz 1974; Petersen and Rajan 1997). Yet, in trusting and working with larger organisations, and particularly state-owned organisations, entrepreneurs often become vulnerable due to power asymmetry and the tendency for delayed payments from state organisations.

Sharing Market Information

Communication among partners has a direct positive impact on supply chain partnerships (Chu 2006). Entrepreneurs in Ghana regard the sharing of information with customers to be another very important trust expectation. The majority of entrepreneurs explained that the sharing of information with customers enhances flexibility and quick responses to changes in domestic, West African, and international markets. In particular, it enables them to respond to fluctuations in market demands regarding pricing, timing, and export volumes, which helps to maximise profits and avoid losses (Amoako 2012). To share information, entrepreneurs use information and communication technologies (ICTs) including the internet, mobile phones, and emails. The sharing of information and good communication between exchange partners promotes what Sako (1998) and Lewicki and Bunker (1996) call goodwill trust and knowledge-based trust respectively.

6.4.7 Trustworthiness in Supplier Relationships

Within supplier relationships in domestic, West African, and international markets, honesty remains the most important trust expectation. Honesty is important as honest suppliers keep promises regarding product and service specifications in terms of quality, quantity, and delivery times. Honest suppliers do not take advantage of entrepreneurs or defraud them by manipulating contracts or misusing trade credit extended to them for the supply of goods/services for other purposes.

Quality Products/Service

To Ghanaian internationally trading entrepreneurs, another important supplier trust expectation is quality of products/services. The supply of quality products/services is important for both exporter-supplier and exporter-customer relations in all sectors, but more so for international markets. This is due to the international supplier-buyer value chains in which customers expect adherence to very high product specifications, breaches of which may entail penalties. Poor quality goods/services from suppliers put the reputation of smaller businesses at risk. To mitigate this challenge, some entrepreneurs develop trust-based relationships with suppliers by offering training and technical support to enable them to meet the high specifications required by international customers. This is particularly common in the agriculture sector where the competitive nature of global market demands, and strict regulations on food due to health and environmental concerns, have given rise to interdependence, cooperation, and mutual trust between entrepreneurs and their suppliers (Amoako 2012). Therefore, in the agriculture and food sector, entrepreneurs lean on farmers and suppliers in order to meet their obligations to their customers and this form of trust is similar to what Nooteboom (1996) and Sako (1998) term 'competence trust'.

Punctuality

Another important expectation of supplier trust that is critical to the competitiveness of entrepreneurs in international markets is punctuality: that is, meeting delivery deadlines.

Punctuality is linked to the competitive nature of international trading as entrepreneurs are expected to meet supply deadlines and, based on this demand, they in turn expect their suppliers to meet delivery deadlines. Yet, while punctuality could be a major issue to entrepreneurs in all sectors, it is more important for those involved in trading in fresh produce, such as food, due to the short shelf life of their produce. The challenges of punctuality relate to cultural-specific norms of 'African punctuality', which refers to the flexible use of time in Ghanaian and African contexts (see Chap. 4). To reduce this challenge, internationally trading entrepreneurs develop trust-based collaborations with their suppliers in order to meet the stringent deadlines imposed on them by their international partners. This process involves the learning of new norms of punctuality (Amoako 2012; Amoako and Matlay 2015) and thereby, as actors, not yielding to existing norms and institutions. Punctuality as an expectation of reliability requires that exchange partners meet their obligations in export transactions and again Nooteboom (1996) and Sako (1998) describe this as 'competence trust'.

Trade Credit from Suppliers

Entrepreneurs trading in domestic, West African, and international markets recognise that trade credit to or from suppliers is a critical expectation in entrepreneurial relationships (Amoako et al. 2018). Thus, entrepreneurs receive trade credit from suppliers who are trustworthy. Similarly, they extend trade credit to trusted suppliers. In competitive sectors, entrepreneurs who refuse to offer trade credit to suppliers when expected to do so may lose suppliers to competitors who are prepared to offer it. Yet, the potential for opportunism exists as suppliers can default and/or divert goods or services to another buyer. For example, in the food and agricultural sector, there is scope for opportunism, particularly when competitors offer farmers higher prices than those the entrepreneur had offered initially through trade credit. However, farmers who receive trade credit from entrepreneurs rarely divert their produce. Thus, trade credit enables entrepreneurs to work closely with partners to develop supplier trust. This dimension of trustworthiness relates closely to 'leanability' based on reciprocity and obligations to provide support to family members based on the traditional family system (Amoako 2012).

Sharing of Information by Suppliers

Sharing of information remains a key dimension of supplier trust in domestic, West African, and international markets. Within supplier relationships, the sharing of information with regard to changes in prices, volumes, deadlines, and quality enables entrepreneurs to quickly respond to changes in domestic, West African, and international markets. Timely information sharing on market prices and demand also allows entrepreneurs to maximise profits and avoid losses (Amoako 2012). Suppliers share information via face-to-face meetings and ICTs (notably mobile phones for calls, text messages, and emails).

Reputation

The reputation of supplier firms is an important attribute that also enhances supplier trust in Ghana. Entrepreneurs prefer buying supplies from well-established and known entrepreneurs and companies that have been in existence for a while, and as a result have a track record. Entrepreneurs often seek references from personal and business networks to identify such organisations (see Chap. 5). The reputation of a supplier serves as an assurance of product specifications regarding quality and reliable supplies. Firms with a good reputation may also offer competitive prices to entrepreneurs. However, cheap supplies may compromise quality and damage the reputation of the entrepreneur's business and so the key issue in such transactions is related to value for money. However, reputable companies may require the payment of deposits which may adversely affect the cash flow of small businesses.

The customer and supplier trusts described above are, however, underpinned by personal trust developed between trading partners. Personal trust originates from previous exchanges and from the initial knowledge of the exchange partner and his or her demonstration of trustworthiness (Zucker 1986; Mayer et al. 1995; Chang et al. 2016). It may also originate from social networks and long-standing bilateral business relationships involving organisations (Welter and Smallbone 2006).

Ghanaian entrepreneurs, like their counterparts from other African countries, rely mostly on personal trust to enhance economic activity (Lyon 2003, 2005; Amoako and Lyon 2014). Entrepreneurs develop personal trust with other entrepreneurs and managers of key partner companies in order to develop or grow their businesses. Based on personal trust, entrepreneurs may receive trade credit, quality products, and timely delivery, all based on flexible arrangements using oral contracts that do not involve a lawyer. This is particularly important in weak institutional contexts such as Ghana where entrepreneurs have limited access to resources from formal institutions.

Case 6.2 demonstrates how entrepreneurs in weak institutional contexts may perceive trustworthiness based on the actions and behaviour of exchange partners. This case also shows how entrepreneurs draw on the logics of indigenous cultural institutions in trust development.

Case 6.2 Personal/Organisational Trust Development

Gifty is a dynamic and ambitious Ghanaian female entrepreneur who learnt her skills as an exporter after working with her sister in the clothing export industry. Later on she received training from the Ghana Export Promotion Authority and founded Top Creativity Industries in 2000, registering the firm in 2002. The company is located at Tema, the industrial hub of Ghana, where she manufactures and exports natural cocoa powder—Life Gold Natural Cocoa Powder—to Nigeria, Togo, and Benin in West Africa and to the United States. Gifty is a member of the Assorted Foodstuff Exporters Association and maintains good relationships with the Ghana Export Promotion Authority (GEPA), the state institution that supports SME exporters operating in the formal sector. GEPA organises training and trade fairs for small-scale exporters in the formal sector. Gifty also works closely with the Cocoa Processing Company, her main supplier. She has developed close working relationships with her customers in West African countries. She does not have a contract with any of her customers or suppliers but instead relies on trust by accepting and placing orders for products and raw materials via the telephone. She works closely with customers who are trustworthy; according to her these customers are 'honest, truthful and God-fearing; when they say [in] two weeks I will pay the money they pay, they keep the promises and send the money'. Similarly, she has worked closely with her suppliers because 'their quality is very good and the manager I deal with is very honest too'.

Gifty offers trade credit to her customers in West African markets to enable her to increase sales and grow her business. However, before offering trade credit to customers, she tests them based on timely payments for a number of previous transactions. Furthermore, before advancing trade credit to customers in West African markets, she visits their workplaces or homes to collect information on their reputation and assets including equipment, machinery, and property. During the visits, she may talk to employees, family members, and at times members and leaders of the community. She also offers gifts to the spouses and children of customers when she visits. Interestingly, often customers who request trade credit invite her to their homes and workplaces. According to her, the invitations enhance trust development because they enable her to trace potential trade debtors in cases of default. However, occasionally she takes a risk by offering small quantities of her products to customers who are relatively new and whose homes and workplaces she does not know and this happens when she perceives the customer to be God-fearing. Gifty therefore develops trust based on cognition, calculation, and at times habituation to build trade credit relationships. In 2017, she acquired a 4 acre-piece of land near Accra and registered a new company, Life Star Cocoa Processing Ltd., to take advantage of the high demand for processed cocoa from local and foreign customers. Currently, she is searching for trustworthy partners to invest in her new company. She is also looking for customers in China, Japan, and Dubai.

6.5 Trust Outcomes

The literature on entrepreneurship confirms that interorganisational trust directly or indirectly offers a variety of positive outcomes for interfirm relationships (see Welter and Smallbone 2006) and this is no different in Ghana. Personal trust with family/kinship contributes in cash and in kind to businesses in the start-up stage through inheritance, apprenticeships, or start-up capital (Clark 1994; Buame 2012). Furthermore, entrepreneurs access resources such as ideas, informal finance, larger networks, and market knowledge, from family/kinship. Family members may also become trusted business partners or apprentices and may also assist in conflict resolution (Amoako 2012; Lyon 2005). Similarly, there is a consensus among entrepreneurs that personal trust between entrepreneurs and their key partners enhances cooperation that in turn facilitate access to ideas, trade credit, larger networks, and market knowledge. Parallel institutional trust with trade associations also enhances legitimacy, advocacy, and access to markets, social security, and conflict resolution. Nonetheless, there is evidence that entrepreneurs experience trust violations and Chap. 7 will explore this in detail.

6.6 Conclusion

This chapter set out to examine the institutional logics that shape trust development, how entrepreneurs perceive trustworthiness, and the forms of trust developed in contexts of weak institutions. The discussions show that institutional logics of a range of societal institutional orders provide the basis of trust (see Fig. 6.1). The logics of weak legal systems and enterprise support institutions underpin the limited institutional trust in state and market institutions. In response, entrepreneurs mainly rely on logics of indigenous cultural institutions to develop personalised trust that enhances stronger obligations and reciprocity in working relationships. Entrepreneurs draw stronger elements of obligation in economic relationships from logics of language, oral contracts, trade associations, family/kinship and friendship, religion, punctuality, gift giving, and traditional justice systems embedded in chieftaincy. As a result, sociocultural institutions underpin trust development (Saunders et al. 2010; Li 2016; Chang et al. 2016) and therefore trust can be habitual and routinised (Zucker 1986). The logics of some indigenous institutions that run side-by-side with state institutions provide the basis of trust that substitutes for limited institutional trust and the author refers to this form of trust as 'parallel institutional trust'. In particular, trade associations provide parallel institutional trust that facilitates entrepreneurship by providing many critical services including advocacy, legitimacy, business information, training, welfare and opportunities for networking to members, and settling commercial disputes between members, and members and their trading partners. Not surprisingly, most entrepreneurs regard membership of these associations as crucial for survival as they enable entrepreneurs to take on some of the risk in a relationship. Some trade associations draw on a hybrid of traditional norms of chieftaincy and

Western notions of organisation with leadership structures that include a queen or chief and a secretary.

Yet, relationships and interactions with officials of institutions, family/kinship and friendship, and customers and suppliers also shape entrepreneurs' trusting behaviour. In these relationships, entrepreneurs base the trustworthiness of trustees primarily on the actions and behaviour of the trustee (Mayer et al. 1995; Zaheer et al. 1998). As a result, the actions and behaviour of officials of a state enterprise support institution, leaders of trade associations, or entrepreneurs owning and managing the partner SME influences trust development.

Thus, within working relationships with customers and suppliers, the entrepreneur's trusting behaviour is shaped mainly by the trustworthiness and expectations of the partner (trustee) owning the micro or smaller business, or the manager or key boundary spanner of the larger organisation (Zaheer et al. 1998). As a result, the distinction between personal/organisational trust remains complex and unclear. This may differ in larger organisational contexts where the number of employees is higher and a number of managers may be involved in decision making. It may also differ in other economies where there is less power distance and in contexts where SMEs may have a larger number of employees.

This chapter shows that entrepreneurs draw on logics of cultural institutions to develop trust. However, it is also clear that as actors, entrepreneurs do not necessarily yield to institutions. For example, the development of new norms of punctuality and refusal to work with family members who are not trustworthy due to opportunistic behaviour (Amoako and Lyon 2014; Amoako and Matlay 2015), show how as actors, entrepreneurs in Ghana have the capacity to reflect and act in ways to counter the constraints and taken-for-granted assumptions prescribed by institutions (Abebrese and Smith 2014).

Trust enables entrepreneurs to access critical resources needed for start-up and enterprise development. These resources include start-up capital, apprenticeships (Clark 1994; Buame 2012), ideas, information, informal finance, larger networks, market knowledge, trusted business partners, and social security (Amoako 2012; Lyon 2005). Furthermore, trust enhances legitimacy, advocacy, access to markets, and conflict resolution in domestic and distant markets.

This chapter contributes to the literature in four ways. First, by presenting a framework that visualises a holistic approach to trust development in SME interorganisational relationships in an emerging economy and African context based on the entrepreneur (trustor), his or her trading partner (trustee), their relationship, and the external cultural norms that shape trust processes within relationships. Second, by reconceptualising the role of state and market institutions and identifying cultural-specific institutions that provide the logics that underpin trust development in entrepreneurial relationships in an African context. Third, by showing how personal/interorganisational trust comingles in SME contexts due to the dominant role of the entrepreneur who as an actor may develop trust in relationships in order to mitigate institutional weaknesses in Ghana. Fourth, by showing how as actors entrepreneurs do not necessarily yield to formal institutional constraints but respond by relying on alternative indigenous institutions.

Yet, notwithstanding these advantages, all the entrepreneurs shared experiences about violations of trust some of which greatly damaged relationships. The next chapter (Chap. 7) discusses trust violations in entrepreneurial relationships in the Ghanaian context.

References

Abebrese, A., and R. Smith. 2014. Developing a phenomenological understanding of cultural survival mechanisms as institutional artefacts in shaping indigenous enterprise culture: A Ghanaian perspective. *Amity Business Journal* 3 (1). Available at SSRN https://ssrn.com/abstract=2456089.

Abor, J., and P. Quartey. 2010. Issues in SME development in Ghana and South Africa. *International Research Journal of Finance and Economics* 39: 218–228.

Acquaah, M. 2008. Perspectives, social capital, the benefits, potential costs and prospects. *Journal of Microfinance/ESR Review* 10 (2): 12–18.

Altinay, L., M.N.K. Saunders, and C.L. Wang. 2014. The influence of culture on trust judgements in customer relationship development by ethnic minority small businesses. *Journal of Small Business Management* 52 (1): 59–78.

Amoako, I.O. 2012. *Trust in exporting relationships: The case of SMEs in Ghana*, Published PhD thesis. Center for Economic and Enterprise Development

Research (CEEDR) Middlesex University, London. http://eprints.mdx. ac.uk/12419/.

Amoako, I.O., and F. Lyon. 2014. We don't deal with courts': Cooperation and alternative institutions shaping exporting relationships of SMEs in Ghana. *International Small Business Journal* 32 (2): 117–139.

Amoako, I.O., and H. Matlay. 2015. Norms and trust-shaping relationships among food- exporting SMEs in Ghana. (Eds) Quinn, B., Dunn, A., McAdam, R., and McKitterick, L. Special Issue on "The Competitiveness of SMEs in the Food Sector: Exploring Possibilities for Growth". *The International Journal of Entrepreneurship and Innovation* 16 (2): 123–124.

Amoako, I. O., Akwei, C., & Damoah, I. S. (2018, forthcoming). "We know their house, family and work place": Trust in entrepreneurs' trade credit relationships in weak institutions. *Journal of Small Business Management.* https://doi.org/10.1111/JSBM.12488.

Aronoff, C.E., and J.L. Ward. 2000. *Family business values: How to assure legacy of continuity and success,* Family business leadership series, no. 12. Marietta: Business Owner Resources.

Arrow, K. 1974. *Limits of economic organization.* New York: Norton.

Bachmann, R., and A. Inkpen. 2011. Understanding institutional-based trust building processes in inter-organisational relationships. *Organization Studies* 32 (2): 281–300.

Bachmann, R., and A. Zaheer. 2013. *Handbook of advances in trust research.* Cheltenham: Edward Elgar.

Besharov, M., and W. Smith. 2014. Multiple logics in organizations: Explaining their varied nature and implications. *Academy of Management Review* 39 (3): 364–381.

Buame, S. K. 1996. Entrepreneurship: A contextual perspective. Discourses and praxis of entrepreneurial activities within institutional context of Ghana. Lund: Lund University Press.

———. 2012. *Entrepreneurship: Entrepreneurial education, venture creation and SME management in Ghana.* Weija-Accra: Big Mike's Publication Ltd.

Burns, Paul. 2016. *Entrepreneurship and small business.* London: Palgrave Macmillan Limited.

Central Intelligence Agency. 2016. Ghana in the world factbook. http://cia.gov/ library/publications.the-worldfactbook/geos/gh.html. Accessed 1 June 2018.

Chang, C.-C., S.-N. Yao, S.-A. Chen, J.-T. King, and C. Liang. 2016. Imagining garage startups: Interactive effects of imaginative capabilities on technopreneurship intention. *Creativity Research Journal* 28 (3): 289–297.

Chu, S.Y. 2006. Exploring the relationships of trust and commitment in supply chain management. *The Journal of American Academy of Business* 9 (1): 224–228.

Clark, G. 1994. *Onions are my husband: Survival and accumulation by west African market women*. London: University of Chicago Press.

Damoah, I.S., C.A. Akwei, I.A. Amoako, and D. Botchie. 2018. Corruption as a source of government project failure in developing countries: Evidence from Ghana. *Project Management Journal* 49 (3): 17–33.

Dana, L.P. 2010. Introduction: Religion as an explanatory variable for entrepreneurship. In *Entrepreneurship and religion*, ed. L.P. Dana, 1–24. Cheltenham: Edward Elgar Publishing Ltd.

Deutsch, Yuval, Thomas Keil, and Tomi Laamanen. 2011. A dual agency view of board compensation: The joint effects of outside director and CEO stock options on firm risk. *Strategic Management Journal* 32 (2): 212–227.

Drakopoulou Dodd, S., and G. Gotsis. 2007. The interrelationships between entrepreneurship and religion. *The International Journal of Entrepreneurship and Innovation* 8 (2): 93–104.

Drakopoulou Dodd, S., and P.T. Seaman. 1998. Religion and enterprise: An introductory exploration. *Entrepreneurship Theory and Practice* 23 (1): 71–86.

Durand, R., B. Szostak, J. Jourdan, and P. Thornton. 2013. Institutional logics as strategic resources. In *Institutional logics in Action. Part A: Research in the sociology of organizations*, ed. M. Lounsbury and E. Boxenbaum, vol. 39, 9th ed., 165–201. Bingley: Emerald Group Publishing.

Etebefia, O.S., and B.W. Akinkumi. 2013. The contribution of small scale industries to the national economy. *Standard Research Journal of Business Management* 1 (2): 60–71.

Fink, M., and A. Kessler. 2010. Cooperation, trust, and performance: Empirical results from three countries. *British Journal of Management* 21: 469–483.

Fukuyama, F. 1995. *Trust: The social virtues and the creation of prosperity*. London: Hamish Hamilton.

Ghanaian Times. 2018. Ghana's population hits 29.6 million. *Ghanaian Times*, Accra, March 12.

Gambetta, D., ed. 1988. *Trust: Making and breaking cooperative relations*. Oxford/New York: Basil Blackwell.

Gillespie, N., and G. Dietz. 2009. Trust repair after an organization level failure. *Academy of Management Review* 34 (1): 127–145.

GSS. 2010. *Population & housing census: Summary report of final results*. Accra: Ghana Statistical Service.

————. 2016. 2016 regional spatial business report, the Ghana statistical service, Accra.

————. *Provisional 2017 Annual Gross Domestic Product*. April ed. Accra: Ghana Statistical Service (GSS).

Kayanula, D., and P. Quartey. 2000. *The policy environment for promoting small and medium-sized enterprises in Ghana and Malawi*, Paper no. 15. Institute for Development Policy and Management (IDPM), University of Manchester.

Kenyatta, J. 1965. *Facing Mount Kenya: The tribal life of the Gikuyu*, 253–258. New York: Vintage Books.

Kuada, J., and G. Thomsen. 2005. Culture, learning, and the internationalisation of Ghanaian firms. In *Internationalisation and enterprise development in Ghana*, ed. J. Kuada, 271–292. London: Adonis and Abbey Publishers Ltd.

Lassen, A. 2016. Re-engaging the unequal distribution of rewards: A study of trust among actors in the Yam and cassava value chain in Ghana. PhD Thesis, Aalborg, Aalborg University.

Lewicki, R.J., and B.B. Bunker. 1996. Developing and maintaining trust in work relationships. In *Trust in organizations: Frontiers of theory and research*, ed. R. Kramer and T.R. Tyler. Thousand Oaks: Sage.

Lewicki, R.J., E.C. Tomlinson, and N. Gillespie. 2006. Models of interpersonal trust development: Theoretical approaches, empirical evidence, and future directions. *Journal of Management* 32: 9.

Li, P.P. 2016. The holistic and contextual natures of trust: Past, present and future research. *Journal of Trust Research* 6 (1): 1–6.

Lyon, F. 2003. Trader associations and urban food systems in Ghana: Institutionalist approaches to understanding urban collective action. *International Journal of Urban and Regional Research* 27 (1): 11–23.

————. 2005. Managing co-operation: Trust and power in Ghanaian associations. *Organization Studies* 27 (1): 31–52.

Lyon, F., M. Guido, and M.N.K. Saunders. 2012. *Handbook of research methods on trust*, 85–93. Cheltenham: Edward Elgar.

Mayer, R., J. Davis, and F. Schoorman. 1995. An integrative model of organisational trust. *Academy of Management Review* 20: 709–734.

Miller, D., J. Lee, S. Chang, and I. Le Breton-Miller. 2009. Filling the institutional void: The social behavior and performance of family vs non-family technology firms in emerging markets. *Journal of International Business Studies* 40: 802–817.

Misztal, B.A. 1996. *Trust in modern societies*. Cambridge: Polity Press.

Mitchell, C.E. 1999. Violating public trust: The ethical and moral obligations of government officials. *Public Personnel Management* 28 (1): 27.

Möllering, G. 2006. *Trust: Reason, routine, reflexivity*. Amsterdam: Elsevier.

Myers, Samuel L. 1992. Crime, entrepreneurship, and labor force withdrawal. *Contemporary Economic Policy* 10 (2): 84–97.

New York Times. 2018. Whats is the worlds fastest-growing economy? Ghana contends for the crown. *New York Times*, March 10.

Ninsin, A.K. 1989. Planning for the growth of small-scale industries in the informal sector: The realities and challenges of the Ghanaian situation. In *Planning African growth and development: Some current issues*, ed. E. Aryeetey, Proceedings of ISSER/UNDP International Conference on Planning for Growth and Development for Africa, University of Ghana, Legon.

Nooteboom, B. 1996. Trust, opportunism, and governance: A process and control model. *Organization Studies* 17: 985–1010.

Nooteboom, B., H. Berger, and N.G. Noorderhaven. 1997. Effects of trust and governance on relational risk. *Academy of Management Journal* 40 (2): 308–338.

Nowak, M., R. Basanti, B. Horvath, K. Kocharr, and R. Prem. 1996. Ghana 1983-1991. In *Adjustment for growth; The African experience* IMF Occasional Working Paper, No. 143, ed. M.T. Hadjimichael. Washington, DC: International Monetary Fund.

Osei-Hwedie, K., and M.J. Rankopo. 2012. Indigenous conflict resolution in Africa: The case of Ghana and Botswana, IPSHU. *English Research Report Series* 29 (3): 33–51 Institute of Peace Studies: Hiroshima University.

Oviatt, B., and P. McDougall. 2005. The internationalization of entrepreneurship. *Journal of International Business Studies* 36: 2–8.

Owusu Kwaning, C., K. Nyantakyi, and B. Kyereh. 2015. The challenges behind SMEs access to debt financing in the Ghanaian financial market. *International Journal of Small Business and Entrepreneurship Research* 3 (2): 16–30.

Palmer, R. 2004. *The informal economy in Sub-Saharan Africa: Unresolved issues of concept, character and measurement*, Occasional paper no. 98. Edinburgh: CAS.

Petersen, M.A., and R.G. Rajan. 1997. Trade credit: Theories and evidence. *The Review of Financial Studies* 10 (3): 661–691.

Platteau, J.P. 1994. Behind the market stage where real societies exist – Part II the role of moral norms. *Journal of Development Studies* 30 (4): 753–817.

PWc. 2017. Global economic growth in 2018 on track to be fastest since 2011. https://press.pwc.com/Newsreleases/global-economic-growth-in-2018-on-track-to-befastest-since-2011%2D%2D-pwc/s/60b3c7e4-c088-4574-995e132dd74d7dac.

Quartey, P., E. Turkson, J. Abor, and A. Iddrisu. 2017. Financing the growth of SMEs in Africa: What are the constraints to the SME financing within ECOWAS? *Review of Development Finance.* https://doi.org/10.1016/j.rdf.2017.03.001.

Reveley, James. 2012. Wartime price control and maritime industry corporatism: The case of New Zealand coastal shipping. *International Journal of Maritime History* 24 (2): 1–20.

Robson, P.J., and B.A. Obeng. 2008. The barriers to growth in Ghana. *Small Business Economics* 30: 385–403.

Rotter, J.B. 1967. A new scale for the measurement of interpersonal trust. *Journal of Personality* 35 (4): 651–665.

Rousseau, D., S. Sitkin, R.S. Burt, and C. Camerer. 1998. Not different after all: A cross-discipline view of trust. *Academy of Management Review* 23 (3): 393–404.

Sako, M. 1998. The information requirements of trust in supplier relations: Evidence from Japan, Europe and the United States. In *Trust and economic learning*, ed. N. Lazaric and Edward Lorenz. Cheltenham: Edward Elgar.

Saunders, Mark, Skinner Denise, Gillespie Nicole, Dietz Graham, and Lewicki Roy. 2010. *Organization trust – A cultural perspective.* Cambridge: New York University Press.

Schulze, W.S., M.H. Lubatkin, R.H. Dino, and A.K. Buchholtz. 2001. Agency relationships in family firms: Theory and evidence. *Organisation Science* 12: 99–116.

Schwartz, R.A. 1974. An economic model of trade credit. *The Journal of Financial and Quantitative Analysis* 9 (4): 643–657.

Smith, K., S. Carroll, and S. Ashford. 1995. Intra and Interorganizational cooperation: Toward a research agenda. *Academy of Management Journal* 39: 7–23.

Tanis, M., and T. Postmes. 2005. A social identity approach to trust: Interpersonal perception, group membership and trusting behaviour. *European Journal of Social Psychology* 35: 413–424.

Teal, F. 2002. *A note on data for Ghanaian manufacturing firms: 1991–1997.* Oxford: Centre for the Study of African Economies, University of Oxford.

Tesfom, G., C.H.M. Lutz, and P.N. Ghauri. 2004. Comparing export marketing channels: Developed versus developing countries. *International Marketing Review* 21 (4–5): 409–442.

Tillmar, M. 2006. Swedish tribalism and Tanzanian entrepreneurship: Preconditions for trust formation. *Entrepreneurship and Regional Development* 18 (2): 91–108.

Tokarczyk, J., E. Hansen, M. Green, and J. Down. 2007. A resource-based view and market orientation theory examination of the role of "familiness" in family business success. *Family Business Review* 20 (1): 17–31.

Trading Economics. 2018. Ghana interest rate 2002–2018. Available at https://tradingeconomics.com/ghana/in.

Vanneste, B.S. 2016. From interpersonal to interorganizational trust: The role of indirect reciprocity. *Journal of Trust Research* 6 (1): 7–36.

Ville, Simon. 2007. Rent seeking or market strengthening? Industry associations in New Zealand wool broking. *The Business History Review* 81 (2): 297–321.

Vinten, G. 2000. Business theology. *Management Decision* 38 (3): 209–215.

Weiwei, T. 2007. Impact of corporate image and corporate reputation on customer loyalty: A review. *Management Science and Engineering* 1 (2): 57–62.

Welter, F., and D. Smallbone. 2006. Exploring the role of trust in entrepreneurial activity. *Entrepreneurship Theory and Practice* 30 (4): 465–475.

Welter, F., M. Asp, and Holmström Ch. 2005. Knowledge creation in small firms: An exploratory study of its influence on growth and performance. In *Informations- und Wissens management in KMU*, Jahrbuch der KMU-Forschung und –praxis 2005, ed. J.-A. Meyer, 37–53. Lohmar/Köln: Eul.

World Bank. 2004. *Skills development in sub-Saharan Africa*. Washington, DC: World Bank.

Wu, W., M. Firth, and O.M. Rui. 2014. Trust and the provision of trade credit. *Journal of Banking and Finance* 39: 146–159.

Yanga, M.L., and I.O. Amoako. 2013. Legitimizing dishonesty in organizations: A survey of managers in four Sub-Sahara African countries. In *(Dis)Honesty in management*, Advanced series in management, ed. Tiia Vissak and Maaja Vadi, vol. 10, 243–268. Bingley: Emerald Group Publishing.

Zaheer, A., B. McEvily, and V. Perrone. 1998. Does trust matter? Exploring the effects of interorganizational and interpersonal trust on performance. *Organization Science* 9 (2): 141–159.

Zucker, L.G. 1986. Production of trust. Institutional sources of economic structure, 1840–1920. *Research in Organisation Behaviour* 8: 53–111.

7

Trust Violations in Entrepreneurial Relationships in an African Context

7.1 Introduction

Trust is important as it binds partners together and reduces uncertainty by promoting long-term cooperation in interorganisational relationships (Fink and Kessler 2010). Yet, trust is fragile as it may take years to develop in relationships, but can be destroyed within a short time if one party engages in a behaviour that violates the trust between the parties (Lewicki and Bunker 1996). All the same, trust violations are common at individual, organisational, and institutional levels (Gillespie and Dietz 2009; Kramer and Lewicki 2010). In interpersonal relationships, trust violations result from the behaviour of individual partners. Similarly, in organisational and institutional settings the behaviour of boundary spanners and officials primarily determine when and how trust is violated since, in the end, it is individuals that trust and not organisations per se (Ring and Van de Ven 1992; Zaheer et al. 1998). Yet, organisational systems and processes may also fail resulting in trust being violated by organisations (Gillespie and Dietz 2009).

Lewicki (2006) explains that trust violations originate from information that differs from a trustor's expectations of a trusteee's behaviour.

© The Author(s) 2019

I. O. Amoako, *Trust, Institutions and Managing Entrepreneurial Relationships in Africa*,
Palgrave Studies in Entrepreneurship in Africa,
https://doi.org/10.1007/978-3-319-98395-0_7

However, it is not only unacceptable behaviour that can influence trust violation, the perceptions that drive frustrations and feelings of violations can also influence trust violations. Trust violation can have serious implications for individuals, organisations, and society at large (Bachman et al. 2015). It can result in a reduction of trust and cooperation and may cause great damage to relationships between exchange partners (Lewicki and Bunker 1996; Dirks et al. 2009; Bachman et al. 2015). In the context of business, trust violations may lead to considerable consequences. For example, when trust is violated between a buyer and a seller or between firms collaborating in a horizontal relationship, the firm that becomes the victim may suddenly be in a situation that threatens their very existence (Bell et al. 2002; Bachmann 2001).

In spite of the potential serious consequences, currently, there are few studies that have investigated trust violations in organisational settings and at the institutional level (Bachman et al. 2015). Surprisingly, among the few existing studies, most adopt experimental and rationalist calculative approaches that emphasise the role of agency based on Mayer et al.'s (1995) dimensions of ability, benevolence, and integrity (Kim et al. 2004; Dirks et al. 2009; Gillespie and Dietz 2009). Despite the significant contributions made by these studies, the influence of context is ignored. Different contexts influence the processes of trust development by providing different forms of embeddedness that encourage or discourage trustworthy behaviour (Li 2016; Rousseau et al. 1998; Möllering 2006). Hence, it is expected that the processes of trust violations may differ based on the differences in expectations within different contexts (Saunders et al. 2010; Amoako 2012). Yet, scholars have done very little work to enhance our understanding of how context influences trust violations (Bachman et al. 2015; Amoako and Lyon 2012). Context in this book include state and market institutions, cultural institutions, networks and relationships, sector and industry, and markets.

The aim of this chapter is to explore and extend our understanding of how weak state and market institutions, cultural institutions, personal and working relationships, industry, and markets shape the processes of trust violations in entrepreneurial relationships in Ghana (Amoako and Lyon 2014; Bachmann 2010).

Entrepreneurs and small and medium-sized enterprises (SMEs) in Ghana, as in other African countries, operate in countries with limited institutional trust in state and market institutions. As a result, parallel institutional trust from cultural institutions (Amoako and Lyon 2014), trade associations, and industry-specific norms in addition to personal trust in networks and relationships enhance economic activity (Amoako and Matlay 2015; Hyden 1980; McDade and Spring 2005).

The analysis and discussions in this chapter focus on the entrepreneur, and how the logics of societal institutional orders such as weak legal systems, family/kinship, religion, trade associations, and industry shape the processes and interpretations of trust violations in an African context.

The discussions are based on three core questions: (1) 'How is trust violated in entrepreneurial relationships?', (2) 'What institutional logics influence interpretations of trust violations in entrepreneurial relationships and how?' and (3) 'What are the outcomes of trust violations?'

This chapter shows that trust violation occurs when the entrepreneur's (trustor's) initial trust expectations are not met by the partner's (trustee's) actions and behaviour. Nonetheless, the interpretation of trust violations is not clear as it is influenced by institutional logics which may differ between markets, sectors, and industries. In spite of the lack of clarity of what constitutes trust violation, entrepreneurs admit that trust violations lead to outcomes including the loss of resources, termination of relationships, and, at times, personal grief. The analysis and discussions in this chapter are summarised in Fig. 7.1 and the rest of the chapter offers an in-depth explanations of the processes of trust violations portrayed in the framework.

This chapter contributes to our understanding of how entrepreneurs owning and managing smaller businesses in Africa experience and interpret trust violations. It presents a framework that incorporates the trustor, trustee, institutions, relationships, and industry that shape the processes of trust violations. Currently, such a holistic approach is lacking in the literature. It also draws attention to how the concept of trust violations remains unclear due to the logics of: culturally specific institutions, and of relationships and industry that shape interpretations of trust violations in entrepreneurial relationships. It further highlights that trust violations can lead to varying negative financial, psychological and social costs to entrepreneurs and yet the literature has not paid attention to these outcomes. The rest of the chapter is organised as follows: Sect. 7.2 discusses the entrepreneur's initial trust. Section 7.3 focuses on how trustees violate trust and the different levels and forms of trust violations. Section 7.4 examines the institutional logics that shape entrepreneurs' interpretations of trust violations. Section 7.5 presents the outcomes of trust violations and Sect. 7.6 offers the conclusion.

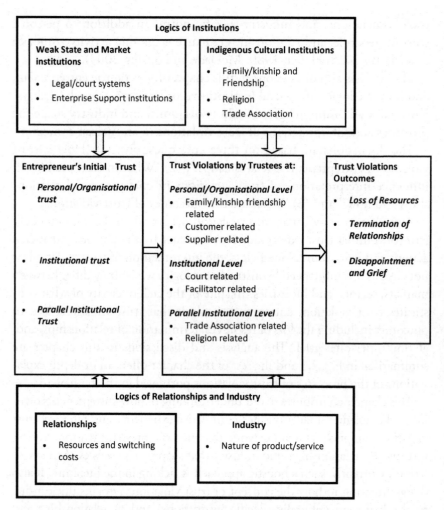

Fig. 7.1 Trust violation in entrepreneurial relationships. (Source: Own research)

7.2   Entrepreneur's Initial Trust

Entrepreneur's initial trust expectations are based on their expectations of the actions and behaviour of the trustee that allows him or her to be more or less trusted (McKnight et al. 1998; Mayer et al. 1995;

Rousseau et al. 1998). Within entrepreneurial relationships in Ghana, the actions and behaviour of the partner entrepreneur or the key boundary spanner of the larger organisation or institution forms the basis on which the entrepreneur (trustor) becomes willing to be vulnerable.

At the personal/organisational level, an entrepreneur's initial trust is shaped by the logics of weak legal systems and those of family/kinship and friendship. An important initial trust expectation is that a key business partner who may be a family member or regarded as a 'family' member must be willing to be relied on or to support the entrepreneur in economic exchanges.

Initial trust at the institutional level is based on trust in state and market institutions such as government, legal and justice systems, the tax system, and other enterprise support institutions that offer incentives in the institutional environment (Zucker 1986; North 1990; Welter and Smallbone 2010). While the processes, culture, and systems of institutions are important for institutional trust development, it is often the character, actions, and behaviour of officials and the key boundary spanners of institutions, and how consistent they are regarding the rules, regulations, and objectives of those institutions that determine trust in those institutions (Mitchell 1999).

Initial parallel institutional trust refers to trust in the officials and the institutions that run parallel to state institutions, notably trade associations and religion. The honesty of the leaders of trade associations and the logics of social capital based on regulation, conflict resolution, advocacy, legitimacy, networking, market information, references regarding reputation and creditworthiness, developing skills of members, and providing welfare to members in times of crisis form the basis of parallel institutional trust. Similarly, honesty, brotherliness, shared values, and caring for one another based on logics of religion also provide the basis of parallel institutional trust. Based on these logics, more informal personalised relationships are developed to enhance economic activity. As a result, initial trust expectations in Ghana may have stronger elements of obligation between exchange partners than in other countries, particularly in the West where the emphasis is more on individualism (see Chap. 6). Trust violations therefore result from breaches in these expectations.

7.3   Trust Violations by Trustees

Evidence in Ghana shows that entrepreneurs experience trust violations in different forms. Some family members, customers, suppliers, facilitators, and officials of state institutions as well as trade association leaders violate the trust reposed in them. Amoako and Lyon (2011; 2012) examine how trust is violated in entrepreneurial relationships in Ghana and entrepreneurs identify different types of incidents of trust violations. At the personal/organisational level, the discussions focus on family/kinship-related, customer-related and supplier-related violations. The discussion of breaches of trust at the institutional level centres on court-related and facilitator-related incidents while violations at the parallel institutional level are based on trade association-related violations. In this chapter, the discussions focus on trustees not meeting the expectations of entrepreneurs based on promises made and norms of institutions. Table 7.1 presents a summary of the forms of trust violations as well as the incidents of violations.

7.3.1   Personal/Organisational Trust Violations

In this section the author discusses personal/organisational trust violations based mostly on empirical data. It is important to remember that in Chaps. 3 and 6 we saw that in the context of SMEs in Africa, the distinction between interpersonal trust and interorganisational trust is ambiguous since entrepreneurs owning SMEs remain the key boundary spanners and decision makers for their organisations (Amoako 2012; Kuada and Thomsen 2005). As a result, in this book, interpersonal trust and interorganisational trust are not regarded as distinct even though they may be different in the context of larger organisations where a number of managers and boundary spanners may be involved in trust development processes. Similarly, interpersonal trust violations and interorganisational trust violations are not distinct but regarded to comingle at personal/organisational levels.

Table 7.1 Forms and incidents of trust violations in entrepreneurial relationships in an African context

Type of trust violated	Forms of violation	Incidents of violations
Personal and organisational trust	Family-related	Family members misappropriating funds
		Family members as poor trade creditors and borrowers
		Family members not adhering to contract terms
	Customer-related	Disappearing after receiving goods on trade credit from entrepreneurs
		Reducing the agreed price of goods already supplied on trade credit
		Not paying for goods supplied on trade credit on time
		Not paying for goods supplied on trade credit at all
		Telling lies about the timing of depositing money at the bank for entrepreneurs
		Going behind the back of entrepreneurs to establish a warehouse and competing directly
		Exploiting loopholes in contracts to take advantage of entrepreneurs
	Supplier-related	Disappearing after receiving trade credit to supply goods
		Diverting money advanced for the supply of goods to other uses
		Not supplying goods already paid for on time
		Supplying poor quality products
		Supplying a smaller quantity of the goods already paid for
Institutional trust	Facilitator-related	Perceptions of state-backed bodies involved in nepotism and corruption
	Court-related	A court in Ghana allegedly brought forward the time of a case without telling the entrepreneur
		Inability to pursue customers in the European Union due to lack of jurisdiction of courts in Ghana
		A land dispute pending more than six years after the first hearing
Parallel institutional trust	Trade association-related	Leaders of trade associations exploiting opportunities for themselves
		Agents in West African markets delaying payments against the norms of the efiewura system
	Religion-related	Belief in the use of black magic and juju by competitors to destroy businesses
		Exploitation by fake and unscrupulous religious leaders

Adapted from Amoako (2012)

Interpersonal Trust Violations Interpersonal trust violations has been conceptualised in different forms. For example, Kim et al. (2004) and Janowicz-Panjaitan and Noorderhaven (2009) draw on trust dimensions of ability, integrity, and benevolence (Mayer et al. 1995) to suggest that violations of trust involve breaches of ability, integrity, and benevolence. Breaches of integrity refers to violations in which the perpetrator purposefully engages in acts that differ from the ethical or moral expectations of the trustor. Kim et al. (2004) suggest further that violations of integrity lead to more decline in trust than perceived breaches in benevolence (Kim et al. 2004; Dirks et al. 2009). Accordingly, perceived violations of integrity or values may be generalised across other dimensions of trust due to assumptions that people with integrity will refrain from dishonest behaviour in any situation, whereas those with low integrity may exhibit either dishonest or honest behaviour depending on their incentives and opportunities. Competence violations refer to when the trustee unintentionally engages in an incompetent act due to lack of ability to do an activity correctly or when a mistake is committed. However, as argued earlier in Chap. 3 and in the introduction to this chapter, most of the existing studies downplay the complex relationships between calculation and context (Amoako 2012).

In interorganisational relationships, the conceptualisation of trust violations becomes complex because of the multiple levels of organisational trust. Gillespie and Dietz (2009) and Dirks et al. (2009) corroborate that organisations are multilevel systems and the various components contribute to perceptions of an organisation's trustworthiness as well as to failures (Gillespie and Dietz 2009; Dirks et al. 2009). Even though some dimensions of trust can be covered in written contracts or agreements it is the soft criteria that exist in mutual beliefs, perceptions, and informal obligations in a buyer-supplier relationship that form the psychological contract and when breached trust is also violated (Hill et al. 2009).

At the personal/organisational level, trust violation occurs when the actions and behaviour of individual family/kinship members and friend who are partners involved in the business, or managers and leaders owning and managing partner customer or supplier SMEs or larger organisations do not meet the expectations of the entrepreneur.

Family/Kinship Related Violations Violations of trust by family members in business is common in Ghana. Amoako and Lyon (2014) report that in spite of the benefits of the family in enhancing entrepreneurship (see Chaps. 4, 5 and 6), entrepreneurs often encounter challenges in enforcing agreements with family members. Family members may also embezzle funds when employed in businesses (Amoako and Matlay 2015). Hart (2000) posits that kinsfolk may often make poor borrowers in Ghana. Interestingly, the paradoxical role of family/kinship is not limited to Ghana but instead it is a common observation across a number of African countries. These violations relate closely to the norms of obligations of the family/kinship systems in Ghana and Africa which oblige entrepreneurs to provide for members of the extended family. Nonetheless, there are a number of very successful family businesses in Ghana and these are guarded by values that encourage commitment, accountability, and trustworthiness.

Customer-Related Violations Customer-related trust violations are quite common in Ghanaian and West African markets. An entrepreneur's customer expectations are based on honesty, reputation of the customer, access to trade credit, observing norms of trade credit, and sharing market information. However, breaches of these expectations are also quite common (Amoako 2012; Amoako and Lyon 2011).

In the domestic markets, trust violations relating to breaches of honesty occur when a customer does not keep promises regarding oral or written contract arrangements. For example, some customers may tell lies about the quality of products already supplied in order to reduce the agreed price of the goods. At times, other customers may renege on pledges to pay money at the agreed time. A few dishonest customers may not pay the money at all and, in rare and extreme cases, other dishonest customers could disappear after receiving goods/services on credit.

While incidents of trust violations are also quite common in the West African markets, trade associations, families, and religious organisations offer the safety net that often protects entrepreneurs from these opportunistic traders. In the face of these risks, entrepreneurs often test and observe how customers keep promises regarding agreements. Particularly, violations of promises to pay trade credit for goods or services supplied is taken very seriously and may lead to a reduction or abrogation of the trade credit arrangement. Furthermore, entrepreneurs rely on trade association membership as a guarantee of help to get their money back in cases of default in West African markets. Similarly, leaders and members of families and religious bodies may also intervene to enforce contracts. These conflict resolution methods will be discussed in more details in Chap. 8.

Similarly in international markets, customer-related violations of trust range from dishonest customers telling lies about the quality of products already exported in order not to pay the agreed full price of the goods already supplied, delaying payments, breaching the terms of legal contracts and memorandums of understanding (MOUs), exploiting loopholes in contracts, including non-enforceable clauses in agreements, to covertly seeking changes to contract terms in order to take advantage of SME exporters. Customers may also violate trust by not sharing information relating to changes in market demand and prices. However, trust violations relating to reputation is rarely mentioned probably because entrepreneurs may not start a trust-based relationship with customers whose reputations are knowingly tarnished.

Supplier-Related Violations Suppliers' trust expectations are based on honesty, supplying quality products/services, punctuality relating to meeting supply deadlines, access to trade credit and observing the norms of trade credit, the reputation of the supplier, and sharing market information. Yet, supplier-related trust violations are common in domestic, West African, and international markets. Entrepreneurs may experience breaches of honesty from some suppliers who may attempt to take advantage or defraud them by not keeping promises regarding contracts, product and service specifications, the right quality and quantity, and delivery times, or misusing trade credit for purposes other than supplying the goods/services already paid for.

To Ghanaian internationally trading entrepreneurs, another key supplier-related trust violation is being supplied with poor quality products/service. In particular, when expectations based on previously agreed specifications are not met. Yet, supplier-related violations concerning poor-quality products/services may not necessarily result from dishonesty but from other factors such as poor equipment or poor practices, which may not be intentional. In such instances, some entrepreneurs offer training and technical support to enable suppliers to meet the high specifications required. In contrast, dishonest suppliers may intentionally attempt to conceal the defects of their products, particularly when transactions are one off. Yet in either case, the supply of poor quality products/services puts the reputation of smaller businesses at risk and may result in loss of contracts with customers.

Another supplier-related trust violation relates to punctuality; that is, missing delivery deadlines. Entrepreneurs have expectations of punctuality in order to meet their obligations to their customers in local, West African, and international transactions. Yet, some suppliers, especially those without experience of Western business norms, may underestimate meeting the stringent deadlines required by entrepreneurs due to the norms of African punctuality. As discussed in Chap. 4, the cultural-specific norms of 'African punctuality', which refers to the flexible use of time in Ghanaian and African contexts, could be a major issue in relationship building in Ghana and Africa. Nonetheless, as stated in Chap. 6, entrepreneurs do not yield to these norms but instead respond by teaching new suppliers new norms of punctuality (Amoako 2012; Amoako and Matlay 2015).

One more supplier-related trust violation is the breach of trade credit terms. As discussed in Chap. 6, in competitive sectors entrepreneurs advance trade credit to suppliers. The expectation is that suppliers will keep the terms of trade credit by supplying the right quantity of goods/services at the right time. Yet, opportunistic suppliers may default and/or divert goods or services to another buyer. In extreme but rare cases, some suppliers apparently disappear after receiving payment advances for the supply of goods/services. To mitigate this, entrepreneurs often visit homes and workplaces and involve third parties such as family members and long-term customers or suppliers as witnesses to trade credit agreements.

7.3.2   Institutional Level Trust Violations

Institutional level trust violations originate from breaches of the processes, culture, and systems of institutions that are important for institutional trust development. Nonetheless, it is often the dishonesty and corruption of officials and the key boundary spanners of state and market institutions that determine trust in those institutions (Mitchell 1999).

Court-Related Violations Entrepreneurs widely perceive the judiciary and legal systems and the courts to be weak and corrupt (Amoako and Lyon 2014). In particular, allegations of corruption in the judiciary and courts is common in the domestic market. These allegations relate to demands for bribes by dishonest officials and judges to the long processes involved in court resolution of commercial disputes. In the context of international trade, the main concerns of entrepreneurs centre on the inability of the courts to resolve disputes with international partners who do not live in Ghana. The courts in West African countries are equally perceived to be corrupt and entrepreneurs raise security concerns as well.

Facilitator-Related Violations The forms of violations dubbed facilitator related refer to breaches of trust by officials of state-backed enterprise-support institutions. In Ghana, incidents of institutional trust violations also relate to officials of state institutions involved in enterprise support breaching trust. Allegations of dishonesty, bribery and corruption, and/or favouritism are cited by entrepreneurs as violations of trust by officials of state-backed enterprise-support institutions like the Ghana Export Promotion Authority (GEPA), National Board for Small Scale Industries (NBSSI). For example, there are allegations that money and support meant for internationally trading entrepreneurs are at times diverted by unscrupulous officials to their cronies who may not be involved in international business (Amoako 2012).

7.3.3   Parallel Institutional Trust Violations

Trade Association Related Violations While trade associations serve as parallel institutions to the courts and provide some certainty to entrepreneurs in Ghana, there are allegations of violations of trust in some of the associations. Amoako and Lyon (2012) cite instances where some leaders of trade associations abuse their positions by exploiting opportunities for themselves instead of making them known to their members. Parallel institutional trust violations also result from allegations of the misuse of association funds and fraudulent accounting systems by association leaders (Amoako 2012).

Religion-Related Violations Religious norms that encourage superstition are widespread in Africa and Ghana and can lead to violations of trust in entrepreneurial relationships (Amoako 2012). In particular, these violations may result from perceptions that customers or partners are able to exploit or abuse through the use of black magic, locally referred to as *juju*, to take advantage of their creditors or sponsors. Furthermore, there are perceptions that competitors can also destroy the businesses of others with *juju* and witchcraft. Hence some entrepreneurs often make references to God, Allah, the smaller gods, and prayers as bastions of protection for themselves and for their businesses.

Religion-related violations of trust also include the activities of fake religious leaders exploiting some entrepreneurs who may be followers. There are instances where Christian, Muslim, and Africanist religious leaders make claims to authority and authenticity by fraudulently faking miracles and connections to the spirits in order to deceive and defraud entrepreneurs and other followers in order to enrich themselves. De Witte (2013) cites instances where some Pentecostal pastors use electric touch machines to fake the transmission of divine power from the holy spirit to followers. Table 7.1 presents a summary of incidents of trust violations and the levels at which they occur.

7.4   Logics of Institutions Influencing Interpretations of Trust Violations in Ghana

A key challenge in understanding trust violation in entrepreneurial relationships is how context and particularly institutional logics influence interpretations of violations. The challenge is based on the premise that logics of weak state and market institutions, relationships, industry, and cultural institutions provide the cognitive filters or frames and inferential sets that actors utilise in the selection and interpretation of information (Kostova 1997; Gibson et al. 2009). In this chapter, the logics include: norms relating to relationships, sectors, and industry; and cultural institutions that are used to interpret what constitutes a violation (Amoako and Lyon 2011; Amoako 2012). Therefore, the definition of what constitutes trust violations in entrepreneurial relationships remains vague as it is predominantly shaped by norms of weak legal and support institutions, family/kinship, religion, trade association/industry norms, and power based on the nature of products/services, the nature of benefits derived, and individual agency. As a result, one party may perceive that trust has been violated while the other party may not realise this, particularly where there are differences in culture and expectations.

Logics of State and Market Institutions

Weak Legal Systems/Courts and Support Institutions

Interpretations of trust violations by internationally trading SME entrepreneurs in Ghana are influenced by the logics of weak judiciary and court systems and enterprise support institutions including the financial institutions. In a context where entrepreneurs seldom use the courts due to perceived corruption, long delays, cumbersome processes, and high costs, often violations of trust are either ignored or regarded as acceptable as the resources involved in pursuing legal redress for a breach of trust may be costly while the outcome may often be limited. Similarly, perceptions of inaccessible and unaffordable legal systems in both West Africa and international markets discourage entrepreneurs from using the courts in these markets. Entrepreneurs exporting to international markets also perceive the legal systems to be expensive due to high costs of travelling abroad and the legal fees (Amoako and Lyon 2014; Amoako 2012).

Yet, apart from the weak legal/court influences, a number of cultural-specific norms shape interpretations of trust violations.

Case 7.1 Ghanaian Court Trust Violations

Ama is a Ghanaian female entrepreneur who lived in the United States where she became familiar with the market demand for shea butter. When she returned to Ghana in 2002, she founded a company that processes shea butter for export to the United States. After operating for three years, the business started growing and so she acquired a piece of land to build a new plant. However, Ama encountered problems with the documentation for the property and so she went to court to seek redress. However, to her surprise, the case was in court for six years and was still pending at the time of the interview. Accordingly, Ama has decided not to deal with the courts in Ghana any more. She lamented that, 'If I start dealing with you and I realize that you will end the relationship in court I stop'.

Source: *from an interview with an anonymised respondent.*

Logics of Indigenous Cultural Institutions

The limited institutional support from the courts and state institutions render it necessary to develop and manage personalised networks and relationships to enhance access to resources and affordable credit and conflict resolution. Family/kinship norms of reciprocity and obligations linked to real family members and business partners regarded as family members within relationships allow some of the entrepreneurs to either ignore violations or to regard violations as acceptable. Nevertheless, as stated in Chaps. 5 and 6, a number of entrepreneurs do not internalise these norms and may decide not to work with family members due to past negative experiences.

Religious norms serve as filters used in interpreting trust violations and enable some entrepreneurs to continue working with partners who may abuse the trust placed in them by the entrepreneur. For example, religious norms based on fatalism may inform entrepreneurs' interpretations of trust violation by attributing violations to God, Allah, or the gods. Similarly, norms of forgiveness found in religion occasionally influence entrepreneurs' decisions to ignore violations of trade credit agreements. The evidence therefore suggests that religion impacts on entrepreneurs' interpretations of trust violations.

Norms of trade associations determine the expectations of the acceptable levels of behaviour of members and leaders in relationships with partners. As a result, trust violations are interpreted based on norms which may vary between markets and industries. For example, the dominance of the *efiewura* system in West African markets has empowered actors to dictate the terms of trade with regard to payments timing which may last from a few days to several weeks and yet entrepreneurs accept these norms and usually do not regard delayed payment as a trust violation.

Logics of Relationships

The norms of specific relationships influence interpretations of trust violations. Particularly, when the resources and benefits derived from a specific relationship are substantial, entrepreneurs owning and managing SMEs often consider the switching costs and ignore violations by such partners. For example, entrepreneurs often ignore delayed payments by larger organisations in domestic and international markets (Amoako and Lyon 2011; 2012), in particular, when the larger organisation remains the key customer that buys all or most of the products/services. Similarly, the violation of trust by partners who may fund or provide critical support services such as training on international standards, packaging, and issues pertaining to shipments may be ignored with entrepreneurs having little option but to continue working with the more powerful partners. Similarly, powerful suppliers such as small-scale mining companies supplying gold are able to default without entrepreneurs being able to withdraw trade credit deposits. Given the high switching costs, entrepreneurs and SMEs often put up with these challenges and continue to work with their more powerful partners.

Logics of Industry

The nature of the industry and the product/service remains a key factor in perceptions of trust violations. For example, in both West African and international markets entrepreneurs trading in agricultural products are often more vulnerable and more dependent on their customers abroad. Their dependency is due to the lack of refrigeration for fresh agricultural products such as eggs and fresh vegetables which have short shelf lives. This constraint influences the decisions of entrepreneurs to continue to supply their customers who may default in the payment of trade credit. For example, some entrepreneurs producing fresh eggs in Ghana continue to encourage customers who have defaulted to settle their debts by instalments as they continue to supply them, particularly when there is a glut in the domestic market.

This section has demonstrated that perceptions of trust violations are influenced by a number of logics and therefore are subjective and socially constructed. Table 7.2 presents a summary of how specific logics linked to weak formal institutions, cultural institutions, relationships, and industry influence interpretations of trust violations by entrepreneurs owning and managing smaller businesses.

7.5   Outcomes of Trust Violations

Understanding the outcomes of trust violations is important to smaller businesses as they generally operate based on informal flexible agreements underpinned by trust. As stated earlier, trust violation is common in Ghana and in most cases the damage to businesses may be minimal. However in rare but extreme cases trust violation may lead to loss of resources, disappointment and grief, and misunderstanding which in turn may lead to the termination of a contract and relationship. This often happens when trust violations leads to substantial resource losses or when it is attributed to dishonesty. In extreme cases, trust violations may endanger the very existence of the firm (Bachmann 2001), and lead to serious financial, psychological, and social implications for the entrepreneur. It could also lead to a loss of interest in future collaborations by the victim and other entrepreneurs who may hear about the negative experiences of the victim.

Table 7.2 Logics shaping perceptions of trust violations

Logics of	Description of impact on perceptions of trust violation
Legal/courts system	Due to allegations and incidents of corruption by some judiciary and court officials, most entrepreneurs do not go to court but instead either ignore or regard violations as acceptable
Enterprise support institutions	Some entrepreneurs respond to lack of support from enterprise support institutions by developing personal trust-based relationships within which trust violations may be ignored due to norms of obligation and reciprocity
Family/kinship/ friendships	Family members, kinsmen, friends, and community leaders draw on family norms of obligation and forgiveness to influence and at times coerce entrepreneurs to ignore trust violations in cases concerning a 'family member', friend or community member.
Religion	Religious-fatalistic beliefs influence some entrepreneurs' perceptions that God or Allah causes violations when, for example, a customer absconds without paying for trade credit on goods already supplied
Trade association	Industry or sector association specific norms determine what constitutes acceptable behaviour in the industry or association. For example, norms of payment of trade credit differ based on industry and association
Relationships	The switching costs associated with particular relationships influence some entrepreneurs' decision to continue working with existing partners who may default on credit payments
	Receiving benefits such as training on international standards, packaging, shipments, and fair trade branding influence some entrepreneurs to continue working with a partner in spite of breaches of contract terms
Industry	The short shelf life and perishability of fresh agricultural products such as eggs and fresh vegetables influence some entrepreneurs to continue to supply their customers who may default on payments

Source: Adapted from Amoako (2012)

Loss of Resources

Trust violations may lead to loss of resources including working capital, sales, and time. This happens in particular when entrepreneurs are over-reliant on specific customers or suppliers. For example, when a key customer violates a promise to buy from an SME, the business that has fallen victim may run into very serious liquidity problems that may threaten its survival. Similarly, supplier-related violations by a key supplier can threaten the survival of small businesses. For example, when partners supply poor-quality products that do not meet the specifications for customers, entrepreneurs may end up losing customers, market share, and destroying the brand in the long term. Trust breaches related to missing supply deadlines by suppliers can in turn lead to the loss of sales and possibly penalties based on clauses in MOUs and contracts. Another important resource that may be lost is time. The amount of time involved in seeking solutions after violations, and in repairing trust and building new relationships when relationships break down can be massive and may negatively impact on businesses since many entrepreneurs are time constrained.

Disappointment and Grief

Trust violations can also cause disappointment and grief to entrepreneurs especially when the betrayal was least expected and in circumstances where the loss is very damaging to the business. In such cases, entrepreneurs may experience painful emotions, self-blame, and uncertainty resulting from financial, psychological, and social costs. Particularly for smaller businesses, the entrepreneur as owner/manager and sole trader may be liable for the losses of his or her business (Bittker and Eustice 1994): hence a significant financial loss can be very traumatic. Similarly, due to the emotional relationship entrepreneurs have with their businesses (Shepherd 2003), the collapse of the business can also be very distressing. Psychological costs can also involve. entrepreneurs feeling ashamed and blaming themselves for lack of due diligence, sharing too much information, and for over trusting. Social costs can include negative impacts on relationships including marriages, families, and other social networks as well as loss of social status due to the embarrassment of being taken advantage of and often an inability to meet financial commitments to employees and other debtors in extreme cases of trust violations. Yet, researchers have paid little or no attention to disappointment and grief caused by breaches of trust in entrepreneurial relationships. The current focus is on the psychological, financial, and social costs associated with business failure (Shepherd 2003; Cope 2011), but not from trust violations.

Termination of Relationships and Loss of Interest in Future Collaborations

Trust violations involving substantial loss of resources often lead to a termination of relationships. In particularly if entrepreneurs perceive that the violations border on dishonesty and the perpetrator's explanations of the causes of the violation are not deemed tangible This will be discussed in more details in Chap. 8. Negative experiences of trust violations may serve as a disincentive to some entrepreneurs in engaging in future collaborations. Negative experiences may also be shared among entrepreneurs, association members, family members, and communities, mainly by word-of-mouth, and this may discourage other entrepreneurs from engaging with the perpetrators whose reputation may be damaged. However, negative experiences can deter and cause other entrepreneurs who have heard about such experiences to be reluctant to engage in trust-based relationships with other parties, thus confirming existing studies on the negative outcomes of interorganisational trust violations on future trust relationships (Hardin 1996; Das and Teng 1998).

Case 7.2 Trust Violations and Outcomes

Kate is a postgraduate and an experienced entrepreneur who lived and worked in the EU but returned to Ghana in the early 1990s. She established a food processing company after recognising that there was plenty of seasonal fruit in the country during harvest times but fruits became very scarce during other seasons. She admits that as a small business, success to a large extent depends on building trust and relationships with customers, suppliers, and facilitators. However, she cautions that it is important not to trust partners too much. Her caution is based on her negative experiences of violations of trust by some customers and suppliers. Kate recounts two main incidents of trust violation that shaped her current attitude towards trusting her partners. At the early stages of her company she was able to secure an agreement to supply her products to one of the largest public institutions in Ghana. That customer was taking almost all her products, which enabled her company to grow very quickly and, due to the company's limited capacity at that stage, she was not able to supply anybody else. After a couple of years of successful collaboration with the key customer, she run into a major problem when the government was changed and the state institution did not have the funds to pay her. Her company nearly ground to a halt and she had to secure finance from friends, family members, and banks to be able to start operating again. She also recounts another trust violation when a key supplier in the EU supplied junk machinery worth several tens of thousands of dollars to her. In spite of a signed agreement on the deal, the courts in Ghana could not assist her due to lack of jurisdiction since the perpetrator does not live in Ghana. Unfortunately, Kate could not seek redress abroad due to the fees for the courts and lawyers and the associated costs for hotel accommodation, visa fees, and air tickets. She ended up running into serious liquidity problems, laying off her staff, blaming herself, and vowing not to share too much information or trust any partner in future. Apart from the financial and marketing problems, Kate experienced serious emotional problems and grief. She lamented, 'At that time my world fell apart, and I blame myself for trusting them. I lost everything—my working capital, couldn't pay my staff, I was disappointed, embarrassed, and ashamed for not being able to pay and keep my hardworking staff. In fact, I fell ill for some days. But, I learnt a very important lesson. I will not give too much of my goods on credit, keep my eyes wide open in purchasing machinery and will not trust anybody'.

Anonymised case study from a respondent.

7.6   Conclusion

This chapter highlights how trust is violated in entrepreneurial relationships and the institutions and institutional logics that shape interpretations of trust violations. It also draws attention to the outcome of trust violations. The discussions show that trust violations are quite common in entrepreneurial relationships. Trust violations originate from the unmet expectations of actions and behaviour of partner entrepreneurs, managers and key boundary spanners of larger organisations, and state officials (Gillespie and Dietz 2009; Kramer and Lewicki 2010; Mitchell 1999). Customer-related violations range from customers delaying payments for goods supplied, giving excuses to justify not repaying trade credit, lying about the quality of products already supplied, lying about the time of depositing money in the bank, changing telephone numbers, and moving house to disappearing after receiving trade credit. Supplier-related violations involve supplying products/services late, supplying poor-quality products/services, diverting trade credit into other uses, and disappearing after receiving trade credit. Facilitator-related violations are based on allegations of corruption and nepotism by officials of state-sponsored enterprise-support institutions. The courts are also regarded as corrupt, expensive, and a waste of time due to cumbersome and long processes that are not friendly to entrepreneurs and SMEs. Allegations have also been made by association members against some trade association leaders regarding abuse of power, nonetheless, the trade associations are deemed more supportive and trusted than state institutions.

In spite of the occurrence and significance of trust violations in entrepreneurial relationships, the concept of trust violations remains unclear due to the logics of: culturally specific institutions, norms of relationships, and industry that shape interpretations of trust and trust violations in entrepreneurial relationships. The perceptions and interpretations of trust violations are specifically shaped by logics of weak legal institutions, family/kinship, religion, trade associations, and industry relations. Based on these institutional logics, some blatant incidents of trust violations are at times ignored or not acknowledged as trust violations. There are differences in perceptions of violations particularly between actors from different cultural backgrounds, associations, industries, and markets. It is therefore important for economic actors to understand the acceptable levels of trust violation in a relationship as this may vary between cultures, associations, sectors, and markets, and over time (Amoako and Lyon 2012). Due to the influences of these institutions and institutional logics, there is often a degree of acceptance about breaking integrity without violating perceived trust. Yet these logics have received very little empirical investigation in the literature.

This chapter also highlights that trust violations can lead to financial, psychological, and social costs. The outcomes of trust violations could have varying negative impacts on the entrepreneur and smaller businesses ranging from loss of resources, termination of relationships, near collapse of the business (Bachmann 2001), to disappointment and grief. The discussions show that when trust is violated, entrepreneurs and their firms may lose substantial resources including capital which, in extreme cases, can pose liquidity challenges. In cases where entrepreneurs may have suffered substantial financial loss, the disappointment can cause them painful emotions, self-blame, uncertainty, and grief. This happens to entrepreneurs owning smaller businesses due to the emotional relationship they have with their businesses (Shepherd 2003) in which the entrepreneur as a sole trader may also be liable for all the losses of the business (Bittker and Eustice 1994). This in turn may lead to loss of assets, feelings of shame, self-blame, and loss of trust in future collaborations. The time required to deal with the aftermath of the violations can also be significant. Entrepreneurs may spend time in an attempt to repair the relationship and, if unsuccessful, to build new relationships in order to gain access to the vital resources which may be lost as a result of the violation (Amoako 2012). There can be social costs as well; embarrassment can adversely impact on relationships including marriages and those with other social networks. The outcome of trust violations may also deter victims and their close networks from engaging in future collaborations. This may be explained by the role of word-of-mouth and second-hand information about the behaviour of perpetrators and the plight of victims of trust violations (Ajzen 1991). Yet the literature has only focused on the impact of trust violations on the firm rather than the entrepreneur.

This chapter contributes to the literature in four ways. First it presents a framework that attempts to integrate the role of the trustor, trustee, relationships, industry, and institutions in trust violations. Such an holistic view is lacking in the current literature. Second, it discusses the processes and provides examples of how trust is violated in entrepreneurial relationships in Africa. It thereby helps our understanding of how entrepreneurs owning and managing smaller businesses in Africa experience trust violations. Third, it draws attention to how the concept of trust violation remains unclear due to the logics of weak state and market institutions, culturally specific institutions, norms of relationships, and norms of industry that shape interpretations of trust and trust violations in entrepreneurial relationships. It therefore draws attention to the importance of economic actors understanding the acceptable levels of trust violations in a context and relationship as this may vary between cultures, associations, sectors, and markets—and over time. Fourth, it highlights that trust violations can lead to varying negative financial, psychological, and social costs to entrepreneurs. The discussions show that when trust is violated, entrepreneurs and their firms may lose substantial resources including capital, which in extreme cases can pose liquidity challenges. The disappointment caused by trust violations may result in painful emotions, self-blame, uncertainty, and grief to entrepreneurs and yet the literature has not paid attention to these negative impacts on the entrepreneur.

References

Ajzen, I. 1991. The theory of planned behavior. *Organizational Behavior and Human Decision Processes* 50: 179–211.

Amoako, I.O. 2012. *Trust in exporting relationships: The case of SMEs in Ghana*, Published PhD thesis. Center for Economic and Enterprise Development Research (CEEDR) Middlesex University, London. http://eprints.mdx.ac.uk/12419/.

Amoako, I.O., and Lyon F. 2011. Interorganizational trust violations and repairs in a weak legal environment: The case of Ghanian exporting SMEs. Paper presented at the 6th Workshop on Trust within and between organizations. European Group for Organization Studies (EGOS) Conference, Gothenburg, Gothenburg University, July 2011.

———. 2012. Violations and repairs of trust across cultural boundaries: The case of Ghanian exporting SMEs. Paper presented at the 6th Workshop on trust within and between organizations. European Institute for Advanced Studies in Management (EIASM), Milan, Italy, June 14–15.

———. We don't deal with courts: Cooperation and alternative institutions shaping exporting relationships of SMEs in Ghana. *International Small Business Journal* 32 (2): 117–139.

Amoako, I.O., and H. Matlay. 2015. Norms and trust-shaping relationships among food- exporting SMEs in Ghana. (Eds) Quinn, B., Dunn, A., McAdam, R., and McKitterick, L. "Special issue on the competitiveness of SMEs in the food sector: Exploring possibilities for growth". *The International Journal of Entrepreneurship and Innovation* 16 (2): 123–124.

Bachman, Martin, Santiago Uribe-Lewis, Xiaoping Yang, Heather E. Burgess, Mario Iurlaro, Wolf Reik, Adele Murrell, and Shankar Balasubramanian. 2015. 5-Formylcytosine can be a stable DNA modification in mammals. *Nature Chemical Biology* 11 (8): 555.

Bachmann, R. 2001. Trust, power and control in trans-organizational relations. *Organization Studies* 22 (2): 337–365.

———. 2010. Towards a context–sensitive approach to researching trust in interorganizational relationships. In *Organizational trust: A cultural perspective*, ed. M.N.K. in Saunders, D. Skinner, G. Dietz, N. Gillespie, and R.J. Lewicki, 87–106. Cambridge: Cambridge University Press.

Bell, G.G., R.J. Oppenheimer, and A. Bastien. 2002. Trust deterioration in an international buyer–supplier relationship. *Journal of Business Ethics* 36: 65–78. https://doi.org/10.1023/A:1014239812469.

Bittker, B.I., and J.S. Eustice. 1994. *Federal income taxation of corporations and shareholders.* 6th ed. Boston: Warren Graham and Lamont.

Cope, J. 2011. Entrepreneurial learning from failure: An interpretative phenomenological analysis. *Journal of Business Venturing* 26 (6): 604–623.

Das, T.K., and B. Teng. 1998. Between trust and control: Developing confidence in partner cooperation in alliances. *The Academy of Management Review* 23 (3): 491–513.

De Witte, M. 2013. The electric touch machine miracle scam: Body, technology and the (dis)authentication of the pentecostal supernatural. In *Machina: Religion, Technology, and the Things in Between*, ed. Stolow J. Deus. New York: Fordham University Press.

Dirks, K.T., R.J. Lewicki, and A. Zaheer. 2009. Repairing relationships within and between organizations: Building a conceptual foundation. *Academy of Management Review* 34: 401–422.

Fink, M., and A. Kessler. 2010. Cooperation, trust, and performance: Empirical results from three countries. *British Journal of Management* 21: 469–483.

Gibson, C.B., M. Maznevski, and B.L. Kirkman. 2009. When does culture matter? In *Handbook of culture, organizations, and work*, ed. R.S. Bhagat and R.M. Steers. Cambridge: Cambridge University Press.

Gillespie, N., and G. Dietz. 2009. Trust repair after an organization level failure. *Academy of Management Review* 34 (1): 127–145.

Hardin, R. 1996. Trustworthiness. *Ethics* 107: 26–42.

Hart, K. 2000. Kinship, contract, and trust: The economic organization of migrants in an African City slum. In *Trust: Making and breaking cooperative relations*, ed. D. Gambetta, Electronic ed., 176–193. Oxford: Department of Sociology, University of Oxford.

Hill, James, Eckerd Stephanie, Wilson Darryl, and Greer Bertie. 2009. The effect of unethical behavior on trust in buyer-supplier relationship: The mediating role of psychological contract violation. *Journal of Operations Management* 27: 281–293.

Hyden, G. 1980. *Beyond jämää in Tanzania under development and an uncaptured peasantry*. Berkeley/Los Angeles: University of California Press.

Janowicz-Panjaitan, Martyna, and Niels G. Noorderhaven. 2009. Trust, calculation, and interorganizational learning of tacit knowledge: An organizational roles perspective. *Organization Studies* 30 (10): 1021–1044.

Kim, P.H., D.L. Ferrin, C.D. Cooper, and K.T. Dirks. 2004. Removing the shadow of suspicion: The effects of apology versus denial for repairing competence-based versus integrity-based trust violations. *Journal of Applied Psychology* 89 (1): 100118.

Kostova, T. 1997. Country institutional profiles: Concept and measurement. *Academy of Management Proceedings* 1997: 180–184.

Kramer, Roderick M., and J. Lewicki Roy. 2010. Repairing and enhancing trust: Approaches to reducing organizational trust deficits. *Academy of Management Annals* 4 (1): 245–277.

Kuada, J., and G. Thomsen. 2005. Culture, learning, and the internationalisation of Ghanaian firms. In *Internationalisation and enterprise development in Ghana*, ed. J. Kuada, 271–292. London: Adonis and Abbey Publishers Ltd.

Lewicki, R.J. 2006. Trust and distrust. In *The negotiator's fieldbook: The desk reference for the experienced negotiator*, ed. A.K. Schneider and C. Honeyman, 191–202. Chicago: American Bar Association.

Lewicki, R.J., and B.B. Bunker. 1996. Developing and maintaining trust in work relationships. In *Trust in organizations: Frontiers of theory and research*, ed. R. Kramer and T.R. Tyler. Thousand Oaks: Sage.

Li, P.P. 2016. The holistic and contextual natures of trust: Past, present and future research. *Journal of Trust Research* 6 (1): 1–6.

Mayer, R., J. Davis, and F. Schoorman. 1995. An integrative model of organisational trust. *Academy of Management Review* 20: 709–734.

McDade, B.E., and A. Spring. 2005. The new generation of African entrepreneurs: Networking to change the climate for business and private sector-led development. *Entrepreneurship and Regional Development* 17: 17–42.

McKnight, D., L. Harrison Larry Cummings, and L. Norman Chervany. 1998. Initial trust formation in new organizational relationships. *Academy of Management Review* 23 (3): 473–490.

Mitchell, V.-W. 1999. Consumer perceived risk: Conceptualizations and models. *European Journal of Marketing* 33 (1): 163–195.

Möllering, G. 2006. *Trust: Reason, routine, reflexivity.* Amsterdam: Elsevier.

North, D.C. 1990. *Institutions, institutional change and economic performance.* Cambridge: Cambridge University Press.

Ring, P.S., and A.H. Van de Ven. 1992. Structuring cooperative relationships between organizations. *Strategic Management Journal* 13: 483–498.

Rousseau, D., S. Sitkin, R.S. Burt, and C. Camerer. 1998. Not different after all: A crossdiscipline view of trust. *Academy of Management Review* 23 (3): 393–404.

Saunders, M.N.K., D. Skinner, G. Dietz, N. Gillespie, and R.J. Lewicki. 2010. *Organizational trust: A cultural perspective.* Cambridge: Cambridge University Press.

Shepherd, D.A. 2003. Learning from business failure: Propositions of grief recovery for the self-employed. *Academy of Management Review* 28 (2): 318–328.

Welter, F., and D. Smallbone. 2010. The embeddedness of women's entrepreneurship in a transition context. In *Women's entrepreneurship and the global environment for growth: An international perspective*, ed. C. Brush, E. Gatewood, C. Henry, and A. De Bruin, 96–117. Cheltenham: Edward Elgar.

Zaheer, A., B. McEvily, and V. Perrone. 1998. Does trust matter? Exploring the effects of interorganizational and interpersonal trust on performance. *Organization Science* 9 (2): 141–159.

Zucker, L.G. 1986. Production of trust. Institutional sources of economic structure 1840–1920. *Research in Organisation Behaviour* 8: 53–111.

8

Trust Repairs in Entrepreneurial Relationships in an African Context

8.1 Introduction

Trust offers numerous benefits in small and medium-sized enterprises (SMEs) entrepreneurial relationships. Trust often serves as the governance mechanism in SME interorganisational relationships due to a lack of recourse to elaborate contracts and mechanisms for enforcing contracts (Gaur et al. 2011). In these relationships, trust often substitutes for or complements contracts (Frankel et al. 1996; Sydow and Windeler 2003). Yet, trust is fragile and its violation may cause significant damage to relationships and, in very serious circumstances, threaten the existence of the business (Bachmann 2001) and the emotional well-being of the entrepreneur (see Chap. 7). However, trust violations are common in entrepreneurial relationships and may lead to conflict, loss of resources, and the termination of relationships. Hence, one of the main tasks for entrepreneurs following trust violation is finding ways to repair the damage and rebuild personal/interorganisational relationships (Amoako 2012; Janowicz-Panjaitan and Krishnan 2009; Amoaka and Lyon 2014). This is particularly significant against the background of SMEs operating in contexts where legal

© The Author(s) 2019

I. O. Amoako, *Trust, Institutions and Managing Entrepreneurial Relationships in Africa*,
Palgrave Studies of Entrepreneurship in Africa,
https://doi.org/10.1007/978-3-319-98395-0_8

systems and enterprise-support institutions are weak. In these contexts, trust in personalised relationships is the key to doing business and repairing trust in relationships remains critically important.

Yet, there is very little knowledge about how trust is repaired in SME interorganisational relationships. There are only a few studies on trust repair and most are based on theoretical and controlled laboratory experiments (e.g. Lewicki and Bunker 1996; Kim et al. 2004; Gillespie and Dietz 2009; Dirks et al. 2011). Interestingly, most of the studies focus on interpersonal trust repair (e.g. Lewicki and Bunker 1996; Lewicki 2006), paying less attention to trust repair within and between organisations, even though processes of interpersonal trust repair may not work in organisational contexts (Gillespie and Dietz 2009; Bachmann et al. 2015). There is also a lack of studies on how institutional contexts, particularly culture, impact on the processes of trust and trust repairs (Ren and Gray 2009; Bachmann et al. 2015; Gillespie 2017). This is disturbing given the significant impact of context on trust development and perceived trust violations (see Ren and Gray 2009; Saunders et al. 2010; Amoako and Lyon 2014) particularly in entrepreneurial relationships.

There are a few theoretical studies on interorganisational trust repair in developed economies (e.g. Ren and Gray 2009; Gillespie and Dietz 2009), however, there is a dearth of knowledge on interorganisational trust repair in emerging economies involving entrepreneurs owning and managing SMEs (Amoako and Lyon 2011). While entrepreneurs and SMEs in advanced economies have recourse to strong institutions such as affordable courts and mediation bodies set up and supported by the state to assist in conflict resolution, entrepreneurs and SMEs in emerging economies do not have access to affordable and reliable courts and so generally they do not use the courts (see Amoako and Lyon 2014). However, there is very little knowledge, if any, about how entrepreneurs operating smaller businesses in emerging countries characterised by weak legal systems repair trust in interorganisational relationships (Amoako and Lyon 2011; Amoako 2012). This chapter seeks to provide insights on the role of institutions in trust repair in entrepreneurial relationships in emerging economies by addressing two questions: (1) 'How do entrepreneurs owning and managing internationally trading SMEs repair trust?' and (2) 'What institutional logics influence trust repair and how?'

The author draws on the literature on trust repair and theory of institutional logics as well as empirical data from his work on trust repair in entrepreneurial relationships of internationally trading SMEs in Ghana to provide insights into how entrepreneurs repair trust (see Amoako and Lyon 2011; Amoako 2012). Institutional logics is defined as the 'socially constructed, historical patterns of cultural symbols and material practices, including assumptions, values, and beliefs by which individuals and organisations provide meaning to their daily activity, organize time and space and reproduce their lives and experiences' (Thornton et al. 2012, 2). In this chapter, the author examines how societal-level logics of state and indigenous cultural institutions and norms underpin entrepreneur's decisions about trust repair.

This chapter shows that the process of SME interorganisational trust repair begins when the trustor's initial trust is violated. This can occur at the personal/organisational level, institutional level, or at the parallel institutional level. In repairing trust, entrepreneurs deploy a number of tactics at these levels. However, the processes of trust repair are influenced by logics of institutions, the nature of the product/industry, and entrepreneurial agency. This is presented in Fig. 8.1 below, and the rest of the chapter discusses these issues in more detail.

This chapter contributes to the ongoing development of knowledge about trust repair (Dirks et al. 2009) and trust across cultural boundaries (Dietz et al. 2010). It shows how institutional logics of the traditional African justice system embedded in family/kinship, trade associations, communities, and religious bodies shape the processes of trust repair in entrepreneurial relationships in an African economy. By examining businesses operating in contexts with less-formalised institutional environments and legal systems in less-developed countries, it fills a gap in the literature that has previously focused on the developed economies of North America and Europe.

The rest of the chapter is structured as follows. Section 8.2 reviews the different forms and processes of trust violations entrepreneurs encounter in relationships. Section 8.3 discusses the institutional logics shaping the processes of trust repair. Section 8.4 examines the trust repair tactics that entrepreneurs use in restoring trust in entrepreneurial relationships after violations,

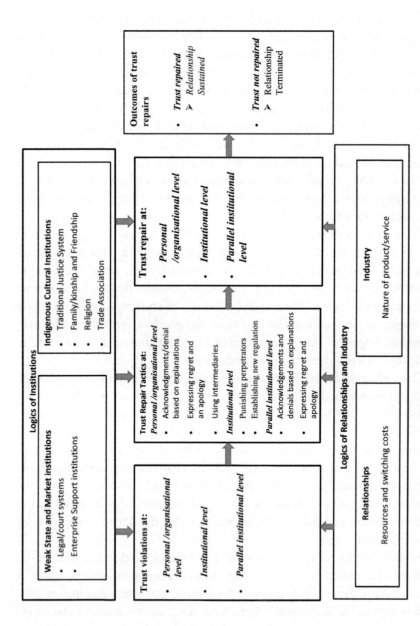

Fig. 8.1 Trust repair in entrepreneurial relationships. (Source: Own research)

Sect. 8.5 discusses the outcomes of trust repair, and Sect. 8.6 concludes the chapter.

8.2 Trust Violations in Entrepreneurial Relationships

Trust repair processes in entrepreneurial relationships may start soon after trust is violated by a family/kinship member or a friend who is a business partner, or an entrepreneur, manager, or leader of a partner SME or larger organisation when his or her actions and behaviour and that of the organisation do not meet the expectations of the entrepreneur. In Ghana trust violations occurs at the personal/organisational level, institutional level, and at the parallel institutional level.

In Ghana trust violations are common at the personal/organisational level. Entrepreneurs may face challenges in enforcing agreements with some family members, kinsfolk, and friends who are business partners and also with some customers and suppliers. At times it can be particularly challenging to get some relatives and friends who receive trade credit from entrepreneurs to pay back the money due to norms of communalism and obligation in the African family system. Amoako and Lyon (2014) report that in spite of the immense benefits of the family in enhancing entrepreneurship some family members make poor exchange partners due to challenges in enforcing agreements with them (see Chaps. 6 and 7). Similarly, some kinsfolk make poor borrowers in Ghana (Hart 2000). This is due to the logics of family/kinship and friendship in Ghana and Africa which oblige entrepreneurs and indeed family members to support and cater for members of the extended family; these logics have been discussed in detail in Sect. 5.2. Nonetheless, there are many successful family businesses managed by family members who are aware of and adhere to values and norms that encourage accountability and trustworthiness.

Trust violations are also common in customer and supplier relationships. Customer-related violations often involve dishonesty relating to breaching promises and norms of trade credit. In domestic, West African, and international markets, breaches of trade credit terms may involve some customers delaying payments or telling lies about the quality of products already supplied in order not to pay the agreed full price of the goods supplied on trade credit. In rare and extreme circumstances, dishonest customers may relocate and thus disappear after receiving goods on credit. Furthermore, in international markets some customers may breach the terms of legal contracts and memorandums of understanding (MOUs), exploit loopholes in contracts and include non-enforceable clauses, and covertly seek changes in contract terms in order to take advantage of entrepreneurs. Supplier-related violations of trust relate to dishonest behaviour regarding violations of promises regarding contracts, product and service specifications, delivery times, or misusing trade credit for purposes other than supplying the goods/services already paid for; and in rare cases some suppliers may relocate after receiving substantial amounts of trade credit from entrepreneurs. However, in a developing economy context like Ghana, where there is a lack of public information on individual identity and addresses, when perpetrators of trust violations relocate it can cause a lot of problems for entrepreneurs and this is a key reason why many entrepreneurs prefer working with family members since they are easy to trace in cases of default.

At the institutional level, trust violations relate to some officials of state institutions and leaders of facilitator organisations involved in enterprise support engaging in and perpetuating corruption and nepotism. There are allegations of demands for bribes by dishonest officials and judges (Amoako and Lyon 2014). Hence, entrepreneurs widely perceive the judiciary/legal systems and the courts to be corrupt, expensive, and time consuming. Yet, these allegations may be difficult to prove and individual entrepreneurs who experience these malpractices may find it challenging to obtain redress. Nonetheless, as actors some entrepreneurs use collective action through, for example, trade associations to lobby and draw the attention of government and the authorities to these violations in th hope of combatting them. Interestingly, in 2015 the investigative activities of an undercover journalist, Anas Aremeyaw Anas, exposed widespread corruption by Ghanaian judges and officials of the judiciary. As a result, the Chief Justice and the government took steps to repair trust even though the government could have done more (Daily Graphic, October 2015).

Case 8.1 shows how this was done and the impact the repair actions have had in rebuilding institutional trust in Ghana.

Due to perceptions of corruption and security concerns, entrepreneurs rarely use the courts in West African markets. In the context of international trade, entrepreneurs often remain helpless when trust is violated in international markets, as local Ghanaian courts lack jurisdiction outside the country and are thus unable to resolve disputes with international partners who do not live in Ghana. Moreover, the legal systems abroad are generally inaccessible and unaffordable to most entrepreneurs (Amoako 2012). Due to these barriers, entrepreneurs in Ghana rarely seek redress from the courts abroad.

Apart from the courts, entrepreneurs report violations of trust by enterprise facilitators. Some state officials are alleged to engage in corruption and favoritism. There are allegations that money and support meant for internationally trading entrepreneurs are at times diverted by unscrupulous officials to their cronies who are not involved in international business.

At the parallel institutional level, although entrepreneurs regard trade associations and their leaders to be more reliable, there are some allegations of trust violations. For example, Amoako and Lyon (2011) cite instances of some leaders of trade associations abusing their positions by exploiting opportunities for themselves instead of making them available to their members. Parallel institutional trust violations also result from allegations of the misuse of association funds and fraudulent accounting systems by a few association leaders (Amoako 2012). Apart from association leaders, religious leaders are also involved in trust violations. There are allegations of fake religious leaders violating trust by exploiting entrepreneurs in Ghana. In addition, there are allegations that some Christian, Muslim, and Africanist religious leaders make claims to authority and authenticity, and fraudulently fake miracles and connections to the spirits in order to deceive and defraud entrepreneurs and other followers. De Witte (2013) cites instances where some Pentecostal pastors use electric touch machines to fake the transmission of divine power—specifically the holy spirit—to followers (see Chaps. 4, 5 and 7). There are also allegations that a few unscrupulous customers or partners have exploited or abused entrepreneurs by using black magic, locally referred to as *juju*, in an attempt to charm and take advantage of their creditors or sponsors. Furthermore, there are perceptions that competitors could also destroy the businesses of others with *juju* and witchcraft. Hence, some entrepreneurs often make references to God, Allah, and the traditional gods as bastions for protection. Amidst these violations, entrepreneurs draw on institutional logics to repair trust at the personal/organisational, institutional, and parallel institutional levels. The next section discusses how institutional logics influence trust repair in Ghana.

8.3   Institutional Logics Shaping Trust Repair Processes

8.3.1   Logics of Weak Legal and Enterprise Support Systems

Institutional trust is important for the proper functioning of markets and is underpinned by the logics of state institutions including the government, justice/legal systems, property rights, the tax system, and other enterprise support institutions that offer incentives in the institutional environment (Zucker 1986; North 1990; Welter and Smallbone 2010). While culture and systems of institutions are important for institutional trust development, it is often the character, actions, and behaviour of officials or the key boundary spanners of institutions, and their inconsistency with the rules, regulations, and objectives of those institutions that determine trust violations in those institutions (Mitchell 1999). In Ghana, incidents of institutional trust violations relate to officials of state institutions and leaders of facilitator organisations involved in enterprise support, such as the judiciary/courts, allegedly practising and perpetuating norms of corruption and thereby breaching trust placed in them. As a result, trust repairs in entrepreneurial relationships in Ghana is influenced by the limited trust in state and market institutions. In particular, there is a lack of trust in the legal/court systems in Ghana due to allegations of corruption, higher costs, and long delays (Amoako and Lyon 2014). Consequently, entrepreneurs prefer the use of the traditional legal system which is less corrupt, less formal, less expensive, and less confrontational. Trust repairs is also shaped by the lack of enterprise support and particularly lack of access to finance, and higher costs of financial debts due to higher interest rates and inflation. As a result, developing trust and managing entrepreneurial relationships with customers, suppliers, and other personal networks is critical to SMEs. This in turn requires that entrepreneurs do not portray themselves as litigants who use the courts as their reputations could be negatively affected since the courts are regarded as expensive and adversarial.

8.3.2   Logics of Indigenous Cultural Institutions

Logics of the Traditional Justice System and Trust Repair

The majority of entrepreneurs rely on the traditional justice system to restore relationships after violations of trust in entrepreneurial relationships. The traditional justice system has been resilient in many communities especially at the grassroots level (Myers 1992). Conflict resolution and trust repair processes start at the family level and involve family heads, elders, queens, chiefs, and others who resolve, stop, and intercept conflict. The process is less formal, less intimidating, and less confrontational while aiming to restore broken relationships, rectify wrongs, and restore justice. The process is underpinned by respect for elders, parents, fellow people, and ancestors as well as internal and external control mechanisms based on shame, fear of supernatural forces, and the behaviour and actions of others that may signify their approval or disapproval (Okrah 2013). It is also grounded on the close ties and social capital between families and kinsfolk, which has however been reduced due to urbanisation. Nonetheless, as discussed in Chap. 4, the system faces additional challenges including negative attitudes from 'modernised Africans' and African governments and constitutions that regard the traditional system to be inferior to the formal judiciary of the state. Also, due to shifts in African traditional economic structures, dispute resolution by elders can be affected by bribery, corruption, and favouritism as the urban young may be significantly richer than the elders whose wealth through land, farming and livestock might have been eroded (see Kariuki 2015). Yet, the system is more enterprise friendly and it manifests itself in a number of

African indigenous institutions used by entrepreneurs in conflict resolution including logics of family/kinship, trade associations, and religion.

Logics of Family/Kinship and Trust Repair

An overwhelming number of entrepreneurs rely on logics of family/kinship in the restoration of violated trust. This is understandable given that the norms of family shape how trust violation is perceived. In instances when biological or business-related 'family members' violate trust, there is the tendency for the entrepreneur to ignore the violation or be coerced by family elders and members not to put money ahead of family and to reconcile and rebuild trust. Yet, these norms of resolving conflict in family businesses are not accepted by a number of entrepreneurs who may decide to withdraw from family businesses or not to work closely with family members in their businesses.

Logics of Trade Associations and Trust Repair

Trade associations play an important role in trust repair in Africa. For example, in West Africa, entrepreneurs prefer using the trade associations rather than the courts due to allegations and perceptions of corruption, higher costs, and long delays (Fafchamps 2004; Lyon and Porter 2009; Amoako and Lyon 2014). In Ghana and West Africa, trade association leaders play a unique role in conflict resolution and therefore in trust repair. Generally, when there is a breach of trust in business, entrepreneurs owning and managing smaller businesses often report incidents of violations to trade association leaders who draw on the norms of the traditional justice system to convene a court and a hearing, guided by the norms of the association, to resolve disagreements between exchange partners. To entrepreneurs, the use of trade association in conflict resolution saves time, is less confrontational and less expensive, and provides evidence that the entrepreneur is not a litigant and wants to resolve the dispute peacefully. This is important as most entrepreneurs and people in business regard the courts to be a route taken by controversial and heartless people to resolve conflicts. This in turn is informed by the amount of time and money, and the injustice, that may result due to corruption in courts.

There are other indigenous trading institutions embedded in the trade associations that are actively involved in conflict resolution in distant domestic and regional trade. For example, in West Africa, the *efiewura* (landlord) system is an indigenous institution that resolves conflicts between entrepreneurs and their trading partners from distant markets. The system is an indigenous institution that may operate as a trade association and yet involves agents (landlords) who sell goods (mostly food and agricultural produce) on behalf of entrepreneurs in distant domestic and regional markets for a commission. The agents take delivery of the goods, check and record the quantity, and then sell them. In addition, the agents also offer many other critical services to entrepreneurs in including bridging language barriers and providing market information, credit references, and accommodation. The landlord system therefore enables entrepreneurs who trade across cultures and borders in West Africa to overcome the 'liability of foreignness' resulting from differences in language and access to market spaces in the various markets. The system is sustained by shared norms of culture, language, payments, and trade associations. As mentioned earlier in Chap. 6, the structures of these indigenous institutions are based on the traditional legal and chieftaincy systems where the elders and chiefs resolve disputes among community members. Therefore, in cases of conflict or disagreement about payments or product quality, leaders are often requested by the parties to convene a court hearing to resolve the dispute. The system predates the colonisation of Africa, and yet still remains dominant in the small business and informal export sectors in the region (Lyon and Porter 2009; Amoako and Lyon 2014) contrary to assumptions that indigenous African institutions do not facilitate arm's-length transactions. The activities of trade associations in managing entrepreneurial relationships and trust building have been explored further in Chaps. 5 and 6 respectively.

Logics of Religion and Trust Repair

Entrepreneurs rely on logics of religion and religious leaders to resolve disputes and repair trust with business partners. Some entrepreneurs request the mediation of ministers of religion—pastors, imams, and clerics—and traditional religious leaders, instead of the courts, to resolve disputes and to enforce agreements between them and their partners. In such interventions, the perpetrators may be requested to abide by their contractual obligations and the entrepreneur may be encouraged to forgive, reconcile, and rebuild trust. This is understandable due to entrepreneurs' belief in supernatural bodies and their ability to reward or take revenge on people based on their actions and behaviour (see Kariuki 2009; Mbiti 1991).

Logics of Industry Shaping Trust Repair Processes

The nature of a product/service and an industry also shape trust repair processes. Yet, currently, there is sparse theory and therefore little understanding of how the nature of an industry and products/services play in trust repair (see Bachmann et al. 2015). In Chaps. 6 and 7 it was highlighted that entrepreneurs exporting agricultural products to West African and international markets are more dependent on their customers abroad and therefore more vulnerable. Their vulnerability accrues from the short shelf life of raw agricultural products such as eggs and fresh vegetables and the lack of refrigeration facilities that can mitigate this limitation. Therefore, entrepreneurs producing vegetables, eggs, and fresh fruit are generally more cautious in their interpretations of trust violations compared to those dealing in manufactured goods. For example, during peak harvesting periods when there is a glut in the fruit industry, entrepreneurs exporting fresh oranges to distant Ghanaian and West African markets encourage their customers who have defaulted to pay their debts by instalments while they continue to supply them. Similarly, the hotel industry is characterised by norms of trade credit with key business customers without whom hotels may not have sustainable revenues. This is due to the perishability of services in the industry which implies that once they are booked they cannot be stored, saved, returned, or resold once the specific booked time has elapsed (O'Neil and Matilla 2004). As a result, long-term customer relationships, customer loyalty and customer retention are critically important to entrepreneurs and SMEs operating in the sector. Hence, norms of payment and interpretations of trust violations due to default are more flexible compared to the manufacturing sector. Therefore, entrepreneurs operating in the sector are keen to keep their key business customers and do not accept that long delays in the payment of trade credit are a violation of trust even though they often make efforts to understand why payments are delayed. This approach to interpretation and repair of trust can be understood given the intangible nature and distinct perishability of some of the services such as hotel accommodation and conferences in the hospitality sector.

8.3.3   Logics of Relationships Shaping Trust Repair

Trust repair processes are primarily influenced by the nature of the relationship based on the benefits and resources received, liquidity concerns, and switching costs. For example, in relationships where the resources and benefits derived are substantial or when the switching costs are high the entrepreneur is more likely to ignore violations of trust. Therefore, trust repair efforts are more common in such relationships. Entrepreneurs rationally calibrate the benefits and switching costs as well as the seriousness of the violations before making a decision about whether to repair violated trust or abrogate a working relationship. Yet, in relationships that are embedded in logics of family and religion, the trust propensity of the entrepreneur influences his or her willingness to repair trust due to norms of obligations and fatalism. In these relationships trust repair is more habituated and routinised.

8.4   Personal/Organisational-Level Trust Repair Tactics

Trust repair at the customer/supplier level aims to restore trust. At the interpersonal level, there has been a number of studies that have delineated strategies for restoring trust after violations. For example, Lewicki and Bunker (1996) suggest that to repair trust, perpetrators must: (1) acknowledge that a violation has occurred; (2) determine the causes of the violation and admit culpability; (3) admit that the violation was destructive; and (4) accept responsibility. However, the weakness in this model relates to the assumptions about the passive role of the victim. Later models recognise trust repair as interactive with the trustor's actions (Kim et al. 2009) and the victim's cognitions of the perpetrator's repentance (Dirks et al. 2011). Kim et al. (2009) suggest that trust repair processes involve three levels where the trustor determines: (1) whether the trustee is guilty or not; (2) if guilty then whether the violation was caused by external situational factors or by the trustee's actions; and (3) if the violation is caused by the trustee's actions then can he or she rectify the wrongdoing that has occurred in the past or meet the trustor's expectations in the future. Kim et al. acknowledge the role of contextual factors in the trust repair process. To repair trust this model suggests three main approaches: (1) the trustee can claim innocence by presenting evidence or deny the breach; (2) the perpetrator may attempt to make attributions of the violations, fully or partly, to external factors in order to claim innocence and to repair trust; or (3) the perpetrator accepts responsibility and make trust repair efforts aimed to rectify the past breach and to offer assurances that future violations will not occur. While these studies and many others have provided huge insights into trust repair at the interpersonal level (e.g. Lewicki and Bunker 1996; Kim et al. 2004), at the organisational level, the conceptualisation of trust repair remains complex because of the multiple levels of organisational trustworthiness and violation (Gillespie and Dietz 2009; Dirks et al. 2009).

Concerning organisational trust repair, Gillespie and Dietz (2009) argue that the target for trust repair may be individuals or groups of individuals that make up an organisation. Consequently, trust repair at the organisational level creates a further degree of uncertainty and may be more difficult due to the multiplicity of organisational membership and the need for individuals to change their views towards the violating organisation. However, larger organisations that have violated trust with key stakeholders based on scandals and corruption may repair trust by tightening organisational rules and processes (Erberl et al. 2015; Gillespie and Dietz 2009).

Yet, there is a dearth of studies on trust repair in interorganisational relationships (IOR) but a notable exception is Janowicz-Panjaitan and Krishnan's (2009) theoretical model for investigating trust repair in larger companies. The model suggests that the nature of trust repair depends on the type of violation. These include whether the violation was integrity based or competence based, whether the violation occurred at the corporate level or the operating level, and the level of constraints limiting the boundary spanner. The model proposes that trust repair at the corporate level involves legalistic measures to repair trust or exit the relationship. Non-legalistic means are only effective when trust violations occur at lower levels—the operating level. Yet the author argues that for entrepreneurs owning and managing SMEs, legalistic modes of trust repair are not generally applicable or affordable to them since IOR are more personalised and informal. The analysis and discussions in this chapter therefore focus on the repair of trust violations in family/kinship and friendships, as well as customer-supplier and facilitator relationships and pays less attention to legalistic modes of trust repair.

8.4.1 Trust Repair in Family/Kinship- and Friendship-Related Violations

When trust is violated by a family member, kinsman/woman or friend who is a business partner, entrepreneurs often draw on the traditional African justice system embedded in the extended family system to contact elders and heads of family/kinship to seek assistance in resolving the dispute and repair trust (Amoako and Lyon 2014). However, based on the logics of the African family system, in instances when biological or business-related 'family members' violate trust, there is a tendency for the entrepreneur to ignore the violation, reconcile, and rebuild trust based on the norms of the African family which require family members to refrain from 'putting money ahead of family'. However, when an entrepreneur decides to seek redress, the first option is the use of the African justice system which begins with the family. An elder (or elders) of the family convenes a hearing and both parties are given the opportunity to tell their side of the story (Okrah 2013; Osei-Hwedie and Rankopo 2012). The perpetrator has the opportunity to acknowledge or deny the violation, and if found culpable to apologise and make a promise to rectify the violation. The system is flexible, less intimidating, quick and cost effective, and less adversarial as the emphasis is on reconciliation (Okrah 2013). Even though entrepreneurs abide mainly by the rulings of the elders, some may decide to withdraw from family businesses or not to work closely with family members in their private businesses after a violation.

8.4.2 Trust Repair with Customers and Suppliers

Trust repair mechanisms within entrepreneurial customer-supplier relationships tend to focus on restoring the observance of agreements and the norms of the relationships. Generally, the perpetrator may initiate repair processes through phone calls, emails, text messages, personal visits, and meetings. In these cases, the entrepreneur (who is the victim) waits until the perpetrator establishes contact. However, the victim may play an active role in the process and may often initiate the repair process. Against the background of SMEs operating in contexts of weak institutions, three main tactics are utilised in repairing trust at the personal/organisational level: (1) acknowledgement or denial based on explanations of causes of violations; (2) showing regret and apologising; and (3) the use of intermediaries.

The first common tactic used in domestic, West African, and international markets in trust repair is the acknowledgement or denial of the violation based on explanations. The violation may be acknowledged or denied. Generally, an acknowledgement of a trust violation facilitates the repair process since it presupposes that the perpetrator empathises with the victim. More importantly, it opens windows of opportunities for explanations of what caused the violations (Amoako 2012).

Generally, explanations of the causes of the violation lead to either denying or accepting responsibility for the violation or denying responsibility by attributing the violation to external causes. This is common as support systems and processes such as logistics, electricity, and banking services may fail in the Ghanaian context. While such attributions may be acceptable in domestic and West African markets, they tend not to be acceptable in international markets.

The second tactic used in repairing trust is the expression of regret and an apology following the violation. In expressing regret and offering an apology, the perpetrators of violations in domestic and West African markets mainly use telephone calls and personal visits. Apologies are particularly important in the restoration of trust after violations (Lewicki and Bunker 1996; Kim et al. 2004) and yet, to be effective, apologies must be timely, credible, and backed up with substantive actions such as punishment and compensation (Gillespie and Dietz 2009; Bottom et al. 2002). Generally, apologies without showing signs of regret do not work effectively as entrepreneurs may think that the incident could be repeated. In international markets, expressions of regret and apologies are often done directly from violator to victim and mostly without recourse to intermediation. An expression of regret and an apology simultaneously open doors for discussions, which may lead to repairing trust (Amoako and Lyon 2011).

The use of intermediaries in trust repair is the third common tactic used in repairing trust in entrepreneurial relationships. Intermediaries often used include friends, family members, community leaders, religious leaders, and trade association leaders. In domestic and West African markets, intermediaries often culturally bridge the distance between parties regarding language and cultural norms associated with pleading for clemency. This practice is more common in domestic and West African markets than in international markets even though there are instances when entrepreneurs rely on embassy staff and the organisers of trade fairs as intermediaries in resolving disputes in overseas markets.

In the domestic markets, entrepreneurs regard the use of intermediaries as more cost effective than going to court. In the process, intermediaries who may know either the perpetrator or the victim are often implored by either of the parties to resolve the dispute and repair trust amicably. These intermediaries may influence either party to compromise or give in to the demands of the other. The use of intermediaries in repairing trust in entrepreneurial relationships is drawn from the traditional legal and chieftaincy systems in which the intermediary (*dwanetoafo* in Akan-Twi) mediates on behalf of the perpetrator for leniency. The intermediary also serves as a witness in case the perpetrator does not cooperate and the victim decides to escalate the demand for redress in the courts since going to court is regarded as an extreme approach adopted by litigants due to its cumbersome nature, high cost, and long delays associated with the process (Amoako and Lyon 2011).

In circumstances when trust is not fully repaired, entrepreneurs may reach an agreement with the perpetrator on reviewing contract terms. In domestic markets, such reviews may penalise the perpetrator. For example, entrepreneurs may either reduce the amount of trade credit or withdraw the trade credit altogether and instead insist on cash payments. Similarly, in West African market entrepreneurs may reduce or withdraw trade credit and insist on cash payments by trade debtors who violate trust. The reduction or withdrawal of trade credit facilities is also common in international markets. However, due to the relatively more frequent use of legal contracts and MOUs in international relationships, compared to local and West African markets, in addition, reviewing the contract terms may include inserting clauses in contracts to impose sanctions and penalties such as payment of money for every day missed in a supply contract. Nonetheless, when all attempts to repair trust fail, and efforts to continue working together under new contract or credit terms, entrepreneurs may terminate the relationship.

8.4.3   Institutional-Level Trust Repair Tactics

Institutional trust is important for the proper functioning of markets. Institutional trust is based on trust in formal institutions including government, justice/legal systems, property rights, the tax system, and other enterprise-support institutions that offer incentives in the institutional environment (Zucker 1986; North 1990; Welter and Smallbone 2010). While culture and systems of institutions are important for institutional trust development, it is often the character, actions, and behaviour of officials or the key boundary spanners of institutions and their inconsistency with the rules, regulations, and objectives of those institutions that determine trust violations in those institutions (Mitchell 1999).

Entrepreneurs widely perceive the judiciary/legal systems and the courts to be weak and corrupt. In particular, allegations of corruption in the judiciary and courts are common in the domestic market. There are allegations of dishonest officials and judges making demands for bribes (Amoako and Lyon 2014). Yet, these allegations may be difficult to prove and, as a result, individual entrepreneurs who experience these malpractices apparently remain victims without recourse to redress. Yet, as actors, some entrepreneurs use collective action through, for example, trade associations to lobby and draw the attention of government and the authorities to these violations, calling for action to combat them. Since 2015, due to the exposure of widespread corruption by judges and staff of the judiciary and the courts, the Chief Justice and the government have taken steps to repair trust even though more could have been done. Case 8.1 shows how this was done and the impact these actions have had in rebuilding institutional trust in Ghana. Within West African markets, repair with the courts is uncommon due to perceived corruption as well as security concerns.

In the context of international trade, for entrepreneurs the main obstacles to lack of engagement concern the inability of the courts in Ghana, due to lack of jurisdiction, to resolve disputes with international partners who do not live in Ghana.

Case 8.1 Trust Repair at the Institutional Level in Ghana

The role of government in repairing institutional trust can be significant, as shown by government action on corruption in the courts in Ghana. On 22 September 2015, videos showing corruption in the judiciary recorded on camera by an undercover journalist Anas Ameriyaw Anas were shown on television revealing lower and high court judges and judicial staff requesting bribes and pay-offs (Daily Graphic, October 6 2015). The videos confirmed widespread violations of trust in the judiciary and courts in the country. To repair trust in the courts, the Chief Justice with the blessing of the President of the Republic of Ghana took dramatic steps by dismissing 20 lower court judges, 19 senior administrative staff, and suspending seven high court judges. In a statement, the Chief Justice sought to rebuild trust by reassuring the public that the judiciary council would take prompt and resolute action to redeem the image of the judiciary. Later, in 2017, the government passed a bill setting up the Office of the Special Prosecutor to combat corruption in the country. The Special Prosecutor will have a mandate to investigate and prosecute cases of alleged corruption-related offences involving political office holders, public officers and their accomplices. Due to the government's actions in rebuilding trust, there seems to be an upsurge of trust in the country, albeit a slow one. The Transparency International Corruption Perception Index (CPI) shows that Ghanaian's perceptions of corruption score of 48 points in 2014 reduced to 40 points in 2017 (Transparency International 2018), thus showing an improvement in trust in the judiciary/courts and in the country.

8.5   Trust Repair Outcomes

The empirical study shows that the outcomes of trust repair are twofold. In the overwhelming majority of cases, trust repair leads to the restoration of trust and entrepreneurs and their partners continue to work together. However, even though relationships may be restored, it is possible that trust violations may be a wake-up call for entrepreneurs to search for other partners. This may lead to the establishment of newer partnerships and, as a result, the level of commitment in relationships prior to violations may not be fully restored. For example, in cases when customers do not take delivery of goods/services, entrepreneurs may look for other customers and, in most cases, the entrepreneur will continue to supply the customer even after the trust violation may be repaired. In such cases, the perpetrators may not receive the quantities they used to receive previously.

Yet, in other cases when trust repair is unsuccessful, entrepreneurs may terminate the relationship. However, depending on the nature of the relationship, entrepreneurs may have to develop new relationships and, as discussed in Chap. 7, this may require a lot of time in identifying new partners and developing new relationships.

8.6   Conclusion

This chapter provides an understanding of how entrepreneurs owning and managing internationally trading SMEs repair trust in interorganisational relationships in Ghana. It also identifies the institutions and the institutional logics that influence trust repair processes. It shows that in SMEs' interorganisational relationships, trust repair processes start after a partner entrepreneur, manager, key boundary spanner of a larger partner organisation, leader of a trade association, or an official of an institution that is expected to facilitate entrepreneurship violates trust. The violations relate to breaches of the entrepreneur's expectations. The chapter also shows how family members (who may be business partners), customers, suppliers, officials of state institutions, and leaders of facilitator organisations involved in enterprise support may violate trust. Furthermore, some trade association leaders may violate trust by breaching the expectations of entrepreneurs who are members of the associations.

Thus trust repair processes within entrepreneurial relationships tend to focus on restoring the observance of agreements, expectations in relationships. In customer- and supplier-related violations, the perpetrator may initiate trust repair processes through telephone calls, emails, text messages, personal visits, and meetings. In these cases, the entrepreneur who is the victim waits until the perpetrator establishes contact. However, the victim may play an active role in the process and may also initiate the trust repair process. Trust repair involves three main tactics at the personal/organisational level and they are: (1) acknowledgement or denial based on explanations for the causes of violations; (2) showing regret and apologising; and (3) the use of intermediaries. This chapter shows regret and apologies as well as explanations facilitate trust repair (Lewicki and Bunker 1996; Kim et al. 2004). It also shows the importance of intermediaries in the trust repair process. This tactic draws on the traditional chieftaincy and judicial systems in which intermediaries plead for clemency for the perpetrator of an offence. However, in institutional trust repair, this chapter shows the challenges that entrepreneurs may face when corrupt officials abuse their positions and violate trust. It also shows the importance of government in repairing trust through sanctioning corrupt officials and restoring trust in state institutions.

The chapter provides a valuable understanding of trust repair in relation to interorganisational relationships for small businesses in an African country and in other emerging economies. It contributes to the ongoing development of knowledge about the importance of culture in trust development, trust violations espoused by Ren and Gray (2009) and Dietz et al. (2010). Yet this chapter also extends knowledge about the role of culture in trust repair processes by pointing to the cultural-specific logics of the traditional African justice system embedded in family/kinship, trade associations, communities, and religious bodies and how these logics shape the process of trust repair in entrepreneurial relationships. It also shows the tactics that entrepreneurs use to repair trust. By examining businesses operating in the context of less-formalised institutional environments and legal systems in less-developed countries, this chapter fills a gap in the literature by showing how specific institutional logics allow trust to be repaired.

Finally, from a practical point of view, the chapter shows that trust violations are common in entrepreneurial relationships, and it is important for entrepreneurs to understand the logics of weak state and market institutions, cultural institutions, industry, and relationships that enable the repair of trust without entrepreneurs resorting to litigation and the courts which can be expensive, a waste of time, and damage their reputation. For policy makers, this chapter shows how government action in tackling corruption is important. By sanctioning corrupt officials of the judiciary and the courts, governments can repair trust in state and market institutions.

References

Amoako, I.O. 2012. *Trust in exporting relationships: The case of SMEs in Ghana*, Published PhD thesis. Center for Economic and Enterprise Development Research (CEEDR) Middlesex University, London. http://eprints.mdx.ac.uk/12419/.

Amoako, I. O., and Lyon, F. 2011. Interorganisational trust violations and repairs in a weak institutional environment: The case of Ghanaian Exporting SMEs. Paper presented at the 27th European Group for Organisational Studies (EGOS) Conference, Gothenburg, University of Gothenburg, July 2011.

———. 2014. We don't deal with courts: Cooperation and alternative institutions shaping exporting relationships of SMEs in Ghana. *International Small Business Journal* 32 (2): 117–139.

Bachmann, R. 2001. Trust, power and control in trans-organizational relations. *Organization Studies* 22 (2): 337–365.

Bachmann, R., N. Gillespie, and R. Priem. 2015. Repairing trust in organizations and institutions: Toward a conceptual framework. *Organization Studies* 36: 1123–1142.

Bottom, W.P., K. Gibson, S. Daniels, and J.K. Munighan. 2002. When talk is not cheap: Substantive penance and expressions of intent in rebuilding cooperation. *Organization Science* 13 (5): 497–513.

Daily Graphic. 2015. *7 High Court judges suspended*, Issued no. 198990. Accra.

De Witte, M. 2013. The electric touch machine miracle scam: Body, technology and the (dis)authentication of the pentecostal supernatural. In *Machina: Religion, Technology, and the Things in Between*, ed. Stolow J. Deus. New York: Fordham University Press.

Dietz, G., N. Gillespie, and G.T. Chao. 2010. Unravelling the complexities of trust and culture. In *Organizational Trust: A cultural Perspective*, ed. M.N.K. Saunders, D. Skinner, G. Dietz, N. Gillespie, and R.J. Lewicki, 3–41. Cambridge: Cambridge University Press.

Dirks, K.T., R.J. Lewicki, and A. Zaheer. 2009. Repairing relationships within and between organizations: Building a conceptual foundation. *Academy of Management Review* 34 (1): 68–84.

Dirks, K.T., P.H. Kim, D.L. Ferrin, and C.D. Cooper. 2011. Understanding the effects of substantive responses on trust following a transgression. *Organizational Behavior and Human Decision Processes* 114: 87–103.

Erberl, P., D. Greiger, and A. Blander. 2015. Repairing trust in an organization after integrity violations: The ambivalence of organization rule adjustments. *Organization Studies* 36: 1205–1235.

Fafchamps, M. 2004. *Market institutions in Sub-Saharan Africa: Theory and evidence*. Cambridge: MIT Press.

Frankel, R., J. Smitz Whipple, and D.J. Frayer. 1996. Formal versus informal contracts: Achieving alliance success. *International Journal of Physical Distribution and Logistics Management* 26 (3): 47–63.

Gaur, A.S., D. Mukherjee, S.S. Gaur, and F. Schmid. 2011. Environmental and firm level influences on inter-organizational trust and SME performance. *Journal of Management Studies* 48: 1752–1781.

Gillespie, John. 2017. *Transplanting commercial law reform: Developing a 'rule of law' in Vietnam*. London: Routledge.

Gillespie, N., and G. Dietz. 2009. Trust repair after an organizational-level failure. *Academy of Management Review* 34 (1): 127–145.

Hart, K. 2000. Kinship, contract, and trust: The economic organization of migrants in an African City slum. In *Trust: Making and breaking cooperative relations*, ed. D. Gambetta, Electronic ed., 176–193. Oxford: Department of Sociology, University of Oxford.

Janowicz-Panjaitan, M., and R. Krishnan. 2009. Measures for dealing with competence and integrity violations of interorganizational trust at the corporate and operating levels of organizational hierarchy. *Journal of Management Studies* 46 (2): 245–268.

Kariuki, F. 2009. Conflict resolution by elders in Africa: Successes, challenges and opportunities. *Journal of Law and Conflict Resolution* 1 (August): 60–67.

Kariuki, F. 2015. Conflict resolution by elders in Africa: Successes, challenges and opportunities. *Alternative Dispute Resolution* 3 (2): 30–53.

Kim, P.H., D.L. Ferrin, C.D. Cooper, and K.T. Dirks. 2004. Removing the shadow of suspicion: The effects of apology versus denial for repairing competence-based versus integrity-based trust violations. *Journal of Applied Psychology* 89 (1): 100–118.

Kim, P.H., K.T. Dirks, and C.D. Cooper. 2009. The repair of trust: A dynamic bilateral perspective and multilevel conceptualization. *Academy of Management Review* 34 (3): 401–422.

Lewicki, R.J. 2006. Trust and distrust. In *The negotiator's fieldbook: The desk reference for the experienced negotiator*, ed. A.K. Schneider and C. Honeyman, 191–202. Chicago: American Bar Association.

Lewicki, R.J., and B.B. Bunker. 1996. Developing and maintaining trust in work relationships. In *Trust in organizations: Frontiers of theory and research*, ed. R. Kramer and T.R. Tyler. Thousand Oaks: Sage.

Lyon, F., and G. Porter. 2009. Market institutions, trust and norms: Exploring moral economies in Nigerian food systems. *Cambridge Journal of Economics* 33 (5): 903–920.

Mbiti, J.S. 1991. *Introduction to African religion*. 2nd ed. Portsmouth: Heinemann.

Mitchell, V.-W. 1999. Consumer perceived risk: Conceptualizations and models. *European Journal of Marketing* 33 (1): 163–195.

Myers, Samuel L. 1992. Crime, entrepreneurship, and labor force withdrawal. *Contemporary Economic Policy* 10 (2): 84–97.

North, D.C. 1990. *Institutions, institutional change and economic performance*. Cambridge: Cambridge University Press.

Okrah, K.A.A. 2013. Toward global conflict resolution: Lessons from Akan traditional judicial system. *Journal of Social Studies Research* 27 (2): 4–3.

O'Neil, J.W., and S.A. Mattila. 2004. Hotel branding strategy: Its relationship to guest satisfaction and room revenue. *Journal of Hospitality and Tourism Research* 28 (2): 156–165.

Osei-Hwedie, K. and M.J. Rankopo 2012. Indigenous conflict resolution in Africa: The case of Ghana and Botswana. *IPSHU English Research Report Series* 29 (3), 33–51, Institute of Peace Studies, Hiroshima University.

Ren, H., and B. Gray. 2009. Repairing relationship conflict: How violation types and culture influence the effectiveness of restoration rituals. *Academy of Management Review* 34 (1): 105–126.

Saunders, M.N.K., D. Skinner, G. Dietz, N. Gillespie, and R.J. Lewicki. 2010. *Organizational trust: A cultural perspective.* Cambridge: Cambridge University Press.

Sydow, J., and A. Windler. 2003. Knowledge, trust, and control: Managing tensions and contradictions in a regional network of service firms. *International Studies of Management and Organization* 33 (2): 69–100.

Thornton, Patricia H., William Ocasio, and Michael Lounsbury. 2012. *The institutional logics perspective: A new approach to culture, structure and processes.* Oxford: Oxford University Press.

Transparency International. 2018. Ghana corruption perception index 2017, Berlin.

Welter, F., and D. Smallbone. 2010. The embeddedness of women's entrepreneurship in a transition context. In *Women's entrepreneurship and the global environment for growth: An international perspective,* ed. C. Brush, E. Gatewood, C. Henry, and A. De Bruin, 96–117. Cheltenham: Edward Elgar.

Zucker, L.G. 1986. Production of trust. Institutional sources of economic structure, 1840–1920. *Research in Organisation Behaviour* 8: 53–111.

Part IV

Conclusions and Implications

9

Conclusion and Implications of Trust, Institutions and Managing Entrepreneurial Relationships in Africa

9.1 Introduction

Africa has achieved considerable economic growth during the past two decades and currently entrepreneurs, investors and businesses, regard the continent as an emerging market destination for businesses to invest and grow (George et al. 2016; Delloitte 2014; Accenture 2010). Hence, entrepreneurs, investors, corporate executives and politicians are showing a keen interest in building networks and relationships with customers and businesses in the continent (BBC News 2018). Yet, despite the huge interest, potential entrepreneurs, investors, and corporate executives are frightened by the lack of trust in doing business in Africa due to numerous weak institutional structures that are highlighted in the literature and reports in the West (World Bank 2018; The Economist 2016; Bruton et al. 2010). These sources emphasise that in African economies transaction costs are higher and trust to invest and engage in entrepreneurship is low due to weak state and market institutions. Yet, these assertions do not fully reflect the nature and role of institutions in entrepreneurship in Africa and in other emerging economies (Peng et al. 2008; Welter and Smallbone 2011). In Africa and other emerging economies, entrepreneurs

© The Author(s) 2019   265
I. O. Amoako, *Trust, Institutions and Managing Entrepreneurial Relationships in Africa*,
Palgrave Studies of Entrepreneurship in Africa,
https://doi.org/10.1007/978-3-319-98395-0_9

as actors do not necessarily yield to state and market institutional barriers but instead draw on cultural institutions to develop trust in order to do business (Welter and Smallbone 2011; Amoako and Lyon 2014). In emerging economies like Africa, the weak formal institutions are often replaced by indigenous cultural institutions to enhance trust development in entrepreneurship. Estrin and Pervezer's (2011) study in Brazil, Russia, India, and China show that in emerging economies cultural institutions replace ineffective state and market institutions leading to enhanced domestic and foreign investment. Unfortunately, there is a lack of knowledge about how entrepreneurs in Africa draw on indigenous cultural institutions that run parallel to institutions of the modern African states (Jackson et al. 2008; Amoako and Lyon 2014; George et al. 2016).

The main aim of this book is to offer an understanding about how entrepreneurs owning and managing small and medium-sized enterprises (SMEs) in Africa draw on local cultural institutions to develop trust in entrepreneurial relationships in the absence of strong state and market institutions. The author uses an abductive approach to combine literature with empirical findings from observations and semi-structured interviews with 50 entrepreneurs owning and managing SMEs in Africa in order to refine or generate theory. The level of analysis is the entrepreneur who owns an SME in Africa. SMEs dominate the economies of African countries, and reflect the impact of local institutions on trust development better than larger organisations. The discussions focus on trust development in entrepreneurial relationships and how the processes are influenced by logics of state and market institutions, cultural institutions, networks, relationships, industry, and markets. Based on the discussions, the author offers novel theoretical and empirical frameworks and elaborations that become the basis of a continued development of these themes regarding entrepreneurship in Africa and other emerging economies.

9.1.1   Trust, Institutions, and Managing Entrepreneurial Relationships

Entrepreneurial behaviour originates from a complex relationship between entrepreneurs as individuals and the environment in which they operate (Schumpeter 1942; Chell 2007). However, traditionally, entrepreneurship scholars have been divided into two streams of studies: one emphasises rational choice perspectives to focus on the individualistic entrepreneurial agent; the other emphasises the macrostructures that influence the entrepreneurial process. Yet, neither of these two perspectives can fully portray the complex processes of entrepreneurship.

The rational choice perspective emphasises that entrepreneurship encompasses discovery, creation, and exploitation of opportunities, and the traditional entrepreneurship literature primarily ascribes the success or failure of these activities to the individual heroic entrepreneur (see Gartner 1988; Shane and Venkataraman 2000). The traditional approach to the study of trust in entrepreneurship therefore focuses on agency and the internal cognitions of individuals as trustors or trustees in terms of their attributes. Thus, trust is seen as rational and calculative with actors primarily focused on their own benefits. However, the rational perspective underestimates the context or institutions (e.g. Gambetta 1988; Williamson 1993).

Hence, critics argue that entrepreneurs are not atomistic but are embedded in institutions and particularly social relations from which they develop trust in order to draw resources to create new firms (North 1990; Granovetter 1985; Chell 2000). By focusing only on the entrepreneur and ignoring institutional forces, the rational or agency approach risks basing entrepreneurship and trust development on the false idea of the atomistic, sometimes maverick, individual. This may lead scholars and would-be entrepreneurs to undervalue the significance of networking and social capital that are very important to the entrepreneurial process, particularly for SMEs (Drakopoulou Dodd and Anderson 2007; Ellis 2000).

Some scholars, on the other hand, have drawn on institutional theory to highlight the impact of environment on trust development in entrepreneurship. A major strength of institutional theory is its emphasis on macroenvironmental factors in offering an understanding about entrepreneurship and entrepreneurial behaviour (Welter 2002). This theory traditionally draws attention to the embeddedness of entrepreneurial behaviour in both formal and informal institutions. Thus, formal institutions including government and legal systems, and informal cultural institutions like norms, values, and attitudes, all influence trust and entrepreneurship (Welter and Smallbone 2011). For example, legal systems and the courts that enforce legislation and contracts or social norms and codes of conduct influence entrepreneurial behaviour. In developed economies where formal institutions like courts are strong, entrepreneurs have a strong trust to invest and innovate due to lower transaction costs (North 1990). Conversely, in emerging economies with weak formal institutions, entrepreneurs have low trust to invest and innovate due to higher transaction costs. Nonetheless, the author argues that these assertions about institutions, trust, and entrepreneurship mainly draw on advanced Western economy contexts to focus on how state and market institutions must facilitate trust development; thereby ignoring entrepreneurship theory and practices particularly in emerging economies (Peng et al. 2008; Welter and Smallbone 2011; Amoako and Lyon 2014). In emerging economies, entrepreneurs and organisations as agents can improve their competitiveness by turning institutional and resource constraints into incentives and assets (Amankwah-Amoah and Debrah 2017). Yet, reports and research on trust in enterprise and investment in Africa often emphasise the weakness of formal institutions in African economies to justify the lack of entrepreneurship (see e.g. The Economist 2016; World Bank, Business 2018; Bruton et al. 2010). While there may not be strong formal institutions in African economies, there are cultural institutions, networks, relationships, and trust—as well as entrepreneurs.

Thus, the Western context-based rationality of institutions and trust building is criticised and scholars have called for further development of institutional theory to take into account the entrepreneur, the firm, and cognitive foundations of entrepreneurial behaviour (Welter 2002). Examining how cognitive foundations influence entrepreneurship is essential as entrepreneurial behaviour regarding trust development originates from complex ongoing influences of the entrepreneur as an actor, the external institutional factors, and organisational characteristics (see Bachmann et al. 2015).

To address the current gaps in institutional theory regarding trust development in entrepreneurship, the author draws on notions of institutional logics to reject both macrostructural theories and individualistic, rational choice perspectives of entrepreneurship (see Thornton et al. 2011). Thornton et al. (2012, 2) define institutional logics as the 'socially constructed, historical patterns of cultural symbols and material practices, including assumptions, values, and beliefs by which individuals and organisations provide meaning to their daily activity, organize time and space and reproduce their lives and experiences'. Thornton et al. (2012) suggest seven core societal institutions and their logics: family, religion, state, market, profession, corporation, and community. The institutional logics perspective further assumes that institutions are historically contingent (Friedland and Alford 1991). Thornton et al. (2012) suggest that the logics of the state, the professions, the corporation, and the market, typically influence modern societies. However, the author argues that these logics do not fully apply to African economies, not because they are not modern, but because of the incongruence and weaknesses of state and market institutions and the relative dominance of SMEs compared to corporations in the continent.

Drawing on the institutional logics perspective, the author categorises institutional orders whose logics influence entrepreneurship and trust development in Africa into two main groups, namely logics of state and markets, and logics of indigenous cultural institutions. The logics of state and market focus on state institutions, particularly the government, legal/court systems, and enterprise-facilitating bodies such as banks, while the logics of cultural institutions focus on the traditional judicial system, trade associations, language, family/kinship, religion, gift giving, and punctuality that have been shown to influence entrepreneurial trust development in Africa.

The author draws from state and market, as well as indigenous cultural institutional orders and their logics, to present frameworks and discussions that show how the embedded African entrepreneur often responds in ways to counter constraints and taken-for-granted assumptions associated with institutions (see Amoako and Lyon 2014; Jackson et al. 2008; George et al. 2016). The frameworks show that entrepreneurs in Africa as actors use logics of weak state and market institutions as well as cultural institutions to interpret and make sense of the world, while the logics offer the norms that influence organisational strategy, behaviour including networking, and the development of relationships and trust.

The institutional logic perspective allows for theorising the fragmented and contradicted nature of entrepreneurship and trust in cultural institutions and state and market institutions at different levels of analysis such as individual or organisational and in specific contexts in which individuals operate (see Thornton 2004). Based on the discussions and frameworks the author makes a number of contributions.

9.2 Implications for Theory

- Chapter 2 provides a theoretical framework that demonstrates a balanced approach to the study of entrepreneurship. The framework recognises the importance of formal and informal institutions, networks, relationships, trust, the entrepreneur, and the firm in entrepreneurship. It therefore refutes assertions in reports and literature that draw on Western models and mainstream economic institutionalist perspectives to suggest that formal institutions are the key to successful entrepreneurship in emerging economies including Africa (e.g. The Economist 2016; World Bank Doing Business Survey; 2018; Bruton et al. 2010). In Africa and other emerging economies, culture plays an important role in entrepreneurship due to its impact on cognition—norms, values, beliefs, network strategies, and trust development (Amoako and Lyon 2014; Wu et al. 2014)—and yet the literature does not pay much attention to the importance of cultural institutions in entrepreneurship in emerging economy contexts.
- The author develops in Chap. 3 a holistic theoretical framework to highlight the processes of trust development across the levels of the individual (trustor and trustee), his or her interactions within relationships, and formal and informal institutions that shape the development processes of interorganisational trust. The model suggests that trust originates from a trustor's propensity to trust and trusting behaviour as well as a trustee's trustworthiness based on ability, integrity, and benevolence (Mayer et al. 1995; Kim et al. 2004). The model shows further that context, namely the formal and cultural institutions, networks and relationships, and interactions with exchange partners, all influence the development of trust and the processes of violation and repair (Granovetter 1985; Möllering 2006; Zucker 1986; Ren and

Gray 2009; Bachmann and Inkpen 2011). This holistic approach is currently lacking in the trust literature (Bachmann et al. 2015; Li 2016).

- In Chap. 4, the author presents a framework to show the institutions that influence trust development in entrepreneurial relationships in Africa. The identified institutions are colonialism, weak state and market institutions, traditional justice systems, trade associations, family/kinship, religion, gift giving, and punctuality. The logics of the indigenous institutions often substitute for or complement the logics of weak state and market institutions in entrepreneurship (Estrin and Pervezer 2011). For example, the traditional justice system and trade associations promote trust and trade in domestic and distant markets by resolving conflicts and disputes among entrepreneurs and thereby providing parallel institutional trust that enables entrepreneurs to mitigate some of the risks involved in doing business in local and distant markets (Amoako and Lyon 2014). This is contrary to assumptions that indigenous institutions do not promote arm's-length exchanges (see Lyon and Porter 2009). Yet, we know very little about these indigenous institutions as most African governments and foreign agencies recognise and support the weak state and market institutions but do not recognise and support the indigenous cultural institutions. This chapter therefore helps to reconceptualise the role of formal and informal institutions in entrepreneurship in Africa.

- In Chap. 5 the author develops empirical frameworks that show entrepreneurial customer attraction strategies and the logics of institutions that influence entrepreneurial relationship management in Africa. This chapter explains how entrepreneurs attract customers through networking and referrals, prospecting for business by using information and communication technologies (ICTs) and through promotions. It shows how entrepreneurs draw on the logics of weak state and market institutions and indigenous cultural institutions such as family/kinships, oral contracts, traditional justice systems, trade associations, religion, punctuality, gift giving, reciprocity, commitment, and mutuality inherent in family/kinship and friendship to manage relationships. By doing so, this chapter provides knowledge about how African entrepreneurs as actors draw on indigenous institutions to develop and manage entrepreneurial relationships across cultures.

- In Chap. 6 the author presents an empirical framework of trust development and how the logics of institutions influence trust development in an African context. The framework shows a range of cultural institutions that are both the basis of personal/organisational trust and can be seen as forms of institutional trust in themselves. It shows how the norms of language, oral contracts, family/kinship and friendship, religion, punctuality, gift giving, and trade associations confer stronger elements of trust in economic relationships. As a result, socio-cultural institutions underpin the development of trust (Saunders et al. 2010; Li 2016; Chang et al. 2016), and therefore trust can be habitual. Yet, the discussions show that entrepreneurs as actors do not necessarily yield to institutions. For example the use of the traditional justice system, the ability to develop new norms of punctuality or to refuse to work members who are not trustworthy shows how as actors, entrepreneurs reflect and act in ways to counter the constraints and taken-for-granted assumptions prescribed by institutions, contrary to traditional institutionalist assertions about the constraining influences of institutions (North 1990; Scott 2005). This chapter shows further that in the context of SMEs, the distinction between personal/organisational trust remains complex and unclear, but this has not received much attention in the literature.

- In Chap. 7, the author provides a holistic framework of trust violations to highlight that entrepreneurs encounter different forms of trust violations in their relationships. Yet, the chapter emphasises that the concept of interorganisational trust violation remains unclear due to contextual factors, particularly culturally specific norms that shape interpretations of trust and trust violations in entrepreneurial relationships. This chapter shows that norms of weak legal institutions, family/kinship, religion, trade associations, and industry shape the perceptions and interpretations of trust violations and the interpretations may differ between associations, sectors, and markets. Based on these influences, at times entrepreneurs ignore or do not acknowledge some blatant incidents of trust violation. This observation shows the challenges of developing and managing trust in entrepreneurial relationships across cultures. Even though the literature acknowledges the potential for differences in interpretations of trust dimensions (e.g. Ren and Gray 2009; Saunders et al. 2010), this chapter extends our knowledge by identifying specific, cultural and other contextual logics that influence interpretations of trust violations in an African context. It also shows that the outcomes of trust violations could have varying negative impacts, not only on businesses but also on entrepreneurs. When exchange partners violate trust, entrepreneurs may suffer financial, psychological, and social costs and disappointment and grief can be profound. Yet the literature has only emphasised how trust violations may adversely impact on business (e.g. Bachmann 2001) while giving no attention to how trust violations may impact entrepreneurs.

- In Chap. 8 the author contributes to the literature by providing an empirical framework of trust repair in SME interorganisational relationships (Dirks et al. 2009) and trust across cultural boundaries (Dietz et al. 2010). The framework explains how entrepreneurs draw on the institutional logics of the traditional African justice system embedded in family/kinship, trade associations, communities, and religious bodies to repair trust in relationships. It also shows the trust repair tactics that enable entrepreneurs to repair trust. For example, it confirms that apologies and explanations facilitate trust repair (Lewicki and Bunker 1996; Kim et al. 2004). However, in African contexts, intermediaries play a key role in trust repair. This tactic draws on the traditional chieftaincy and judicial systems in which intermediaries plead for clemency and mediation for the perpetrator of an offence. Hence this chapter provides an understanding of how institutions influence trust repair in an African and emerging economy context as currently the role of institutions in the process of trust repair is not well understood (Bachmann et al. 2015).

9.3 Implications for Practice

- This book shows the importance of African indigenous cultural institutions, networks, relationships, and trust in contexts where state and market institutions are weak. It also demonstrates how entrepreneurs in Africa rely on logics of indigenous institutions that substitute for and at times complement logics of weak state and market institutions (Estrin and Pervezer 2011). These indigenous institutions provide 'parallel institutional trust' that enables entrepreneurs to develop personal and working relationships in order to access resources (Amoako and Lyon 2014). Thus, entrepreneurs and investors who seek to do business in Africa should endeavour to understand the nature and role of the relevant cultural institutions and how they shape trust development in sectors, industries, and markets, across cultures and over time (Amoako 2012). This is important as the logics of these institutions influence trust development, interpretations, and acceptable levels of trust violation and trust repair tactics in entrepreneurial relationships.

- Given the weaknesses of state and market institutions, entrepreneurs and investors who seek to do business in Africa, as actors, should rely on their agency in developing personal and working relationships based on trust to enhance business development and growth. To African entrepreneurs, this book shows that while family/kinship ties may enable the success of some family businesses, in others, family ties may constrain growth due to lack of trust and the obligations of the African family system. Entrepreneurs therefore need to understand how family values relate to business in order not to ruin their family ties or their businesses.

- The limited support from state and market institutions renders trust an important strategic tool for entrepreneurs who seek resources such as trade credit from trade partners. This book shows that trustworthiness and trust expectations accruing from the behaviour and actions of the entrepreneur or the key boundary spanner of a firm are key determinants of trust. Thus, honesty, truthfulness, keeping promises, making timely payments for trade credit, capacity to pay, reputation, supplying quality products/service, and being punctual with supply deadlines are important trust expectations that underpin an entrepreneur's decisions to offer or not to offer trade credit to prospective partners. It is equally important for entrepreneurs to understand the cultural and industry logics that underpin trust development, interpretations of trust violations, and trust repair. This book shows that logics of weak legal institutions, traditional legal systems, family/kinship, religion, trade associations, industry, and the nature of specific relationships shape the perceptions and interpretations of trust violations. Entrepreneurs therefore need to understand the logics and acceptable norms that underpin trust in relationships as this may vary between associations, sectors, and markets and over time (Amoako and Lyon 2011). Entrepreneurs should also be aware that trust violations could have severe costs including loss of resources, termination of relationships, near collapse of businesses (Bachmann 2001), disappointment and grief. Entrepreneurs should also understand trust repair tactics and the logics of institutions that allow trust to be repaired since in contexts like Africa, trust is critically important for entrepreneurs owning and managing SMEs. It is important for entrepreneurs to be aware that trust violations are common and yet trust is repaired in the overwhelming majority of cases by deploying appropriate repair tactics.

9.4 Implications for Policy

- This book highlights the weaknesses of state and market institutions and the important role of indigenous African institutions in fostering entrepreneurship in Africa. Accordingly, policy makers in Africa should reform the weak state and market institutions such as legal systems, tax systems, and enterprise support systems to enhance entrepreneurship and economic growth. An understanding of local contexts and the institutional logics that enable trust to develop in entrepreneurship should guard these reforms.
- This book also shows the need for African governments, economic development experts and partners, and enterprise education policy makers to consider, recognise, and support local cultural institutions that support entrepreneurship. The case of traditional legal systems and trade associations show the critical importance of such institutions in entrepreneurship and national economic development. Nonetheless, there is a need to reform some aspects of African culture such as attitudes of government officials towards asking for gifts, bribes, and other corrupt practices. It is also important for policy makers to incorporate

local institutions and local knowledge into education curricula. By incorporating the local cultural institutions into enterprise education and curriculum development, the education system can enhance the accelerated development of the continent. Currently, African enterprise education is over-reliant on imported models and concepts, most of which are not fit for purpose in African contexts.

- Last but not the least, governments, policy makers, donors, and international development agencies should desist from imposing interventions that are devoid of local institutional logics and instead base national and international interventions on relevant local knowledge and practices in order to avoid misplaced development programmes that fail to deliver the expected outcomes.

9.5   Researching Trust, Institutions, and Managing Entrepreneurial Relationships

This study sets the stage for further research into the complex cultural and sub-cultural institutions that influence entrepreneurship across African economies and other emerging economies from an institutionalist and cross-cultural perspective. Yet it has some limitations that form the basis of future research.

Given the comparative-static nature of institutional theory (Welter 2002) used in this study, future research should explore longitudinal studies to analyse the changes in the logics of institutions in entrepreneurship over time as entrepreneurship is a dynamic and process-oriented phenomenon. Such approaches will help unravel how the logics of African institutions may change over time in line with notions of historical contingency proposed by Thornton et al. (2012).

The case studies and purposive sampling approaches may lack a basis for scientific generalisation (Yin 2009). Hence, future studies should focus on testing hypotheses about the role of indigenous institutional logics in African countries and in other emerging economies on a larger sample to identify the most significant institutions that provide the logics for entrepreneurship across the continent.

While the literature shows the impact of trust violations on firms (e.g. Bachmann 2001; Gillespie and Dietz 2009), no attention has been paid to the impact of trust violations on the entrepreneur. This study shows that entrepreneurs may experience serious financial, social, and emotional consequences from trust violations and future investigations are needed to help understand the negative impact of trust violations on entrepreneurs. This may in turn help the development of support interventions for distressed entrepreneurs.

There is also a need to understand the role of the entrepreneur as a victim in trust repair as previous research mainly focused on the role of the perpetrator and less on the role of the victim of trust violations in trust repair.

The role of power in shaping interpretations of trust violations and trust repair in entrepreneurial and SME interorganisational relationships deserve attention as entrepreneurs owning SMEs in emerging economies may often be engaged in asymmetrical power and trust relationships. This will enable a clearer understanding of entrepreneurial and small business perspectives regarding the development of trust, networks, and relationships.

Even though this study contributes to an understanding of the relationship between individual entrepreneurs as actors in relation to institutions based on the institutional logics approach, there is still very little known about how entrepreneurs as actors draw on institutional incentives and constraints in Africa and in other emerging economies. Future studies should continue to investigate how entrepreneurs relate to institutional challenges across African countries and other emerging economies as there may be variations across the different cultural contexts and over time.

Currently, there is very little understanding about how institutions shape trust development, trust violations, and trust repair in entrepreneurship and in international business across different cultural contexts. Hence, future studies should explore trust development, trust violations, and trust repair within entrepreneurial relationships across different cultures.

References

Accenture. 2010. Africa: The new frontier for growth. Online access on 13 Feb 2012. http://nstore.accenture.com/pdf/Accenture_Africa_The_New_Frontier_for_Growth.pdf.

Amankwah-Amoah, J., and Y. Debrah. 2017. Toward a construct of liability of origin. *Industrial and Corporate Change* 26 (2): 211–231.

Amoako, I.O. 2012. *Trust in exporting relationships: The case of SMEs in Ghana*, Published PhD thesis. Center for Economic and Enterprise Development Research (CEEDR) Middlesex University, London. http://eprints.mdx.ac.uk/12419/.

Amoako I.O., and Lyon F. 2011. Interorganisational trust violations and repairs in a weak legal environment: Evidence from Ghanaian Exporting SMEs. Paper presented at the European Group of Organisational Studies (EGOS) Conference, Gothenburg, Gothenburg University, July 7–9.

Amoako, I.O., and F. Lyon. 2014. We don't deal with courts: Cooperation and alternative institutions shaping exporting relationships of SMEs in Ghana. *International Small Business Journal* 32 (2): 117–139.

Bachmann, R. 2001. Trust, power and control in trans-organizational relations. *Organization Studies* 22 (2): 337–365.

Bachmann, R., and A. Inkpen. 2011. Understanding institutional-based trust building processes in inter-organisational relationships. *Organization Studies* 32 (2): 281–300.

Bachmann, R., N. Gillespie, and R. Priem. 2015. Repairing trust in organizations and institutions: Toward a conceptual framework. *Organization Studies* 36 (9): 1123–1142.

BBC News. 2018. May in Africa; UK Prime Minister's mission to woo continent after Brexit. 28th August 2018. http://www.bbc.co.uk/news/world-africa-45298656

Bruton, G.D., D. Ahlstrom, and H.-L. Li. 2010. Institutional theory and entrepreneurship: Where are we now and where do we need to move in the future? *Entrepreneurship Theory and Practice* 34 (3): 421–440.

Chang, C.-C., S.-N. Yao, S.-A. Chen, J.-T. King, and C. Liang. 2016. Imagining garage startups: Interactive effects of imaginative capabilities on technopreneurship intention. *Creativity Research Journal* 28 (3): 289–297.

Chell, E. 2000. Towards researching the 'opportunistic entrepreneur': A social constructionist approach and research agenda. *European Journal of Work and Organizational Psychology* 9 (1): 63–80.

Chell, E. 2007. Social enterprise and entrepreneurship: Towards a convergent theory of entrepreneurial process. *International Small Business Journal* 25 (1): 5–26.

Delloitte. 2014. The Delloitte consumer review Africa: A 21st century view, London.

Dietz, G., N. Gillespie, and G.T. Chao. 2010. Unravelling the complexities of trust and culture. In *Organizational trust: A cultural perspective*, ed. M.N.K. Saunders, D. Skinner, G. Dietz, N. Gillespie, and R.J. Lewicki. Cambridge: Cambridge University Press.

Dirks, K.T., R.J. Lewicki, and A. Zaheer. 2009. Repairing relationships within and between organizations: Building a conceptual foundation. *Academy of Management Review* 34: 68–84.

Drakopoulou Dodd, S., and A.R. Anderson. 2007. Mumpsimus and the mything of the individualistic entrepreneur. *International Small Business Journal* 25 (4): 341–360.

Ellis, P. 2000. Social ties and foreign market entry. *Journal of International Business Studies* 31 (3): 443–470.

Estrin, S., and M. Pervezer. 2011. The role of informal institutions in corporate governance: Brazil, Russia, India, and China compared. *Asia Pacific Journal of Management* 28 (1): 41–67.

Friedland, R., and R.R. Alford. 1991. Bringing society back in: Symbols, practices, and institutional contradictions. In *The new institutionalism in organizational analysis*, ed. W.W. Powell and P.J. DiMaggio, 17th ed., 232–263. Chicago: University of Chicago Press.

Gambetta, D. 1988. *Trust: Making and breaking cooperative relations*. Oxford/New York: Basil Blackwell.

Gartner, W.B. 1988. Who is an entrepreneur? Is the wrong question. *American Journal of Small Business* 12 (4): 11–32.

George, G., J.N.O. Khayesi, and M.R.T. Haas. 2016. Bringing Africa in: Promising directions for management research. *Academy of Management Journal* 59 (2): 377–393.

Gillespie, N., and G. Dietz. 2009. Trust repair after an organization level failure. *Academy of Management Review* 34 (1): 127–145.

Granovetter, M.S. 1985. Economic action and social structure: The problem of embeddedness. *American Journal of Sociology* 91 (3): 481–510.

Jackson, T., K. Amaeshi, and S. Yavuz. 2008. Untangling African indigenous management: Multiple influences on the success of SMEs in Kenya. *Journal of World Business* 43 (3): 400–416.

Kim, P.H., D.L. Ferrin, C.D. Cooper, and K.T. Dirks. 2004. Removing the shadow of suspicion: The effects of apology versus denial for repairing competence-based versus integrity-based trust violations. *Journal of Applied Psychology* 89 (1): 100–118.

Lewicki, R.J., and B.B. Bunker. 1996. Developing and maintaining trust in work relationships. In *Trust in organizations: Frontiers of theory and research*, ed. R. Kramer and T.R. Tyler. Thousand Oaks: Sage.

Li, P.P. 2016. The holistic and contextual natures of trust: Past, present and future research. *Journal of Trust Research* 6 (1): 1–6.

Lyon, F., and G. Porter. 2009. Market institutions, trust and norms: Exploring moral economies in Nigerian food systems. *Cambridge Journal of Economics* 33 (5): 903–920.

Mayer, R., J. Davis, and F. Schoorman. 1995. An integrative model of organisational trust. *Academy of Management Review* 20: 709–734.

Möllering, G. 2006. *Trust: Reason, routine, reflexivity*. Amsterdam: Elsevier.

North, D.C. 1990. *Institutions, institutional change and economic performance*. Cambridge: Cambridge University Press.

Peng, M.W., D.Y.L. Wang, and J. Yi. 2008. An institution-based view of international business strategy: A focus on emerging economies. *Journal of International Business Studies* 39: 920–936.

Ren, H., and B. Gray. 2009. Repairing relationship conflict: How violation types and culture influence the effectiveness of restoration rituals. *Academy of Management Review* 34 (1): 105–126.

Saunders, M.N.K., D. Skinner, G. Dietz, N. Gillespie, and R.J. Lewicki. 2010. *Organizational trust: A cultural perspective*. Cambridge: Cambridge University Press.

Scott, W.R. 2005. Institutional theory: Contributing to a theoretical research programme. In *Great minds in management: The process theory development*, ed. M.A. Hitt and K.G. Smith. Oxford: Oxford University Press.

Schumpeter, J. 1942. *Capitalism, socialism and democracy*. London: Allen & Unwin.

Shane, S., and S. Venkataraman. 2000. The promise of entrepreneurship as a field of research. *Academy of Management Review* 25 (1): 217–226.

The Economist. 2016. Special report: Business in Africa, 1.2 billion opportunities. http://www.economist.com/news/special-report/21696792-commodity-boom-may-beover and barriers-doing-business-are-everywhere-africas.

Thornton, P. 2004. *Markets from culture: Institutional logics and organisational decision in higher educational publishing*. Stanford: Stanford University Press.

Thornton, P.H., D. Ribeiroi-Soriano, and D. Urbano. 2011. Socio-cultural logics and entrepreneurial activity: An overview. *International Small Business Journal* 29 (2): 105–118.

Thornton, P., W. Ocasio, and M. Loundbury. 2012. *The institutional logics perspective: A new approach to culture, structure and process.* Oxford: Oxford University Press.

Welter, F. 2002. Trust, Institutions and Entrepreneurial Behaviour. In *Entrepreneurial Strategies in East and West European Environments. Concepts and Considerations,* ed. H.H. Hohmann and F. Welter, 37–42. Bremenr: Forschungsstelle Osteuropa.

Welter, F., and D. Smallbone. 2011. Institutional perspectives on entrepreneurial behaviour in challenging environments. *Journal of Small Business Management* 49 (1): 395–406.

Williamson, O. 1993. Calculativeness, trust and economic organization. *Journal of Law and Economics* 36: 453–486.

World Bank. 2018. *Doing Business 2018.* Washington, DC: World Bank.

Wu, W., M. Firth, and O.M. Rui. 2014. Trust and the provision of trade credit. *Journal of Banking & Finance* 39: 146–159.

Yin, R.K. 2009. *Case study research: Design and methods.* Beverly Hills: Sage.

Zucker, L.G. 1986. Production of trust. Institutional sources of economic structure, 1840–1920. *Research in Organisation Behaviour* 8: 53–111.

Index

© The Author(s) 2019
I. O. Amoako, *Trust, Institutions and Managing Entrepreneurial Relationships in Africa*,
Palgrave Studies of Entrepreneurship in Africa,
https://doi.org/10.1007/978-3-319-98395-0